Bob Vila's Guide to
Historic Homes of the Mid-Atlantic

Bob Vila's Guides to Historic Homes of America

Bob Vila's
Guide to Historic Homes of the Mid-Atlantic

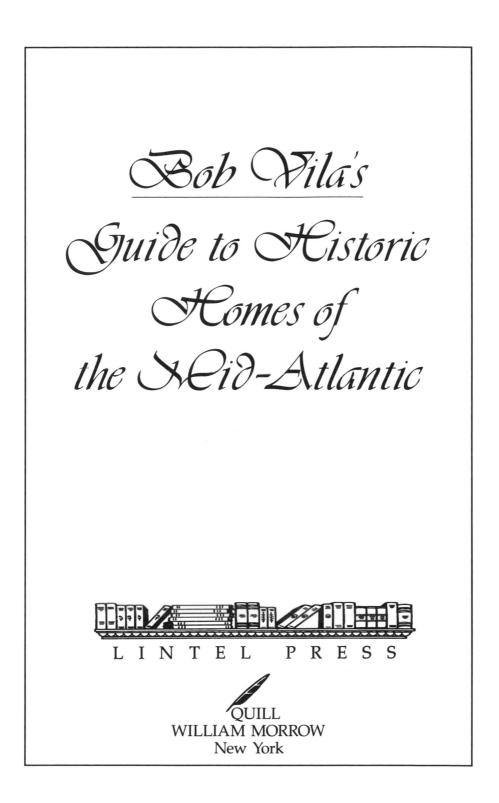

LINTEL PRESS

QUILL
WILLIAM MORROW
New York

Bob Vila's guide to historic homes of the Mid-Atlantic.

Library of Congress Catalog Card Number 93-083606

ISBN 0-688-12494-1

Printed in the United States of America

First Quill Edition

1 2 3 4 5 6 7 8 9 10

MANAGING EDITOR—SUSAN RYAN
LAYOUT AND DESIGN BY EVA JAKUBOWSKI

Acknowledgment

I would like to acknowledge all of the people who helped make the idea of this book become a reality. To my wife Deborah who shares my enthusiasm for everything about history and whose idea of a vacation is incomplete without visiting every historic house along the way. Her encouragement and determination to see every room in every house gave me the idea for this series of guides.

To Ron Feiner who brought us all together long ago and by doing so enriched us all. To Bob Sann and Hugh Howard whose path findings led us to our publishers, a special thanks for enabling us to be spared the normative agony of attempting to get published. Through Hugh's excellent relationships we hope to benefit all.

To my brother, whose expertise in the publishing business facilitated my limited understanding of the industry.

To Susan Ryan and Kim Whelan who worked so tirelessly and professionally to make this a reality. I could not have found more skillful people whose strengths complemented my weaknesses.

To my partner Barry Weiner, whose unfailing support allowed us to open the checkbook when the possibility of returns were vague.

To Eva Jakubowski, who makes books and computers come together. If I ever figured out what you do I'd probably thank you even more.

And finally, to my mother, who aside from being a librarian demonstrated to me at a very early age that a universe of knowledge could be found between the covers of that most marvelous and wonderful of all things...books.

— *Jonathan Russo*
Lintel Press

Table of Contents

Publisher's Note

We hope that this book will serve as more than a conventional guide to historic homes. For while we set out to create a detailed, informative, and unique guide, devoted exclusively to historic houses, we also had higher goals. For those among you who enjoy, and are devoted to, preservation, architecture, decorative and fine arts, what we have attempted will be self-evident. For those who are first becoming interested in the world of historic Americana, we will try to give you a helping hand. For all those venturing across these historic thresholds, we invite you in, knowing that you will not be disappointed.

The following pages contain a wealth of information on the fascinating people—both the famous and not so famous—who lived in these houses, as well as descriptions of the houses and their remarkable collections. What can also be found within this book, beyond the listings of locations, hours, and tour information, is the most elusive of all things—wonder. For behind each and every house listing lies a world of wonder. Not the manufactured kind, packaged and sold to replace the imagination. Not the superficial kind which manipulates the emotions at the expense of the intellect. But wonder on a higher plane.

The first wonder is that any of these houses still exist and that anyone cares at all. Our society has often achieved its enviable position of affluence by focusing on the new and disposing with the old. The desire for the latest architectural styles, furnishings, and conveniences has often meant a bulldozing of the past, to the point where even the recent past is endangered. Of course, this has always been so; Colonial homes were remodeled into Greek Revivals at the expense of their original architecture. But the changes are far more devastating now, instead of remodeling the houses, we are tearing them down altogether. Time after time, when we went to a historic house in a small city or village, our guide's first statement was that the historic society had been formed to prevent the house from being torn down, often to make room for a parking lot. Historic houses have been made into rooming houses, beauty parlors, or high rises. As we walked through a fifteen room, four-story house built in 1840, complete with irreplaceable architectural details, the enormity of the "let's tear it down" mentality became overwhelming.

Of course the houses themselves possess more wonder than anything else. It is a sorrowfully calloused person who cannot experience the past in a historic house. To tour the prosperous ship captain's house in historic Newport, Rhode Island is to wonder at the riches of furniture, decorations, textiles and food stuffs that ships and winds provided. To tour the 18th-century stone houses of Washington, Pennsylvania with their two-foot thick walls is to wonder at the fortitude of their inhabitants as they struggled against attacks and defended themselves against the cold winters. The very cosmopolitanism of mercantile families in Greenwich Village, New York permeates the air of the historic houses there. One can sense the refinement these people must have felt when they sipped brandy and smoked cigars in their impressive parlors. To be told why people used fireplace screens —so that the wax women used as a cosmetic to fill in their pockmarked faces would not melt—is an explanation of a common object that brings the past alive in a personal and wonderful way. The treasures of art, architectural details, furniture, household implements, and costumes contained in these homes also makes us pause in reflection. Things were viewed very differently when they were made by hand and scarce. There is an education for all of us living in a throw-away culture.

So it is to the individuals, organizations and societies who are saving, preserving and displaying historic America that our sense of wonder and gratitude is directed. Sometimes, we would drive by a mall and see endless cars, stores and shoppers, and know that the energy of the town was now clearly centered at the mall. Then we would arrive at our destination, the local historic house, and find we were the only visitors. Despite this daunting competition from today's faster paced entertainments, our guide was cheerful, patient and full of enthusiasm for the wonder of the house.

We admire the volunteers who fundraise, lobby, catalogue, lecture, and guide their fellow citizens. As visitors, we enrich ourselves because of the efforts of the organizations and individuals who have labored to restore and revitalize these fine houses. We wish to thank the individuals who have given us their time and energy on these tours, and have given us their cooperation in putting this book together. If, in some small way, this guide helps you in your efforts, please consider it a thank you.

— *Jonathan Russo*
Lintel Press

Editor's Note

Thanks to everyone who filled out our questionnaire and sent the vast amounts of brochures and booklets which provided the basis for the book. All of the information about the houses has been supplied by the historical organizations and societies themselves; we have tried to reproduce the descriptions, biographical information, and schedule information as accurately as possible. Since many of the houses are subject to uncertain funding, and their hours and activities for visitors vary from season to season, we encourage people to call in advance to verify the information. Wherever possible, we have mentioned other houses located in the same town or village for which we do not have a complete listing. Finally, please contact us if there are other houses you would like to see listed in the next edition.

Introduction

All buildings have character, some seem friendly while others have a forbidding feel. Many big buildings demand your attention, while more than a few small ones seem content to let you pass by them unnoticed. Buildings can be eccentric, exotic, familiar, unassuming, warm and welcoming, or cold and sinister; but their individuality is there for all who choose to recognize it.

Since the Bicentennial celebration, millions of Americans have come to appreciate another element of the architectural personality. Like people of a certain age, antique buildings have survived wars and changes and visitors, wanted and unwanted alike. Their very characters are reflections of times past. Some buildings, like some people, have aged gracefully; some have seen happy and sad times, but all of them have something to teach us, about their histories and even ourselves. The truth is that all old houses have something in common with your house and mine.

I fell in love with houses and buildings early in my life—I studied architecture long before *This Old House* and *Bob Vila's Home Again* introduced millions to some intriguing rehabilitation jobs with which I've been involved. My fondness for buildings in general and my experience with old houses in particular only heightens my appreciation of the houses you'll meet in these pages, and the uncompromising approach the many historical societies, community organizations, individuals, and groups have taken to getting the houses restored just right.

These houses represent an immense range of the American experience. Every one has a story to tell, whether it's of the people who built the house or those who lived there; the community that is the context for the place; or even the events that led to its preservation; which so often involve battles with developers or others insensitive to the value and merit in a tumbledown, antique structure.

Each of these houses provides a unique opportunity to step back in time, to learn about how our ancestors lived. Which is another way of saying, these houses offer a glimpse of history, that wonderful state of mind that explains, in part, why and who we are today. I hope in some way we can help inspire you to visit these houses and those other eras that have so much to teach us.

—*Bob Vila*

Delaware

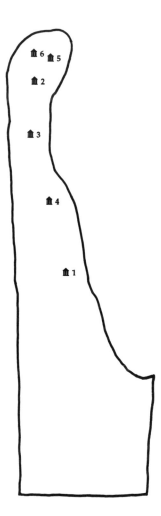

1. Dover
John Dickinson Plantation
Woodburn (The Governor's House)

2. New Castle
George Read II House and Garden
Amstel House
Dutch House

3. Odessa
The Historic Houses of Odessa

4. Smyrna
The Barracks-Smyrna Museum

5. Wilmington
Eleutherian Mills
Lombardy Hall
Hendrickson House
Rockwood Museum

6. Winterthur
Winterthur

John Dickinson Plantation

Rd 3, Box 257
Dover, DE 19901
(302) 739-3277

Contact: Delaware State Museum
Open: Mar.-Dec., Tues.-Sat.
10 a.m.–3:30 p.m., Sun. 1:30–4:30 p.m.;
Jan.-Feb., Tues.-Sat. 10 a.m.–3:30 p.m.
Admission: Free, donations gladly accepted.
Visitor center has an introductory video,
exhibit, and sales area. Guided tours of
house, outbuilding complex and log
dwellings available on advance request.
Suggested Time to View House: 90 minutes
Facilities on Premises: Gift shop

Description of Grounds: Outbuilding
complex is made up of reconstructed
farm buildings of the late 1700s and a
beautiful Colonial Revival garden.
Best Season to View House: Spring
Number of Yearly Visitors: approximately
10,000
Year House Built: 1740
Style of Architecture: Georgian with Federal
interior
Number of Rooms: 10
On-Site Parking: Yes **Wheelchair Access:** Yes

Description of House

The house was constructed in 1740 for Samuel Dickinson, a judge for the Court of Common Pleas in Kent County. John Dickinson, Samuel's eldest son from his second marriage, inherited the house when his father died in 1760. One of America's founding fathers, Dickinson is known in the history books as the "Penman of the Revolution" for his many inspired essays on Colonial rights and liberty. His famed "Letters from a Pennsylvania Farmer..." gained unprecedented public acclaim for his well stated opposition to unjust English taxes. Dickinson's immensely popular "Liberty Song" set his political views to music throughout the land. As a delegate to the federal constitutional convention he helped bring about an important compromise essential to the creation of the Constitution.

This imposing Georgian mansion was built in 1740 and ranks among the largest and most fashionable of 18th-century Delaware. The two-story brick dwelling contains five bay windows along the beautiful St. James River. The main block of the house's facade features Flemish bond brick work with glazed headers, a brick belt course and molded water table. Significant interior details include the circa 1805 staircase with decorative spandrels and a molded handrail.

In contrast to the large home, the site also includes a logged dwelling. The one room log structure and furnishings exhibit the lifestyle of slaves, free blacks and poor whites in the 18th century. The reconstructed farm complex, which includes a smokehouse, granary, double corn crib, stable and barn, sets the stage for interpreting historic farm practices. Domestic activities such as cooking and food storage are discussed in the plantation's log dwellings.

The furnishings include antiques of the period with fine examples of Delaware made pieces, some belonging to the Dickinson family. The log dwelling is furnished with reproductions, based on examples from the collections of Delaware State Museum and excavated pieces from archaeological sites in Delaware.

Notable Collections on Exhibit

The mansion is home to many fascinating historic pieces including an 18th-century London Waystaff Clock, a set of mahogany chairs (c. 1760), fiddle back splat, Queen Anne/Chippendale style; a similar Chippendale style desk (c. 1800), and a working tall case clock (c.1780), with rocking ship. Delicate hurricane globes (c. 1800) and creamware plates belonging to the Dickinson are also on display. Wall hangings include family portraits and a Queen Anne-style mirror.

Additional Information

In addition to the regular tour, the Dickinson Plantation staff offers several special focus tours on African-American history and decorative arts with advance notice. Demonstrations and hands on activities are included in the tours periodically. For more information, please contact the site supervisor.

Woodburn (The Governor's House)

151 Kings Highway
Dover, DE 19901
(302) 739-5656

Contact: Woodburn

Open: Sat. 2–4 p.m.

Suggested Time to View House: 20 minutes

Description of Grounds: Gardens filled with plantings native to Delaware and some interesting exceptions

Best Season to View House: June-fall

Number of Yearly Visitors: 5,000

Year House Built: 1790

Style of Architecture: Georgian

Number of Rooms: 9 rooms, only the downstairs is open to the public

On-Site Parking: Yes **Wheelchair Access:** Yes

Description of House

Built in 1790 by Charles Hillyard, Woodburn has had several notable owners over the last two centuries as well as being home to a series of legends. The Hillyard family occupied the house until 1817. The next occupants, the Cowgill family, lived here for almost one hundred years. Judge Daniel Hastings bought the house in 1912 and stayed until 1918 when he sold to Dr. and Mrs. Frank Sullivan Hall, owners who filled the house with outstanding antiques. In 1966 the house was sold to the state of Delaware for $65,000. Since that time it has been the official residence of five of Delaware's governors.

Woodburn is known as one of the finest, late-18th-century houses in Delaware and is an excellent example of local craftsman's joinery talents. The large scale and good proportions of the three full floors, attic and basement are impressive. The interior is particularly notable for its surviving detailing, including a broad, pine staircase and full interior paneling. The interior design is especially outstanding in the first floor drawing room and the second floor master bedroom. The furnishings comprise a museum collection and are appropriate to the period of the house.

Notable Collections on Exhibit

Woodburn exhibits a fine collection of 19th century furnishings and paintings including Chippendale furniture (a breakfront and a tall case clock among other pieces), a Queen Anne gaming table, an Empire/Sheraton dining room set, and paintings by Henry Lee Tatnall, Edward Moran, and Edward Bannister.

Additional Information

Woodburn has also generated a series of legends over the years related to the house's role in the underground railroad and a raid by Patty Cannon, as detailed in "The Entailed Hat" by George A. Townsend. Also, the house is supposedly haunted by four different ghosts: a little girl in a red-checked gingham dress, an older gentlemen named Mr. Higgins, a chain rattling ghost in the basement, and a wine-tippling spirit.

George Read II House and Garden

42 The Strand
New Castle, DE 19720
(302) 322-8411

Contact: Historical Society of Delaware
Open: March 1-Dec. 31, Tues.-Sat.
10 a.m.–4 p.m.; Sun. 12–4 p.m.; Jan.-Feb.
open regular hours and daily by
appointment
Admission: Adults $4; children $3.50;
seniors $2. Guided tours, special
programs.
Suggested Time to View House: 1 hour
Facilities on Premises: Gift shop
Best Season to View House: Spring-fall
Year House Built: 1797 to 1804

Description of House

George Read II, son of the prominent politician and signer of the Declaration of Independence George Read, was only thirty two years old when he began building this elegant residence. The younger Read had trained as a lawyer in Philadelphia before practicing in Delaware. Despite his father's influence, he was never able to achieve the same political prominence and lost several elections. In many ways, this house represented the culmination of George Read II's success. The dwelling was also occupied by William Couper from 1846 to 1874. Crouper was a merchant involved in the China trade, who decorated the house in a Victorian fashion.

The Read House is constructed in the manner of a Philadelphia townhouse on a narrow lot in New Castle. There are two rooms of equal size on either side of the entrance, thereby creating a five-bay or "double house." The main block of the house has a raised basement, thirteen-foot ceilings on the first and second floors, and a finished garrett with dormer windows. In order to maximize space, the kitchen, laundry, and other service functions were housed in several back buildings attached to the main house and joined together to form a single unit.

Most of the furnishings were collected and are appropriate for the early 19th century. They are well documented by contemporary correspondence and accounts. Three rooms contain the original furnishings of the 1920 Colonial Revival period.

Additional Information

The Read House underwent an extensive restoration program in the late 1970s and 1980s based on the Read family's documents, correspondence, and account books.

Amstel & Dutch Houses

Fourth and Delaware Streets (Amstel)
32 East Third Street (Dutch)
New Castle, DE 19720
(302) 322-2794

Contact: New Castle Historical Society

Open: March-Dec., Tues.-Sat. 11 a.m.–4 p.m., Sun. 1–4 p.m.; Jan.-Feb., Sat. 11 a.m.–4 p.m., Sun. 1–4 p.m.

Admission: $2 per house. Guided tours, Christmas candlelight tours, and seasonal changes.

Suggested Time to View House: 30 minutes per house

Description of Grounds: Restored gardens surround each house

Best Season to View House: Spring

Number of Yearly Visitors: 11,000

Year House Built: 1738 (Amstel); 1700 (Dutch)

Style of Architecture: Georgian (Amstel House); Dutch Colonial (Dutch House)

Description of House

Dr. John Finney built the Amstel House 1738. Later in the 18th century, the house was occupied by Nicholas Van Dyke, Sr., an early governor, whose son Nicholas Van Dyke, Jr. built the house on the opposite side of Delaware Street.

The Amstel House is an excellent example of eighteenth century Georgian architecture. The house contains one of New Castle's earliest fan lights and was among the first with a central hallway. The rooms give visitors the feeling for both the elegance and the hard work which characterized the lives of the early American families. The first floor of the house appears as if the original residents had just stepped out with its complete collection of 18th-century furniture and decorative art objects.

The Dutch House is one of the few survivors of New Castle's 17th-century beginnings. Built around 1700 and restored in 1938, this house is typical of colonial Dutch architecture. The house is furnished throughout with 17th and 18th-century Dutch furniture and artifacts.

Notable Collections on Exhibit

The Dutch House exhibits many items which are characteristic of a Dutch settler's home including a "kas", a hutch table, a 16th-century Dutch Bible and a courting bench. In addition, the house features different exhibits, with the table set with authentic foods and the rooms decorated accordingly. At Christmas, the house displays traditional decorations of the Dutch Twelfth Night celebration.

Additional Information

In addition, the society also maintains the Victorian-style Old Library Museum. This hexagonal structure with a multi-paned three-level skylight houses interpretive exhibits on all aspects of Delaware and New Castle history.

Historic Houses of Odessa

Main Street, P.O. Box 507
Odessa, DE 19730
(302) 378-4069

Contact: Historic Houses of Odessa
Open: Tues.-Sat. 10 a.m.–4 p.m.; Sun.
1–4 p.m.; Closed Mon.
Admission: Adults $3 (single house; $6 all
four); children under 12 free.
Guided tours, yuletide celebrations,
special events.
Suggested Time to View House: 1½–2 hours
Facilities on Premises: Gift shop

Description of Grounds: 15 acres including
Colonial Revival garden and
demonstration herb garden
Best Season to View House: Spring-fall
Number of Yearly Visitors: 10,000
Year House Built: Corbitt-Sharp–1774;
Wilson-Warner–1769;
Collins-Sharp–c. 1700s
Style of Architecture: Georgian;
Collins-Sharpe-Gambrel

Description of House

The village of Odessa, known in the 18th century as Cantwell's Bridge, played a vital role in American commercial life as a busy grain-shipping port. The buildings in Odessa cover a period of over two hundred years with fine examples of Georgian, Colonial and Victorian architecture, and reflect different periods and the vernacular adaptations of these styles.

The stately Corbitt-Sharp House is considered one of the finest examples of mid-Georgian architecture in Delaware. William Corbitt, who operated a tannery on the banks of the Appoquinimink Creek, was the town's leading citizen when he built his handsome Georgian house in 1774. The house remained in the Corbitt family until 1938 when it was acquired by H. Rodney Sharp. He restored the house and donated it to the Winterthur organization for conversion to a house museum. The house is furnished to reflect the lifestyle of the region in the late 18th century and includes both family and regional furniture.

Further down the street, the Wilson-Warner House, built by prosperous merchant David Wilson in 1769, exemplifies Delaware Georgian architecture. The house is completely furnished with items which closely resemble those listed on the Wilson family's 1829 inventory made for bankruptcy proceedings.

The Collins-Sharpe House, one of Delaware's oldest houses, dates to the early 18th century. The picturesque log and frame structure is the center for educational programming for the village and features living history demonstrations of open hearth cooking and other activities.

Notable Collections on Exhibit

In addition to the fine period furnishings on display, the Brick Hotel Gallery, a Federal-style building, is also located in the village and houses an impressive collection. The hotel holds the country's largest display of Victorian furniture made in the style of J.H. Belter and illustrates the best American furniture craftsmanship of the mid-19th century.

Additional Information

There are many annual events that take place at the houses including the Odessa Spring Festival, Independence Day Concert and Fireworks, and the Delaware Decoy Show and Carving Championship.

The Barracks-Smyrna Museum

11 South Main Street
Smyrna, DE 19977
(302) 653-1320

Contact: Duck Creek Historical Society
Open: Sat. 1–4 p.m., other times by
appointment
Admission: Free. Guided tours.
Suggested Time to View House: 30 minutes

Number of Yearly Visitors: 600
Year House Built: Late 1790s
Style of Architecture: Late Georgian
Number of Rooms: 7

Description of House

This modest brick dwelling was never lived in by its first known owner,
widow Susannah Holliday Wilson. Instead, it appears that she rented the
house to local merchants. In in the 1806 tax assessment of Duck Creek, the
building was listed as one of her fifteen properties and was called the barric.
Later the name apperared as the bare ox and finally as the Barracks, the name
by which it is known today. Since that time the house has had a number of
owners including James Hoffecker and the Webb family.

The actual date of construction is unknown, but it appears to be sometime in the late 1790s based on the configuration of the house, the bond of
the brick, and other architectural features found in the basement or cellar
and the attic. The house was unusual for its time in that most other structures
were built of frame construction, while the Barracks is made of brick. The
house used a a modified Quaker Hall and parlour plan with a room on either
side of the central hall. The furnishings are collected and arranged to reflect
the periods from 1800 to late Victorian.

Notable Collections on Exhibit

The house is furnished with fine examples of early Victorian furniture
including spindle Windsor chairs and a painted iron stone punch bowl.
There are also many original oil paintings and a unique collection of pitchers
in the dining room. The display room exhibits artifacts related to Smyrna
history.

Eleutherian Mills

P.O. Box 3630, Route 141
Wilmington, DE 19807
(302) 658-2400

Contact: Hagley Museum and Library

Open: March 15-Dec. 30, daily
9:30 a.m.–4:30 p.m.; Jan.-March 14,
guided tour at 1:30 p.m., weekends
9:30 a.m.–4:30 p.m.

Admission: Adults $9.75; senior citizens
and students $7.50; children (6-14) $3.50;
children (under 6) free. Please call for a
schedule of the numerous activities.

Suggested Time to View House: 1 hour

Description of Grounds: The 240 acres
includes mill buildings, machine shop,
workers community, French gardens
and barn.

Best Season to View House: All seasons

Year House Built: 1803

Number of Rooms: 11 rooms open

Style of Architecture: Georgian

On-Site Parking: Yes **Wheelchair Access:** Yes

Description of House

Eleuthere Irene du Pont, founder of E.I du Pont de Nemours and Co., a family enterprise for the manufacture of black powder, built the house in 1803. This impressive house was occupied by family members until 1890. In 1893, it was converted into a clubhouse for company workman and later became the home of the head of the du Pont Company's farm. In 1923, Henry Algernon du Pont, grandson of E.I du Pont purchased the ancestoral home for his daughter, Mrs. Louisa du Pont Crownshield. In 1852, the residence was given to the Eleutherian Mills Hagley Foundation by Ms. Crownshield.

The house is an example of Georgian-style architecture. Considered conservative for the time it was built, with a hint of Regency and Federal design, the house features notable details such as its elliptical staircase. The design is characteristic of mid to late 18th-century houses of the Pennsylvania-Delaware area. The building was constructed with stone and stucco. An unusual feature of the house is its proximity to the powder works. In addition, the piazza in the back of the house, the winding stairway and French garden all demonstrate the creative thinking that went into building this extraordinary house. The residence is furnished with antiques and memorabilia of the five generations of du Ponts associated with the home. These include pieces from the Federal, Empire, and Victorian periods.

Notable Collections on Exhibit

Numerous objects are on exhibit including hooked rugs, historic prints, early country furnishings, two large sets of family porcelain, and a collection of pewter. The dining room walls are decorated with authentic French block-printed wallpaper.

Lombardy Hall

PO. Box 7036 (1611 Concord Pike)
Wilmington, DE 19803
(302) 764-2128

Contact: Lombardy Hall Foundation
Open: By appointment only except second
Sat. and Sun. afternoon in Dec. when
decorated for Christmas.
Activities: Guided tours by appointment.

Suggested Time to View House: 90 minutes
Number of Yearly Visitors: 5000 plus
Year House Built: 1750, 1793, 1950
Number of Rooms: 7 plus basement

Description of House

Lombardy Hall was the summer home of American patriot Gunning Bedford Jr. Bedford, a statesman and jurist, and one of five signers of the Constitution from Delaware. Bedford was also one of ten contemporaries of the same name, a fact that has both delighted and confounded historians.

Lombardy Hall is Georgian in style, of native field stone and simple in design. The oldest part of the structure dates from 1750. Bedford expanded it to its present size during the time of his ownership between 1793 and 1812. The house maintains its original moldings, fireplaces and paneling and is furnished with period reproduction furniture.

Notable Collections on Exhibit

The house features exhibits pertaining to Bedford and to Freemasonry.

Hendrickson House

606 Church Street
Wilmington, DE 19801
(302) 652-5629

Contact: Old Swedes Foundation
Open: Mon.-Wed., Fri.-Sat. 1–4 p.m. Closed major holidays
Admission: Free. Guided tours.
Suggested Time to View House: 30–45 minutes
Facilities on Premises: Gift shop, book store

Description of Grounds: Churchyard is always open, self-guided tour possible
Best Season to View House: Spring-fall
Number of Yearly Visitors: 2000
Year House Built: 1690
Number of Rooms: 4
On-Site Parking: Yes **Wheelchair Access:** No

Description of House

Andrew Hendrickson, a Swedish farmer who had settled near Chester, Pennsylvania, built the house in 1690 when he married; he eventually had eight children. The house was occupied by three generations of Hendricksons. They sold it in 1788, and it was used as a house for tenant farmers. A fire in the early 1900s destroyed many wooden parts of the house.

The Hendrickson House was moved to this site in 1958 and restored. The dwelling originally consisting of one large room on the first floor for all the family's daily activities and a large bedroom above, the house was enlarged in the 1790s. The original pine mantel and woodwork around the large fireplace were considered up-scale for the time. The floorboards were taken from a Massachusetts farmhouse of the same period. The restoration included making the pine ceiling beams by hand, and reconstructing the curved staircase in accordance with marks on the wall. The furniture in the Hendrickson House dates from 1690 to 1800, but none of it was original to the house.

Notable Collections on Exhibit

Hendrickson House exhibits a fine collection of early American furniture with a Dutch influence including a kas, a spinning wheel, and pewter dishes and cooking vessels. There are also several early maps, and the will left by Andrew Hendrickson.

Additional Information

Close to the Hendrickson House, the Old Swedes Church still stands and is open to the public. Constructed in 1698, the church is one of the nation's oldest church buildings still in use for regular worship and contains the oldest known pulpit in the country. The church is a designated National Landmark.

Rockwood Museum

610 Shipley Road
Wilmington, DE 19809
(302) 761-4340

Contact: Rockwood Museum
Open: Tues.-Sat. 11 a.m.–4 p.m. (last tour at 3 p.m.)
Admission: Adults $3.50; seniors $2.50; students $1; children (under 5) free. Tours for adults and school children; lectures, workshops, concerts.
Suggested Time to View House: 1 hour
Facilities on Premises: Gift shop
Description of Grounds: 6 acres of gardenesque landscape
Best Season to View House: Spring-fall
Number of Yearly Visitors: 22,000
Year House Built: 1851
Number of Rooms: 54, 16 open to public

Style of Architecture: Rural Gothic
On-Site Parking: Yes **Wheelchair Access:** Yes

Description of House

Rockwood's builder, Joseph Shipley, was the great-grandson of William Shipley, the founder of Wilmington. Joseph made his fortune while working as a merchant banker in Liverpool, England and returned to Delaware to retire and build this lovely home. One of his heirs, Sarah Shipley Bringhurst, later bought the house at auction in 1892, and her family lived in the manor until 1972.

The stone rural gothic manor house, known as Rockwood, was designed in 1851 by English architect George Williams based on the design of a house where Shipley had resided while in England. An integral and unique feature of the house was the addition of a glass and iron conservatory (the earliest of its type still standing) attached to the east end of the mansion. The house also featured other modern innovations such as a central heating system and a bathroom with an interior water closet. To accomodate a larger servant staff, an addition was made between 1855 and 1857. The furnishings are original to the Shipley and Bringhurst families and include 17th through 19th-century English, continental, and American decorative arts.

Notable Collections on Exhibit

The remarkable collection of furniture is notable in that it represents the documented possessions of one family. Within this collection, noteworthy pieces include about 100 pieces of overlay glass, the largest assortment in America of documented pieces from Gillows Company, London.

Additional Information

Rockwood is known for its magnificent gardenesque landscaping, a design which was first popular in England in the mid-1800s and later became fashionable in the United States. Rockwood's grounds intermingle native and exotic plants including ginko, weeping beech, sourgum, and other champion trees.

Winterthur

Winterthur
Winterthur, DE 19735
(302) 888-4600

Contact: Winterthur Museum, Garden and Library

Open: Tues.-Sat. 9:30 a.m.–5 p.m., Sun. 12–5 p.m. Closed Mon., Jan. 1, Thankgiving and Christmas.

Admission: Adults $6; children $1.50; seniors $4.50. Guided tours of the period rooms and gardens, specialized tours available on request, Yuletide tour in Dec.

Suggested Time to View House: 45–60 minutes

Facilities on Premises: Gift shop, bookstore, garden shop, cafeteria.

Description of Grounds: 1,000 acres

Best Season to View House: Spring

Number of Yearly Visitors: 169,400

Year House Built: 1839, additions made in 1929, 1959, 1969, as well as current construction on the galleries

Style of Architecture: Greek Revival

Number of Rooms: 196

On-Site Parking: Yes **Wheelchair Access:** Yes

Description of House

Winterthur was Henry Francis du Pont's home from 1880 until 1951, and visitors will see the his vision and exquisite taste upon entering the home. The main house was originally built in 1839 by James Antoine Biderman and his wife Evelina du Pont, a daughter of E. I. du Pont de Nemours, founder of the Du Pont Company. They named the house Winterthur after the Biderman ancestral home in Switzerland. In 1866, Henry du Pont Sr. purchased Winterthur from his nephew, James Irenee Biderman (son of James and Evelina Biderman). Henry Francis DuPont was born here in 1880 and inherited the house in 1925.

Nestled in the picturesque countryside of the Brandywine Valley, the main house evolved from its original Greek Revival structure and today houses 196 period room settings. This extraordinary house-museum has the world's largest collection of decorative arts made or used in America for the period 1640 to 1860; these include furniture, textiles, paintings, prints, silver, needlework and glass. The collection was assembled by Henry Francis du Pont who had a passion for American decorative arts. Several of the rooms have interior architecture from 18th and 19th-century homes. Each of the original thirteen colonies are represented by at least one period room.

Notable Collections on Exhibit

Winterthur's collection numbers more than 89,000 objects including textiles, clocks, silver, needlework, porcelain, Oriental rugs, and paintings. Notable items include Chippendale furniture, a set of six silver tankers by Paul Revere, John Trumbull's portrait of George Washington at Verplanck's Point, and a sixty-six piece dinner service made for George Washington.

Additional Information

In addition to his love of decorative arts, Du Pont also had a passion for horticulture which is evident in Winterthur's gardens. The grounds feature a Quarry Garden with an unusual assortment of bog and rock plants, the Azalea Woods, and the Pinetum, regarded as the most extensive collection of rare conifers in the eastern United States. Also, visitors to Winterthur are encourage to visit the nearby Nemours Mansion, a Louis XVI-style chateau, which was home to Alfred DuPont.

Maryland

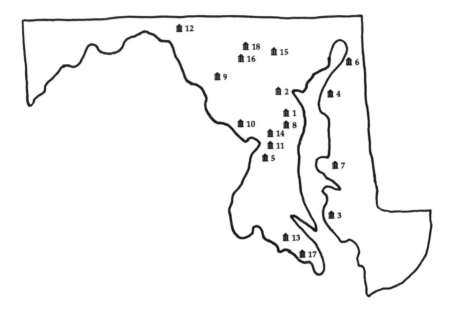

1. **Annapolis**
   Chase-Lloyd House
   Hammond-Harwood House

2. **Baltimore**
   Ballestone Manor
   Carroll Mansion
   Evergreen House
   The Rectory

3. **Cambridge**
   Meredith House

4. **Chestertown**
   Geddes-Piper House

5. **Clinton**
   Surratt House Museum

6. **Earleville**
   Mount Harmon Plantation

7. **Easton**
   *Joseph Neall House &
   James Neall House*

8. **Edgewater**
   London Town Publik House

9. **Fredrick**
   Home of Chief Justice Taney

10. **Glen Echo**
    *Clara Barton National
    Historic Site*

11. **Glenndale**
    Marietta

12. **Hagerstown**
    *Jonathan Hager House &
    Museum*
    Miller House

13. **Hollywood**
    Sotterly Mansion

14. **Laurel**
    Montpelier Mansion

15. **Monkton**
    Ladew House &Topiary Gardens

16. **New Windsor**
    *John Evans House–
    Robert Strawbridge House*

17. **St. Mary's City**
    Historic St. Mary's City

18. **Westminster**
    Carroll County Farm Museum
    Sherman-Fisher-Shellman House

Hammond-Harwood House

19 Maryland Avenue
Annapolis, MD 21401
(410) 269-1714

Contact: Hammond-Harwood House Association, Inc.

Open: Nov.-March, Mon., Wed.-Sat. 10 a.m.-4 p.m.; Sun. 12-4 p.m.; April-Oct., Mon., Wed.-Sat. 10 a.m.-5 p.m.; Sun. 12-5 p.m.

Admission: Adults $3.50; students (6-18) $2.50; under 6 free. Call for group rates. Guided tours, special events and programming.

Suggested Time to View House: 45-60 minutes

Facilities on Premises: Museum gift shop and garden open to the public

Description of Grounds: The garden is filled with trees, shrubs and flowers that reflect the indigenous flora of the region.

Best Season to View House: Spring and summer

Number of Yearly Visitors: 12,000

Year House Built: 1774

Style of Architecture: Georgian

Number of Rooms: 20, 12 open to public

On-Site Parking: No **Wheelchair Access:** Yes

Description of House

In 1774, Mathias Hammond (1748-1786) contracted with William Buckland to design and build his town house. Hammond was a fourth generation planter and patriot who had recently been elected to the Maryland legislature. Hammond's lawyer, Judge Jeremiah Townley Chase, purchased the house in 1811. Upon Judge Chase's death, the house was passed down to his heirs.

The Hammond-Harwood House, a National Historic Landmark, is an outstanding example of American colonial Georgian architecture. Constructed by the architect Willian Buckland, this elegant brick house uses the Palladian five-part plan popular in the Colonial Chesapeake region. Unlike many Colonial houses in America, this house is considered one of the most flawlessly proportioned Palladian-style houses. In addition to its matchless grace and proportioning, the architectural embellishments are outstanding and include exquisitely carved doorcases with a bull's-eye window. Period furnishings (1750-1820) fill the house, many of which belonged to the Harwood family and subsequent residents.

Notable Collections on Exhibit

The house exhibits an outstanding collection of 18th-century decorative arts featuring a display of Maryland furniture. These include many labeled pieces by John Shaw of Annapolis and portraits of the Harwood family and other famous Marylanders by the renowned artist, Charles Willson Peale. There are many other fine pieces in the collection encompassing 18th and 19th-century paintings, furniture, silver, ceramics, glass and textiles.

Chase-Lloyd House

22 Maryland Avenue
Annapolis, MD
(410) 263-2723

Contact: Chase-Lloyd Corporation
Open: March-Dec., Tues.-Sat. 2–4 p.m.;
Jan.-Feb., Thurs.-Sat. 2–4 p.m.
Admission: $1. Guided tours.
Suggested Time to View House:
20 minutes
Year House Built: 1769
Style of Architecture: Georgian
Number of Rooms: 15, 3 open to public
On-Site Parking: No
Wheelchair Access: No

Description of House

Construction of this gracious home was begun for Samuel Chase, one of the signers of the Declaration of Independence. The house was complete for the Lloyd family who lived here for seventy-three years. Mary Lloyd married Francis Scott Key, author of "The Star Spangled Banner" in this house in 1802. Another son, Edward Lloyd V, was governor of Maryland from 1809 to 1811. The house returned to the Chase family in 1845.

This large 18th-century Georgian-style house maintains many of its original features. The interior contains an elaborate cantilevered double staircase, hand-carved window surrounds, and all the original doors and shutters. One of the rooms features an Italian marble fireplace which was quite elaborate for the period. The house holds furnishings which represent a variety of styles from different periods and include several pieces that belonged to the Chase family.

Notable Collections on Exhibit

In addition to the collection of furniture, the house also exhibits personal objects belonging to Horatio Sharpe, governor of the colony in 1753, including a desk, tall clock and sword.

Ballestone Manor

Contact: Ballestone Preservation Society

Open: June-Aug., Sun. 2–5 p.m., other times by appointment

Admission: Free, donations accepted. Guided tours, living history weekend in Sept., Holly tours in December, June open house.

Suggested Time to View House: 30 minutes

Facilities on Premises: Gift shop

Best Season to View House: Spring-summer

Number of yearly visitors: 5000

Year House Built: 1780

On-Site Parking: Yes

Wheelchair Access: Yes

Style of Architecture: Federal

Description of House

Ballestone Manor stands on land which was part of an original land grant from Lord Baltimore to William Ball, the great-grandfather of George Washington. The early section of the house is credited to Dixon Stansbury, the grandson of a prominent Maryland family that had lived in the area since 1658. The nearby cemetery has the tombstones of many of the family members.

The elegant two-and-a-half story manor was constructed in the Federal-style of Flemish bond brick. Later additions in 1820 and 1850 nearly doubled the size of the house. In 1880, a two-story porch was added to the front facade. The furnishings have been purchased or borrowed over the years to reflect the period of 1780 to 1880 in American decorative arts. Costumed docents also represent this period during the guided tours and special exhibitions.

Notable Collections on Exhibit

The manor features specialized exhibits devoted to a variety of topics ranging from wedding gowns and vintage period clothing to lighting devices and quilts. The large exhibitions usually take place during the Holly Tour in December.

Additional Information

The grounds surrounding Ballestone are well-suited for the living history reenactments which take place on a regular basis. Each year Civil War scenes, and Revolutionary skirmishes are acted out on the lawn.

Carroll Mansion

800 East Lombard Street
Baltimore, MD 21202
(410) 396-3524

Contact: Baltimore City Life Museums
Open: Tues.-Sun. 10 a.m.–5 p.m.;
Nov.-March closes at 4 p.m.
Admission: Adults $1.75; discounts for
seniors and children. Self-guided tours,
docent-led tours, and living history
presentations.
Suggested Time to View House: 45 minutes
Facilities on Premises: Gift shop
Number of Yearly Visitors: 20,000
Year House Built: 1812
Style of Architecture: Federal
Number of Rooms: 7 open to public
On-Site Parking: Yes
Wheelchair Access: No

Description of House

This was the winter home of Charles Carroll between 1818 and 1832.
Carroll was was best known as a patriot and the last surviving signer of the
Declaration of Independence. Considered one of the largest and wealthiest
households in the city, Carroll lived here with his daughter and son-in-law
and a considerable number of servants.

Constructed in 1808 in the Federal style, Carroll Mansion was extensively renovated by Christopher Dershon in 1812 and again in 1818. The
house suffered deterioration over the years, but in the early 1960s, the house
was saved from destruction by concerned citizens of Maryland. Visitors
today will a striking entrance hall with a marble floor and impressive
staircase leading to the second floor along with several other furnished
period rooms. These include the hospitality room and office on the first floor
and the parlor, dining room, drawing room and library on the second.

The mansion is furnished with antiques in the style of the period from
1818 to 1832 when Charles Carroll lived here. Three objects have histories
of ownership in the Carroll family: a blue-upholstered shield-back side
chair, a red velvet armchair and a Sheffield silver entree dish.

Evergreen House

Contact: Johns Hopkins University
Open: Mon.-Fri. 10 a.m.–4 p.m.
Admission: Adults $5; children $2.50;
seniors $4. Guided tours, seasonal
symposia, concert series.
Suggested Time to View House: 90 minutes
Facilities on Premises: Museum shop,
garden tour
Description of Grounds: 26 acres of
park-like grounds
Best Season to View House: Spring and fall
Number of Yearly Visitors: 10,000
Year House Built: 1850s
Style of Architecture: Italianate
Number of Rooms: 48
On-Site Parking: Yes
Wheelchair Access: Yes

Description of House

This beautiful Italianate structure was built by the Broadbent family in the 1850s. John Garrett, president of the Baltimore and Ohio Railroad, purchased the house in 1878 for his son T. Harrison Garrett and his family. They expanded the house considerably over the years. John Work Garrett (1872-1942) inherited the house in 1920 and in the family tradition, continued with his wife, Alice Warder Garrett (1877-1952), to modify and expand Evergreen to it present status. During the 1920s and 1930s, the house was a center for cultural and civic pursuits in Baltimore. Distinguished statesmen, diplomats, authors, artists, and musicians, including Leopold Stowkowski and Alma Gluck, were guests of the Garretts.

This forty-eight room mansion reflects Italianate architecture with classical revival additions. The renovations of the 1880s led to the addition of a port-cochere and north wing which held a gymnasium, a bowling alley, a billiard room, gymnasium, and school rooms. The gymnasium was later converted to a theater by the famous Russian costume designer Leon Bakst known for his work with the Ballet Russe. In 1928, a rare book library was constructed to house 8,000 volumes collected by John Garrett and his father. Evergreen's furnishings are original to both generations of the Garrett family; the collection reflects their diverse personalities.

Notable Collections on Exhibit

Evergreen houses a notable collection of impressionist paintings (primarily French), rare books including Audobons, Goulds and other natural history works, and an outstanding collection of Tiffany chandeliers.

The Rectory

24 West Saratoga Street
Baltimore, MD 21201
(410) 685-2886

Contact: Preservation Maryland

Open: By appointment anytime or every first Thur. of the month 5:30–7:30 p.m.

Activities: Guided tours, special tours as requested

Suggested Time to View House: 25 minutes–1 hour

Facilities on Premises: Church

Description of Grounds: Very accessible to the public-also handicap accessible with ramp

Best Season to View House: Spring or fall

Year House Built: 1791

Style of Architecture: Federal-Late Georgian

Number of Rooms: 9

On-Site Parking: Yes **Wheelchair Access:** Yes

Description of House

First occupied in 1791, this magnificent landmark has recently been restored to its original beauty. The Rectory was built as a stately and gracious home for the sixth rector of Old St. Paul's Church (founded in 1692) and since 1791 it has served as home to nine other rectors and and their families.

This 18th-century structure is the oldest, freestanding residence left in Baltimore. The smaller original house was T-shaped; its materials, detailing and craftsmanship were all marks of construction of the highest order. Some of the notable details of the structure include a Palladium window, original pine floors, and an octagonally shaped bay with a winding staircase. There have been various additions and modifications over the years. The existing moldings, fireplaces, mantel shelves and window casings date from about 1815. The Rectory's furnishings reflect the late neoclassical period, most of them date from the late 1820s and 1830s with a concentration on Baltimore-made furniture.

Meredith House

**902 LaGrange Ave PO. Box 361
Cambridge, MD 21613
(410) 228-7953**

Contact: Dorchester County Historical
Society

Open: Thur., Fri., Sat. 10 a.m.–4 p.m., or by
appointment

Admission: Donation; large group $2 per
person. Guided tours.

Suggested Time to View House:
30–45 minutes

Facilities on Premises: Colonial style herb
garden on site

Best Season to View House: Spring,
summer, fall

Number of Yearly Visitors: 1000

Year House Built: 1760

Number of Rooms: 8

Style of Architecture: Georgian

On-Site Parking: Yes **Wheelchair Access:** No

Description of House

John Woolford, a successful farmer, built this lovely home in 1760. The next resident, Dr. William H. Muse, a highly respected physician and landowner, owned the property from 1847 to 1860 and renamed it LaGrange. A later occupant, Russell P. Smith, owned the property from 1921 to 1958. He was active in community, business, and govermental affairs, and served collectors of customs for the port of Baltimore during World War II. Meredith House takes its name from a benefactor who made the purchase of the house by the Dorechester Historical Society possible.

The historical society's collections are well represented in this two-and-a-half story brick Georgian dwelling with a gable roof. The house is three bays wide and two bays deep. Most of the interior woodwork is Greek Revival in style and dates to 1850. The interior also features five corner fireplaces, a tiger-stripe maple stair railing and balusters. The original kitchen wing was demolished and has been replaced by a two-story frame wing with gable roof and one central chimney. The furnishings for Meredith House have been collected from many sources and are generally appropriate for the late 18th and early 19th centuries.

Notable Collections on Exhibit

The building exhibits an eclectic series of collections ranging from 19th-century oil portraits of several Dorchester residents, possessions and memorabilia from seven Maryland governors associated with Dorchester county, a large collection of 19th-century dolls and children's toys, and several antique quilts.

Geddes-Piper House

101 Church Alley
Chestertown, MD 21620
(410) 778-3499

Contact: Historical Society of Kent County
Open: May-Oct., Sat.-Sun. 1–4 p.m., and by
   appointment
Admission: $1. Guided tours.
Suggested Time to View House:
   30–45 minutes
Facilities on Premises: Some items for sale
Description of Grounds: Small
   garden-herb garden, back yard
Number of Yearly Visitors: 4,000
Year House Built: Mid 1700s, rear
   addition 1830s
Style of Architecture: Georgian
Number of Rooms: 10 rooms
   (9 open for viewing)
On-Site Parking: No

Description of House

The house was built on a lot originally owned by James Moor, a brick-layer, and remained in the Moor family until 1784. According to research, Moor probably started building the house and then died, leaving its completion to his heirs. The heirs borrowed money to finish the house from William Geddes, a prominent citizen who was a Tory and loyal to the King, who also worked as the local customs collector. He bought the house from the Moors but never lived here. Within two months he sold it to the family of James Piper, a Chestertown merchant. Ownership then passed to the Westscott family who lived here for over eighty years. This impressive townhouse then fell into neglect when the building was converted to an apartment building in the early 20th century.

Today, the three-and-a-half story brick townhouse has been restored to its original elegance. The design of the house is similar to that of the Samuel Powel house and other townhouses built in Philadelphia in the late 1700s. The front portion of the house was built in the late 1700s and the back portion of the house was added in the 1830s. The house is symbolic of the Georgian style of architecture (based on the designs of Andrea Palladio) prevalent in the colonies at that time. Some furnishings are from the 18th century, others are original to the Westscott family; all of them have been donated by residents of Kent County.

Notable Collections on Exhibit

The Geddes-Piper House not only showcases a fine collection of period furniture, it also houses an unusual collection of fans and over thirty teapots from the 1700s. In addition, the house has a library pertaining to Kent County history and genealogy which is open to the public.

Surratt House Museum

9118 Brandywine Road
PO. Box 427
Clinton, MD 20735
(301) 868-1121

Contact: Maryland National Park
Open: March 1-Dec. 15, Thur.-Fri.
11 a.m.–3 p.m., Sat.-Sun. 12–4 p.m.
Admission: Adults $1; children $.50;
seniors $.75. Guided tours with
costumed docents, numerous special
events and exhibits.
Facilities on Premises: Visitors center, gift
shop
Suggested Time to View House: 1 hour
Description of Grounds: Limited grounds
with small herb garden, Picnic area on
grounds
Number of Yearly Visitors: 7000
Year House Built: 1852
Number of Rooms: 10

Style of Architecture: Georgian
On-Site Parking: Yes **Wheelchair Access:** Yes

Description of House

Built in 1852 for the family of John and Mary Surratt, this modest home and tavern has witnessed several historic events. The home served both as a family residence and a public establishment with a tavern and public dining room serving travelers and local gentlemen with sleeping accomodations available at 25 cents a night. The house has an unusual history in that the Surratts (like most of Maryland) sympathized with the South during the Civil War. The house became a safehouse on the Confederate espionage route and was used by numerous members of the Confederate underground which flourished in southern Maryland. In the fall of 1864, the Surratts also became involved with John Wilkes Booth in a scheme to capture Abraham Lincoln, and later helped him after the assassination. For her efforts, Mary Surratt was tried and convicted and holds the dubious distinction of being the first woman executed by the U.S. federal government.

The Surratt House was originally the focal point of a 300-acre plantation. Today, less than three acres still remain as part of the museum complex. All of the furnishings in the house are of the same period with several original Surratt pieces.

Additional Information

The house has a research library and is associated with the Surratt Society, a 900 member organization including prominent researchers and scholars in the Lincoln assassination field.

Mount Harmon Plantation

P.O. Box 65
Earleville, MD 21919
(410) 275-8819

Contact: Natural Lands Trust
Open: April-Oct., Tues.-Thur. 10 a.m.–3 p.m.;
May 15-Oct., Sun. 1–4 p.m., other times
by special arrangement
Admission: $3.75. Guided tours of
plantation house, outside kitchen,
boxwood garden and tobacco Prize
House and Wharf.

Description of Grounds: The 386-acre
Mount Harmon contains formal boxwood
and wisteria gardens reflecting the 1760
to 1810 period and nature trails
Year House Built: 1730
Style of Architecture: Georgian

Description of House

Mount Harmon Plantation began in 1651 as a land grant of 350 acres to Godfrey Harmon by Caecilius Calvert, the second Lord Baltimore, who owned all of Maryland. Over the years it became a typical plantation of the colonial time—an isolated and self-sufficient unit producing tobacco for direct shipment back to England. In later years, from 1760 to 1810, the plantation was owned by the Louttit and George families. James Louttit, Sr., originally from Glasgow, Scotland, and his wife, Mary George bought Mount Harmon and shipped tobacco to Scotland on their schooner, "The Bee." Phoebe George Bradford, their granddaughter, lived at Mount Harmon until 1810. In 1817, when she traded properties with her half sister, the plantation went to another branch of the family. The property belonged to Sidney George Fisher of Philadelphia and his son, until 1927. From 1963 to 1975, Mrs. Harry Clark Boden IV, a direct descendant of the Louttit and George families, expertly restored the manor house and its grounds.

The manor house at Mount Harmon is a three-story, five-bay structure of the Georgian period. There is a separate kitchen furnished with authentic kitchen artifacts of the colonial period. The house stands on a knoll virtually surrounded by creeks and inlets of the Sassafras River. The area is known on early maps as "World's End," and the farm's isolation is perpetuated today by the winding two-mile lane approaching from the highway. From the house, the rolling fields open dramatically to long vistas of the river and Chesapeake Bay. The house is furnished with American, English, Irish and Scottish antiques which reflect the 1760 to 1810 period, the "golden age" of Mount Harmon.

Additional Information

The outbuildings and surrounding grounds make a visit to Mount Harmon especially enjoyable. Visitors will see the original Tobacco Prize House where tobacco was prepared for shipment to England, a chapel hidden in the nearby woods, a nature preserve, and a pair of magnificent yew trees, thought to be the oldest in the United States.

Joseph Neall House & James Neall House

25 S. Washington St., P.O. Box 964
Easton, MD 21601
(410) 822-0773

Contact: The Historical Society of Talbot County

Open: Tues.-Sat. 10 a.m.–4 p.m., closed major holidays

Admission: Adults $2; children $.50; under 6 free. Guide program "Welcome to Talbot County" for groups only. Self guided and supervised tours available.

Suggested Time to View House: 90 minutes to see 3 buildings

Facilities on Premises: Gift shop

Description of Grounds: Federal-style gardens open to public

Best Season to View House: Spring to fall

Style of Architecture: Late Colonial, Federal Townhouse

Year House Built: 1795 and 1810

Number of Yearly Visitors: 6,000

Number of Rooms: Joseph Neall-4, James Neall-7

On-Site Parking: Yes **Wheelchair Access:** Yes

Description of House

The Neall brothers lived side by side in these two buildings which bear their names. Joseph and James Neall were Quakers who worked as cabinetmakers in Easton during the early Federal period. Joseph was a bachelor, while James married and had twelve children. Both took in apprentices and Joseph had four to six helpers at any given time as well as an indentured servant. James lived with his brother in the smaller three room dwelling before building the larger townhouse next door.

The Joseph Neall House is a small Colonial-style dwelling with two rooms downstairs and one upstairs. The house is furnished according to the items listed on the inventory at the time of his death and include a dresser believed to have been made by him.

The James Neall House is a four-story Federal townhouse built between 1804 and 1810. The house had two rooms on each floor as well as a basement used for food storage. In 1813, James addied a breakfast/office room and warming kitchen to the first floor. Later James sold the house to Jabez Caldwell who moved Joseph's house and made structural changes to the townhouse. All of the furnishings are collected and appropriate to the period.

Notable Collections on Exhibit

The society sponsors three or four museum exhibitions each year and also collects furnishings, textiles, other decorative arts, and photographs.

Additional Information

The guided tour is centered around Quaker life in Talbot County and cabinetmaking industry. In addition, the society also runs the nearby "End of Controversie" House Museum built by the well-known architect, historian, and author Dr. H. Chandlee Forman.

London Town Publik House

839 Londontown Road
Edgewater, MD 21037
(410) 222-1919

Contact: London Town Publik House &
Gardens

Admission: Adults $2.50; children $1;
seniors $2. Tours of house, tape tours,
luncheon, seasonal historical events.

Suggested Time to View House:
30-45 minutes

Facilities on Premises: 1–2 hours with
gardens

Description of Grounds: 10 acres
woodhand gardens

Best Season to View House: April, May,
June

Number of Yearly Visitors: 20,000

Year House Built: 1758

Number of Rooms: 18

Style of Architecture: Georgian

On-Site Parking: Yes **Wheelchair Access:** Yes

Description of House

The London Town Publik House is the only surviving structure from one of Maryland's earliest towns. William Brown, a local planter and cabinetmaker, started construction of this large brick house overlooking the ferry landing in 1758 and eventually completed it in the mid-1760s. The Publik House served as an inn into the 1790s, by which time London Town had declined as a port town. Later the building served as a residence for Maryland Governor John Hoskins and others. In 1828, the building was purchased by the country for use as an almshouse and it continued to house indigent residents until 1965.

This impressive brick structure features an exterior of the regionally distinct all-header bond. The building today has been restored to its original Colonial appearance. The mid 18th-century furnishings reflect the many activities of the tavern and the innkeepers household.

Additional Information

In addition to the tavern, visitors may also visit the accompanying London Town Gardens which feature an extensive array of narcissus, magnolias, azaleas and other examples of both common and rare species.

Home of Chief Justice Taney

**121 South Bentz Street
Frederick, MD 21701**

Contact: Francis Scott Key Memorial
Foundation, Inc.

Open: June-Oct. 1, weekends 10 a.m.–4 p.m.

Admission: $2. Guided tours.

Suggested Time to View House: 30 minutes

Facilities on Premises: Gift shop

Best Season to View House: Spring and
summer

Number of Yearly Visitors: 500

Year House Built: 1799

Number of Rooms: 4

Style of Architecture: Saltbox

On-Site Parking: No

Wheelchair Access: No

Description of House

This modest dwelling was home to the noted judge Roger Brooke Taney, author of the Dred Scott decision. Born in Calvert County in 1777, he graduated from Dickinson College and was elected to the legislature. In 1806, he married Anne Key, sister of Francis Scott Key, author of the national anthem. In the following years he became a member of the Maryland senate, state attorney general, attorney general of the United States, secretary of war, secretary of the treasury, and then Chief Justice of the Supreme Court replacing John Marshall. His most famous decision was the celebrated Dred Scott case, the controversial decision favoring the slave owners which was later reversed by the Civil War. He died in 1864 in Washington.

This historic house has several completely furnished period rooms including a drawing room, dining room, a master bedroom, and kitchen as well as a museum devoted to Taney artifacts. There are also separate slave quarters, typical in structure to many others found in the South.

Notable Collections on Exhibit

The house is filled with Judge Taney memorabilia and artifacts and include a painting of the Lincoln's inaugral of 1861, portraits of the seven Presidents Taney swore into office, Taney's Supreme Court robe, the Taney and Key Coats-of-Arms, 18th and early 19th-century lawbooks, and a Queen Anne chair and parlor organ which may have been used by Francis Scott Key.

Clara Barton National Historic Site

5801 Oxford Road
Glen Echo, MD 20812
(301) 492-6245

Contact: National Park Service
Open: Daily 10 a.m.–5 p.m., closed Jan. 1,
Thanksgiving, and Christmas Day
Admission: Free. Guided tours.
Suggested Time to View House: 1 hour
Best Season to View House: Spring-summer
Style of Architecture: Gothic Revival

Facilities on Premises: Gift shop
Year House Built: 1891
On-Site Parking: Yes **Wheelchair Access:** Yes

Description of House

Clara Barton, humanitarian and founder of the American Red Cross, lived here the last fifteen years of her life. Barton devoted her live to serving others, first as an educator and later aiding the wounded in the Civil War. During the Franco-Prussian War, she labored to help the war-stricken civilians of France and Germany. She was so impressed with the Red Cross that she became determined to carry its ideals to the United States. Even after she retired and built this lovely home, she continued to be active and worked on the Cuban battlefields during the Spanish-American war. She died at home on April 12, 1912.

Built specifically for Barton, the house in Glen Echo features a steam-boat-style exterior based on Barton's own preferences. The interior is Gothic Revival in style and features many of Barton's furnishings. In addition, the attractive gardens were also designed according to her specifications.

Marietta

5626 Bell Station Road
Glenndale, MD 20769
(301) 464-5291

Contact: Maryland National Capital Park
Commission

Open: March-Dec., Sun., 12–4pm; groups
by appointment

Admission: Adults $2; seniors $1; children
$.50; school groups free. Guided tours,
special events (Mad Hatters Tea Party,
candlelight tours)

Suggested Time to View House:
45–60 minutes

Facilities on Premises: Gift shop

Description of Grounds: 25 acres of lawns,
historic and champion trees and the
Judge's Law office

Best Season to View House: Spring and fall

Number of Yearly Visitors: 1,200

Year House Built: c. 1812, addition 1832

Number of Rooms: 7

Style of Architecture: Federal

On-Site Parking: Yes **Wheelchair Access:** No

Description of House

This Federal-style house was built by the respected politican Gabriel Duvall (1752-1844) around 1812. Duvall served in many capacities during his career in politics including representative to the Congress, Presidential elector for Thomas Jefferson (1796-1800), and U.S. Supreme Court Justice. The house stayed in the Duvall family until 1902; the last private owners were Margaret Scherer and Paul Scherer from 1945 to 1978.

This brick Federal-style house has two stories plus a basement and dormered attic. The front or south side of the house is Flemish bond. The first story nine-by-nine windows have stone jack arches with a keystone. The interior features a center hall with staircase with a parlor and dining room on either side. Both dining room and parlor have original window saches, fireplaces, doors and woodwork. The second story has two large bedrooms and a small bedroom that was converted into a bathroom in the 20th century.

The furnishings are period antiques (1790-1840) and reproductions as well as a few Duvall family pieces. Marietta also houses a notable collection of Chinese export porcelain owned and used by Judge Duvall.

Additional Information

The historical society's library of county history is on the site and open to the public on Saturday from 12–4 p.m., year round. Gabriel Duvall's remains, along with several family members and tombstones, have been moved to the Marietta property.

Jonathan Hager House & Museum

**19 Key St
Hagerstown, MD 21740
(301) 739-8393**

Contact: City of Hagerstown

Open: Open April-Dec.; Tues.-Sat.
10 a.m.–4 p.m., Sun. 2–5 p.m.

Admission: Adults $2; children (6-12) $1;
group rates on request. Guided tours of
Hager House; adjacent museum
building containing artifacts on site is
on self-guided tour.

Suggested Time to View House: 30 minutes

Facilities on Premises: Gift shop

Description of Grounds: Located in
Hagerstown city park, grounds are
accessible during daylight hours.

Best Season to View House: Late spring
and summer

Number of Yearly Visitors: 20,000

Year House Built: 1739

Number of Rooms: 6 plus 3 cellar rooms

Style of Architecture: German traditional

On-Site Parking: Yes **Wheelchair Access:** No

Description of House

Jonathan Hager, founder of Hagerstown, built this German-style home
in 1739 and lived here with his wife, Elizabeth, until 1745. Hager founded
the city in 1762 and later served on Maryland state assembly 1771 to 1775.

This two-and-a-half story stone house is unique in that it is built over
two still-flowing springs. This gave the Hagers a constant and protected
water supply. The house also served as a "house-fort" where settlers could
come during Indian attacks. All of the furnishings are collected and appropriate for the period of the Hager's residency. They include many 18th-
century German pieces.

Additional Information

An adjacent building, the Hager Museum, contains numerous artifacts
found on the site during restoration and excavation. The Hager House is
surrounded by herbal gardens showcasing plants readily available in 18th
century.

Miller House

135 West Washington Street
Hagerstown, MD 21740
(301) 797-8782

Contact: Washington County Historical Society

Open: Wed.-Fri. 1–4 p.m.; Sat.-Sun. 2–5 p.m. Closed Jan.-March and first week of Dec.

Admission: Adults $2; seniors $1; children free. Guided tours, occasional shows of quilts, needlework, other artifacts.

Suggested Time to View House: 1–3 hours, depending on interest

Facilities on Premises: Gift area

Description of Grounds: A small, early 19th-century-style garden with appropriate varieties of flowers, fruits, herbs, and vegetables

Best Season to View House: May and June

Number of Yearly Visitors: 2000

Year House Built: 1818 and 1825

Style of Architecture: Federal

Number of Rooms: 20

On-Site Parking: No **Wheelchair Access:** No

Description of House

The Bells and their children lived here beginning in 1804 and made pottery for nineteen years. Peter Bell was the father and grandfather of thirteen potters who worked in the Shenandoah Valley from Pennsylvania to Virginia and whose work is of great interest to collectors today. According to family records, Peter Bell Jr. built a new house on this lot in 1818 that now constitutes a back wing. In 1823, the house was sold to prominent attorney and politician William Price (1793-1868). He, in turn, later sold the property to Alexander Neill, Jr. (1808-1864) a U.S. attorney under Presidents Harrison and Tyler, who was also prominent in local politics and banking. The Neill family continued to live in the house until 1912 and the son, Alexander Neill III, was one of the incorporators of the historical society in 1911.

The original dwelling which housed the Bells was probably a log house. The 1818 back wing was constructed in a style known as a flounder house. This two-story brick addition has a half gable roof and is named for the flat fish because its high side is blind (windowless) and normally falls on the property line. The wing is comprised of an entry, a formal dining room, a restored period kitchen, two enclosed stairways, and bedrooms above. The two large drawing rooms with their eleven foot, nine inch ceilings are furnished with pieces made between the 1760s and 1830s. The rest of the furnishings are mostly of the period of the house.

Notable Collections on Exhibit

The Miller House showcases an extensive exhibit of 285 dolls made of china, bisque, wax, wood,cloth, papier mache which range from 1840 to modern by German, French, and American makers. One room also contains artifacts from the Civil War (the Battle of Antietam). There are also over 200 clocks, including eleven tall case clocks from the late 18th and early 19th century (four locally made) on display. A collection of country store items from the 1880s to the 1920s, including an old post office is on the lower level.

Sotterly Mansion

P.O. Box 67
Hollywood, MD 20636
(301) 373-2280

Contact: Sotterly Mansion Foundation, Inc.
Open: June-Oct., Tues.-Sun. 11 a.m.–4 p.m.
Admission: Adult $4, senior citizens $3,
children $2. Guided tours of the
mansion and special plantation exhibit.
Suggested Time to View House: 1 hour
Facilities on Premises: Gift shop
Description of Grounds: The gardens and
grounds are open to the public year
round

Best Season to View House: June-Oct.
Year House Built: c.1715
Number of Rooms: Eight

Number of Yearly Visitors: 17,500
Style of Architecture: Georgian
On-Site Parking: Yes **Wheelchair Access:** Yes

Description of House

The site of Sotterly was included in a 1650 manorial grant from Lord
Baltimore to Thomas Cornwallis, but James Bowles, son of London merchant and an influential Maryland officeholder, was the first to construct a
house here, circa 1717. In 1729, his widow married George Plater II (1695-
1755) and thereby began an important dynasty that would own Sotterly,
named after the ancient family home in Suffolk, England for nearly a
century. The Plater family was made up of wealthy landowners, merchants,
and Colonial officials. After Sotterly passed out of the Plater family in 1822,
it was occupied by Dr. Walter Hanson Stone Briscoe and his descendants
until 1910. The Satterlee family purchased the house in 1910 and were
responsible for its restoration and preservation in this century.

The main house or mansion is one of the only wooden plantation great
houses open to the public on the eastern seaboard, and is one of only a
handful, public or private, that have survived the ravages of time. When the
Platers expanded Sotterly, they hired Richard Boulton to build the Chinese
Chippendale staircase and to carve the exquisite woodwork in the drawing
room ranked as one of the "100 most beautiful rooms in America." This
distinctive mansion may have served as an architectural model for George
Washington's Mount Vernon. Sotterly is still a working plantation, and as
such is a microcosm of 300 years of America's cultural history. The furnishings are an eclectic mixture of almost three centuries of residency.

Montpelier Mansion

9402 Montpelier Drive
Laurel, MD 20708
(301) 953-1376

Contact: Maryland National Park &
Planning Commission

Open: Open March–1st week in Dec., Sun.
12–4 p.m. Closed holidays.

Admission: Adults $1.50; children $.50;
seniors $1. Guided tours

Suggested Time to View House: 45–60
minutes

Facilities on Premises: Gift Shop

Best Season to View House: Spring and fall

Number of Yearly Visitors: 8,000

Year House Built: 1781 to 1783

Style of Architecture: Georgian Style

Number of Rooms: 15

Description of House

Montpelier was built by Major Thomas Snowden and remained in the hands of the Snowden family until 1888. In the years following 1888 the estate passed in quick succession to the Davis-Chollar, Taylor and Blakeman families. In 1901, the land was purchased by Edmund H. Pendleton. Ownership was then followed by Emmanuel Havenith, envoy extraordinaire and minister to the U.S. from Belgium. Montpelier was held briefly by Mrs. Eleanor Fitzgibbon in 1918. Miss Nelly, as she was called, worked diligently to restore the agricultural heritage of the estate.

The house is Georgian style with a five part composition—main block, two wings and two hyphens—exhibiting the formal symmetry and balance of architecture of the mid to late 18th century. The 18th-century portion of the house has fifteen rooms excluding the attic, cellar, and early 20th-century additions.

Montpelier's furnishings are based on an inventory of Nicholas Snowden's taken after his death in 1831. Select rooms have been researched and furnished as they may have appeared from 1800 to 1830. Several pieces have been donated by the Snowden family but the majoritty of the furnishings are of the proper period and not original to the house.

Ladew House & Topiary Gardens

3535 Jarrettsville Pike
Monkton, MD 21111
(410) 557-9570

Contact: Ladew Topiary Gardens Inc.

Open: Group reservations, Christmas open house

Activities: Guided tours, self guided tours

Suggested Time to View House: House 45 minutes; gardens 1 hour

Facilities on Premises: Gift shop; Carriage Museum cafe

Description of Grounds: 22 acres of theme and topiary gardens

Best Season to View House: Spring-fall

Year House Built: 1750-1850 post 1929 3 sections

Style of Architecture: Country Manor style

Number of Rooms: 10

Number of Yearly Visitors: 35,000

On-Site Parking: Yes **Wheelchair Access:** No

Description of House

The house and gardens are named after the most famous occupant of the estate, Harvey Smith Ladew (1886-1976). Ladew was born into wealth and learned at an early age to cultivate his tastes in collecting and gardening. He was a man accustomed to living in mansions and manor houses and ended up devoting a good part of his life (from 1929 to 1977) in this simple, clapboard house in Pleasant Valley.

Ladew transformed this modest farmhouse, built during the late 1700s and early 1800s, into an English manor house to suit his lifestyle of hunting and collecting. The interior was renovated using the skills of New York architect James O'Connor. The architectural details of the drawing room, the broken pediments and molding, were copied from the Hammond-Harwood House in Annapolis. The Oval Library, considered one of 100 most beautiful rooms in America, was constructed specifically to house an oval Chippendale desk which Ladew had acquired. He also built a room to house rare Elizabethan paneling found in an antique shop in London. The house and gardens are listed on the National Register of Historic Places.

Notable Collections on Exhibit

The house is filled with paintings related to Ladew's passions, hunting and sporting, by a number of well-known artists. Because of Ladew's tastes and travels the collections are eclectic—there is everything ranging from a display of Staffordshire figurines to an ancient bronze Buddha to a china set with hand-painted hunt scenes.

Additional Information

The gardens utilize an unusual balance of topiary and natural plants, water, architecture and sculpture and reflect Ladew's extraordinary horticultural perception. The crowning glory of the twenty-two acres is the topiary—trees and shrubs trained and trimmed to create ornamental shapes.

John Evans House-
Robert Strawbridge House

2650 Strawbridge Lane
New Windsor, MD 21776
(410) 635-2600

Contact: Strawbridge Shrine Association

Open: Daily 10 a.m.–5 p.m.; groups by
appointment

Admission: Free. Guided tours.

Suggested Time to View House: 20 minutes

Description of Grounds: Farm buildings
(18th-19th Century)

Best Season to View House: All

Number of Yearly Visitors: 1000

Year House Built: Evans-c. 1764,
Strawbridge-c. 1768

Style of Architecture: Log Cabins

Number of Rooms: Evans-4, Strawbridge-7

On-Site Parking: Yes **Wheelchair Access:** No

Description of House

These two, unpretentious log cabins were home to the origins of a major American religious denomination, Methodism, during a period of national turmoil, the American Revolution. While living in the four-room log structure from 1760 to 1776, Robert Strawbridge began the Methodist movement in America, and the structure is considered the founding place of American Methodism. Strawbridge purchased the fifty-acre property from the landlord in 1773. The most recent owners (1919-1973) were the Haines family, the last of whom still resides in the Strawbridge House. The last occupant sold the property to Strawbridge Shrine Association in 1973.

The Evans house has been relocated to the present site. Not a conventional dwelling, the house served as the meeting place of the first Methodists from 1768 to 1809. This log meetinghouse today is furnished with early 19th-century benches and a replica of an 18th-century pulpit. Currently, exhibits for both of the structures are being assembled by the association.

Historic St. Mary's City

Route 5, P.O. Box 39
St. Mary's City, MD 20686
(301) 862-0990

Contact: Historic St.Mary's City
Open: March-Nov., Wed.-Sun.
    10 a.m.–5 p.m.
Admission: Adults $5; children $2
Suggested Time to View House: 2 hours
Facilities on Premises: Gift shop
Number of Yearly Visitors: 60,000 plus
Year House Built: Varied:1680 to 1840
On-Site Parking: Yes
Wheelchair Access: Yes

Description of House

St. Mary's City was founded in 1634 as the capital city of Lord Baltimore's new Maryland colony. In its short heydey of little more than sixty years, the city was host to many significant events. These historic events included the establishment of the first Catholic Church in English America, the vote of the first black, Mathias de Sousa, in a legislature, and the first woman to request a vote in 1647, Mistress Margaret Brent, lived here. Today, St. Mary's City is a living history museum with historic structures (some original, some reconstructed) and demonstrations of 17th-century life.

There are several fascinating homes and related structures for visitors to see today. Because St. Mary's was the capital of a growing colony, there were a number of taverns and inns where travelers could spend time. The Van Sweringen site represents the site of a colonial lodging house of the 1680s. Van Sweringen's has been partially reconstructed, and one can view portions of the 17th-century brick floor of the tavern where members of the Governor's Council used to meet.

Structures of a later period are also represented in this historic city. The Brome-Howard House is a beautiful example of Greek Revival architecture. Built in 1840 by Dr. John Brome, this restored plantation house interprets 19th-century St. Mary's City in its exhibits and furnishings.

In addition, the town also contains a recreation of a 1660s tobacco plantation, a reconstructed State House from 1676, and an authentic working recreation of a 1630s square-rigged ship, the "Maryland Dove". St. Mary's is unique in that it presents both living history and on-going archeological excavations to uncover more of the city's history. Visitors will be able to see remains of the first Catholic chapel, the home of the first governor, and other evidence of the rich historical treasure which awaits further excavation and discovery.

Carroll County Farm Museum

500 South Center Street
Westminster, MD 21157
(410) 848-7775

Contact: Carroll County Farm Museum
Open: May-Oct., weekends 12–5 p.m.;
  July-Aug, Tues.-Fri. 10 a.m.–4 p.m.
Admission: Adults $3; children $2.
Suggested Time to View House: 20–40
  minutes
Facilities on Premises: Nature trail, gardens,
  farm exhibit buildings, craft shops

Best Season to View House: June
Number of Yearly Visitors: 90,000
Year House Built: 1852-53
Style of Architecture: Rural modified-
  Georgian
Number of Rooms: 6 open to public
Wheelchair Access: Yes

Description of House

The farmhouse was the county almshouse from 1853 to 1965. This three-story, brick house was laid out in the symmetrical style of a Georgian house. Today, only the first floor is open to the public. The farmhouse maintains many of its original features, and visitors may also see the original stenciling on the walls of several of the rooms. The house is decorated as a single family farmhouse of the 1800s and is filled with period pieces which convey the lifestyle of a farm. There are also several family portraits of the Wagner family (former occupants) hanging on the walls.

Notable Collections on Exhibit

The house exhibits several displays related to agriculture which include the Linwood Feedmill records, Palmer Pump paraphernalia, 19th and early 20th-century veterinary equipment, and farming equipment.

Sherman-Fisher-Shellman House

210 East Main Stret
Westminster, MD 21157
(410) 848-6494

Contact: Historical Society of Carroll County

Admission: Adults $2.50; seniors $2; students $1; children (under 6) free. Guided tours, audiovisual presentations and special programs.

Suggested Time to View House: 1 hour

Facilities on Premises: Gift shop

Best Season to View House: Spring-summer

Number of Yearly Visitors: 600

Year House Built: 1807

Style of Architecture: Early Georgian

Description of House

Although located in Maryland, this house was first home to a typical Pennsylvania German household headed by Jacob Sherman. It is believed that Sherman built this house when he retired from innkeeping in 1807. Although rumored to have been a wedding present for his daughter Eva and her husband David, it was very common practice at the time for the newlyweds to take possession of the house in which the parents still lived. In May 1807, the house was deeded to the young couple, and Jacob and his wife, Elizabeth, continued to live there until his death in 1822. During the rest of the 19th century the house had several owners including John Fisher and Catherine Jones Shellman. The house witnessed several skirmishes during the Civil War and was occupied briefly by Confederate soldiers in 1864.

When the Sherman-Fisher-Shellman house was constructed in 1807, it was the most impressive structure along Westminster's main street. This regional farmhouse's architecture is rooted in the style and cultural traditions of the Pennsylvania Germans. This style is distinguished by an L-shaped plan with an ell that serves as a service wing to the residential main block. The rear of the house shows the double-tiered porch that was a popular feature of this style.. Other architectural features of the house are very refined and display Anglo-American influences that portray the affluence of the first owner, Jacob Sherman.

Several details distinguish the house from others in the area. Particularly striking is the large size and proportions of the main facade with its over-sized windows and molded serpentine brick cornice. The architecture incorporates a number of innovations, included the counter-balanced windows, built-in cupboards, and kitchen waste water drain of quarried stone. The house features a number of furnished period rooms, decorated with furniture owned by the Shermans and the Shellmans.

New Jersey

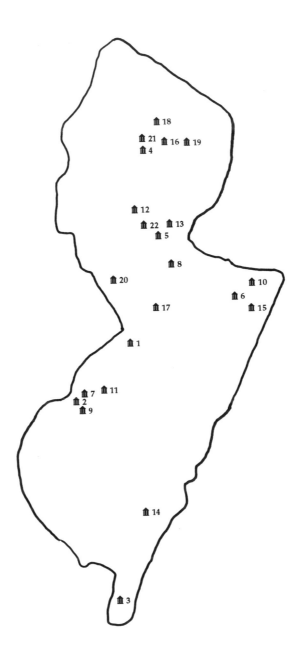

1. **Burlington**
   Captain James Lawrence House
   Cooper House
   Pearson-How House

2. **Camden**
   Pomona Hall
   Walt Whitman House

3. **Cape May**
   Emlen Physick Estate

4. **Cedar Grove**
   Canfield-Morgan House

5. **Clark**
   Dr. William Robinson Plantation House

6. **Freehold**
   Craig House

7. **Haddonfield**
   Greenfield Hall

8. **Jamesburg**
   'Lakeview' The Buckelew Mansion

9. **Laurel Springs**
   Whitman-Stafford Farmhouse

10. **Lincroft**
    Longstreet Farmhouse

11. **Moorestown**
    Smith-Cadbury Mansion

12. **Morristown**
    Macculloch Hall Historical Museum

13. **Newark**
    The Ballantine House

14. **Northfield**
    Risley Homestead

15. **Ocean Grove**
    Centennial Cottage

16. **Paterson**
    Lambert Castle

17. **Princeton**
    Bainbridge House
    Thomas Clarke House

18. **Ridgewood**
    Ringwood Manor

19. **River Edge**
    The Steuben House
    Campbell-Christie House

20. **Titusville**
    Johnson Ferry House

21. **Wayne**
    Dey Mansion/Washington's Headquarters Museum

22. **Westfield**
    Miller-Cory House Museum

Captain James Lawrence House

459 High Street
Burlington, NJ 08016
(609) 286-4773

Contact: Burlington County Historical
Society
Open: Sun. 2–4 p.m.; Mon.-Thur. 1–4 p.m.;
groups by reservation only.
Admission: Donations accepted. Guided
tours.
Suggested Time to View House: 20 minutes
Facilities on Premises: Gift shop, library
Number of Yearly Visitors: 900
Year House Built: c. 1742, remodeled 1820
(Federal style)
Style of Architecture: Colonial
Number of Rooms: 5

On-Site Parking: No **Wheelchair Access:** No

Description of House

James Lawrence was born on the first of October, 1781 at at this modest home on High Street. He was the youngest son of John Brown Lawrence and his second wife, Martha Tallman. Prior to the Revolution, John Lawrence was one of Burlington's most prominent citizens. Martha bore ten children, seven girls and three boys, but died shortly after the birth of James. James attended law school in Woodbury but returned to Burlington to learn navigation and naval tactics. Lawrence distinguished himself during the battle of Tripoli, and continued his naval career by commanding the Vixen, Wasp, Argus, and Hornet. Lawrence is best known, however, for uttering the famous cry "Don't give up the ship!" during his battle against Shannon in the War of 1812 when he was fatally wounded.

The two-story, brick Lawrence house was built in two sections, the first in 1742, the second in 1767. Later in 1844, the house was covered with stucco. The furnishings were collected from the late 18th century, and early 19th century. Several items—fancy Sheraton chairs with rush bottom seats—are said to have belonged to the Lawrence family.

Notable Collections on Exhibit

An exhibit of children's toys and a costume exhibit are displayed on the second floor. The costume exhibit changes frequently. The house also features a tall case clock crafted by Morgan Hollinshead with a painted dial depicting a mourning scene. The Fenimore family piano (c. 1840-1870), manufactured by the A.H. Gale Company, is on display in the music room along with mandolins and a zither (c. 1880).

Pearson-How House

453 High Street
Burlington, NJ 08016
(609) 286-4773

Contact: Burlington County Historical
Society
Open: Sun. 2–4 p.m.; Mon.-Thur. 1–4 p.m.;
groups by reservation only.
Admission: Donations accepted. Guided
tours.
Suggested Time to View House: 20 minutes
Facilities on Premises: Gift shop, library
Number of Yearly Visitors: 900
Year House Built: circ. 1705; addition 1725
Style of Architecture: Colonial
Number of Rooms: 8
On-Site Parking: No
Wheelchair Access: No

Description of House

Built in 1705, the Pearson-How House is the oldest of the structures run by the historical society. This lovely two-and-a-half, brick Colonial dwelling is an excellent example of the provincial vernacular Georgian style, prevalent in South Jersey during the early 18th century. Visitors will not be disappointed by the fine array of period furnishings which have been collected for display in the house.

Notable Collections on Exhibit

Among the many notable items on display is a fine example of one of Isaac Pearson's (a prominent Burlington County clockmaker) tall case clocks. The rest of the home is furnished with decorative arts from the 18th century.

Cooper House

457 High Street
Burlington, NJ 08016
(609) 286-4773

Contact: Burlington County Historical
Society

Open: Sun. 2–4 p.m.; Mon.-Thur. 1–4 p.m.;
groups by reservation only.

Admission: Donations accepted. Guided
tours

Suggested Time to View House: 20 minutes

Facilities on Premises: Gift shop, library

Number of Yearly Visitors: 900

Year House Built: c. 1780

Style of Architecture: Colonial

Number of Rooms: 4

On-Site Parking: No

Wheelchair Access: No

Description of House

Author James Fenimore Cooper, son of William Cooper and Elizabeth Fenimore, was born in this house on September 15, 1789. James Fenimore Cooper is known as America's first novelist and the author of *The Last of the Mohicans* and *The Deerslayer*.

The two-and-a-half story Cooper House was erected circa 1780 by Samual How. The exterior features stuccoed brick. Architecturally, the house combines a mixture of Greek and Federal elements. The building houses four separate museum rooms displaying Cooper artifacts and period furnishings. There is also a separate room devoted to exhibiting furnishings owned by Joseph Bonaparte, the brother of Napoleon Bonaparte.

Notable Collections on Exhibit

Among the many Cooper artifacts on display is a pen and ink sketch of Cooper as a young man of seventeen years drawn by Wesley Jarvis in 1806. The Bonaparte furnishings, which were moved from his estate known as "Point Breeze" in Bordentown, include a bed, nightstand, and vanity as well as other household items. A Chippendale chest-on-chest (c. 1750) augments the other fine furnishings displayed in this historic house.

Pomona Hall

Park Blvd. and Euclid Avenue
Camden, NJ 08103
(609) 964-3333

Contact: Camden County Historical Society
Open: Mon.-Thurs. 12:30–4:30 p.m.; Sat.
1–4 p.m.; Sun. 2 –4:30 p.m.
Admission: Adults $2; seniors and students
$1; children under 16 free. Guided tours;
videos; open hearth cooking and spinning
demonstrations are also possible by prior
arrangement.

Suggested Time to View House: 90 minutes
Year House Built: 1726
Style of Architecture: Georgian
Number of Rooms: 9
On-Site Parking: No **Wheelchair Access:** Yes

Description of House

Pomona Hall, home to the historical society and its museum of collections, illustrates simple 18th-century elegance. The two story, brick house was built in 1726 by Joseph Cooper, Jr., a prominent Quaker farmer. Later, in 1788, Marmaduke Cooper built an addition to this Georgian-style home.

The furnishings are authentic 18th and 19th-century furnishings; several belonged to the Cooper family. Pomona Hall also features a series of exhibits which represent work, play, and family and community life in southern New Jersey as well as a library with an extensive collection of photographic and print resources.

Notable Collections on Exhibit

The exhibits in the museum part of the house feature reconstructed "shops" found in 18th-century communties. These include the blacksmith's, candlemaker's, cooper's and weavers. There are also displays of early American glass, lighting devices, firefighting equipment, toys and household implements, as well as transportation, military and industrial artifacts. In addition, the library houses a vast collection of printed, photographic and other materials related to Camden County and New Jersey, including 20,000 books plus pamphlets, maps, deeds, slides, photographs, and genealogical records.

Walt Whitman House

330 Mickle Blvd
Camden, NJ 08103
(609) 964-5383

Contact: New Jersey State Park Services
Open: Wed.-Sun., hours vary, please call.
   Closed holidays.
Activities: Guided tours only at this time
Suggested Time to View House: 1 hour
Year House Built: c. 1840s
Number of Rooms: 7

Number of Yearly Visitors: 2-3,000
Style of Architecture: Greek Revival
On-Site Parking: No **Wheelchair Access:** No

Description of House

This two-story frame house is the only home that poet Walt Whitman ever owned. In 1884, Whitman purchased the property from Mrs. Jennie Hare for the sum of $1,750. Sadly, America's leading poet, author of *Leaves of Grass* and other noted works, often supported himself with clerical work and never made a substantial amount from his writing. Prior to moving to the house on Mickle Street, he had lived with his mother until her death in 1873 and then with his brother at another house in Camden. Surprisingly, the seventh edition of *Leaves of Grass* sold extremely well and enabled Whitman to save enough money to buy the house. Several years later, he made the acquaintance of a widow, Mrs. Mary O. Davis, and proposed that she move into his poorly furnished home with her furniture and to keep house for him. She remained his housekeeper until his death on March 26, 1892.

This small Greek Revival structure was built as a free standing house, and is now part of a row of brick homes. The house has been preserved to a great extent as it was in 1892. Very few modifications have been made to the structure other than the removal of one wall on the second floor prior to 1884, to make one large bedroom out of two smaller ones, and the addition of radiators. The furnishings are almost entirely original to the house and were used by Whitman and Mary Davis.

Notable Collections on Exhibit

The Walt Whitman house has a large collection of original letters, photographs, furniture, and tableware which belonged to him and his housekeeper.

Emlen Physick Estate

P.O. Box 1048, Washington Street
Cape May, NJ 08204
(609) 884-5404

Contact: Mid-Atlantic Center for the Arts

Open: Jan.-March, weekends; April-Dec., expanded schedule, July-Aug., extended hours, call for exact hours

Admission: Adults $5; children (3-12) $2.50. Guided tours, visitors may also combine a tour of the estate with trolley tours, Victorian week (each Oct.), several literary weekends.

Suggested Time to View House: 1 hour

Facilities on Premises: Museum shop

Description of Grounds: 2-3 acres of open grounds; grounds are beginning to undergo restoration to their Victorian appearance

Best Season to View House: Summer

Year House Built: 1879

Number of Rooms: 18

Number of Yearly Visitors: 35,000

Style of Architecture: Stick-style

On-Site Parking: Yes **Wheelchair Access:** No

Description of House

The estate was built for Dr. Emlen Physick, Jr., whose grandfather, Dr. Philip Syng Physick, is considered the "father of American Surgery". Emlen, a lifelong bachelor, lived in this distinctive mansion with his widowed mother, Mrs. Ralston, and his maiden aunt Emilie. Despite his grandfather's medical accomplishments, Emlen himself never practiced medicine. Instead he lived the life of a country gentlemen and animal breeder and is noted for having the first automobile—and first automobile accident—in Cape May. His great-great-grandfather, Philip Syng, Jr., was a silversmith who designed and executed the inkwell used by the signers of the Declaration of Independence.

The Emlen Physick mansion is the only authentically restored house museum in this National Landmark city. The stick-style structure has been restored to its original 1879 appearance. Attributed to renowned Victorian architect Frank Furness, this is his sole residential design open to the public. The Physick House's exterior is distinguished by the grid-like pattern on its walls, its gigantic, upside-down corbelled chimneys; hooded "jerkin-head" dormers; distorted, oversized features (a Furness trademark); and huge stick-line brackets on the porch. The interior also bears the distinct signature of Furness, who designed many of the moldings, fireplaces, and even furniture, repeating many of the same designs, pattern and details throughout.

Notable Collections on Exhibit

In addition to the architecture, vistors will see the historic inkwell used by the signers of the Declaration of Independence on display as well as many of the original Furness-designed furnishings.

Canfield-Morgan House

903 Pompton Avenue
Cedar Grove, NJ 07009

Contact: Cedar Grove Historical Society
Open: 9 a.m.–5 p.m. during craft boutiques, call for regular hours
Admission: $2. Craft Boutiques and special exhibits.
Suggested Time to View House: 30 minutes

Best Season to View House: Fall (during pumpkin and apple sale)
Number of Yearly Visitors: 5,500
Year House Built: c. 1838-1850
Style of Architecture: Transitional vernacular farmhouse
Number of Rooms: 9

Description of House

Visitors to the Canfield Morgan House will experience the lives of a typical family in mid 19th-century New Jersey. Three generations of the Canfield family lived in this modest farmhouse beginning with Benjamin Canfield and his wife, Sarah Riker. Later generations included John Canfield and another descendant named Benjamin Canfield. The house was sold to the Morgan family in 1910 and two generations occupied the dwelling.

This two-story frame farmhouse is stylish without elaborate detail. There is, however, some elegance in the French doors which lead from the porch from the parlors and attractive moldings at the exterior cornices and interior basebords. A wellhouse, two pergolas, and remnants of family gardens are adjacent to the main house. The furnishings reflect the owner's tastes; many date from the original owners, others have been collected and are appropriate to the period.

Notable Collections on Exhibit

While some of the collections are in storage because restoration is in progress, the collection from the Morgan family is remarkably complete. Everything from invoices, checks, correspondence and photographs to an 18th-century grandfather clock and English lusterware china has been maintained and is on display.

Additional Information

The society plans a historical house museum and educational center on the site. There are also plans for a recreational park on the surrounding fourteen and a half acres of farmland.

Dr. William Robinson Plantation House

593 Madison Hill Road
Clark, NJ 07066
(908) 381-3081

Contact: Clark Historical Society

Open: April to Dec., first Sun. of each month 1–4 p.m.

Admission: Free. Guided tours are conducted by costumed guides.

Suggested Time to View House: 45 minutes

Facilities on Premises: Gift shop

Description of Grounds: The one acre grounds include a barn with attached potting shed, herb garden, corn crib, smoke house, and other unusual details

Best Season to View House: Spring-fall

Number of Yearly Visitors: 800-1000

Year House Built: 1690

Number of Rooms: 3 plus attic and cellar

Style of Architecture: Farmhouse (Tudor details)

On-Site Parking: No **Wheelchair Access:** Yes

Description of House

Dr. William Robinson, a physician and surgeon, built this lovely farmhouse for his home after emigrating to East New Jersey from Bruntisland, Scotland. He was accompanied by his wife, Margaret Allen Carlyle and his children including a son, William, born in 1683 who later inherited the house. The house later passed through a number of hands before being acquired by the town in the 1970s.

The house contains many features of the Tudor period including a steep roof, crenelated chimney, small, diamond-paned casement windows and an overhang on the gable end. The house features many distinctive details such as hand-hewn sills, beams and gunstock posts with champered edges and decoratively carved lamb's tongue and diamond endings to the champher. The building has a huge chestnut summer beam measuring seventeen feet in length and cross supporting beams twenty feet long. The rafters are held together by wooden pegs. The winding staircase is a replica of an original staircase as is the fireplace which has been constructed from bricks found during the restoration. The oak front door is also a reproduction of the original, but it was made with pre-Revolutionary nails and hinges. The house is furnished with period furniture but it appears that nothing dates to the original owners.

Notable Collections on Exhibit

There are many fine examples of 17th and 18th-century furnishings on display including an oak coffer with a handcarved panel (c. 1690), a flax spinning wheel signed by J. Muselman, an 1820 gun made for the New Jersey militia, and a walnut tap table (c. 1790).

Additional Information

The restoration has returned the house to its original beauty and visitors may now see the original post-and-beam walls and floors.

Craig House

Monmouth Battlefield State Park
347 Freehold Englishtown Road
Freehold, NJ 07728
(908) 462-9616

Contact: Department of Enviromental Protection

Open: Mid April-mid Nov., call for hours

Admission: Donations only. Guided tours on weekends.

Suggested Time to View House: 45 minutes

Facilities on Premises: Located at visitor center of Monmouth Battlefield

Description of Grounds: The entire park is opened to the public all year. During the period the house is open, visitors may drive to the house, at other times it is only accessible on foot.

Best Season to View House: Spring and fall

Year House Built: c. 1710, addition c. 1754

Number of Rooms: 6, 3 open to public

Style of Architecture: Dutch frame

On-Site Parking: Yes **Wheelchair Access:** No

Description of House

The house was built by Archibald Craig for his wife and eleven children. Many generations of the family lived here until the house was sold in the early 1940s. The house's main claim to fame is that it withstood the Battle of Monmouth and was used for a short time as a hospital by the British.

The Craig House is a typical colonial farm house of a fairly affluent farm family. The items in this simple dwelling are typical of a Colonial farm house and are collected and appropriate for the period. Several of the rooms are not completely furnished, although the kitchen is fully equipped with artifacts on display.

Additional Information

The visitor's center houses several displays related to the Battle of Monmouth including an electronic scale model map of the area with troop movements indicated. In addition, the site contains a reproduction of the well where Molly Pitcher carried water to Washington's troops.

Greenfield Hall

343 Kings Highway East
Haddonfield, NJ 08033
(609) 429-2462

Contact: Historical Society of Haddonfield
Open: Mon.-Fri. 10 a.m.–12 p.m.; also by
appointment
Admission: Free. Village Fair (first Sat. in
June), Holly Festival (mid Dec.) and
Candlelight Dinner (mid March).
Suggested Time to View House:
30–60 minutes

Description of Grounds: Boxwood garden
dating from the early 19th century
Best Season to View House: Spring
Year House Built: 1841
Style of Architecture: Georgian
Number of Rooms: 12
On-Site Parking: No **Wheelchair Access:** No

Description of House

This gracious mansion was home to six generations of the Gill family, cousins of Elizabeth Haddon, a founder of Haddonfield. Greenfield Hall was built by John Gill IV on the site of an early 1747 Gill family home in which Count Von Donop was quartered the night before the Battle of Red Bank at which he was killed. The Gill family were prominent local Quakers who were farmers and attorneys for seven generations.

This elegant three-story, brick mansion features twelve fireplaces, seven of them marble. The home is furnished with a wide array of pieces from the family and other items of local historical interest. The rooms reflect different periods of occupancy: the front parlor represents the 18th century, a Victorian parlor represents the 1860s, while the rear parlor is decorated in early 19th century fashion. The two bedrooms span the 1800 to 1840s period with some 18th-century pieces. There are also several items owned by Elizabeth Haddon on display.

Notable Collections on Exhibit

Greenfield Hall houses a collection of needlework samplers made by local school girls during the early 19th century. There are also several local tall case clocks from the late 18th to early 19th centuries on display as well as South Jersey glass from the late 18th and early 19th centuries.

"Lakeview" The Buckelew Mansion

203 Buckelew Ave
Jamesburg, NJ 08831
(908) 521-2040

Contact: Jamesburg Historical Association
Open: Buckelew Day, Aug. 15 1–5 p.m.;
Christmas at Lakeview, Dec. 16
2–4:30 p.m.; other times by prior
arrangement
Admission: Free. Guided tours for adults
and school classes, call in advance;
audiovisual program; craft
demonstrations on Buckelew Day;
Christmas musical program
Suggested Time to View House: 1½–2 hours
Facilities on Premises: Gift shop
Description of Grounds: A large lawn area
with concerts and crafts on Buckelew
Day. The grounds also feature an
authentic, restored blacksmith shop, a
farm museum, and a smokehouse.
Year House Built: 1685 with several later
additions (1730, 1832, 1875)
Best Season to View House: May-Oct.

Number of Yearly Visitors: 1200 Approx.
Style of Architecture: Colonial to Victorian
Number of Rooms: 23
On-Site Parking: Yes **Wheelchair Access:** No

Description of House

William Davison, an early settler to the area, built the original one-room house. James Buckelew, for whom the mansion is named, brought the property in 1832. He was well known throughout the state for cultivating large tracts of land (mainly cranberries), for his railroad interests, and for his business which held a team-towing contract for twenty five years on the Delaware Canal.

The original structure was built in 1685 as a one-room farmhouse. Visitors today can still see the original working fireplace and beehive oven. During James Buckelew's residency the structure changed completely. A large, two-story front addition was built in the 1830s with a wide center hallway, spacious double parlors, wide floorboards, mantelpieces, a curving mahogany bannister, and a wide, pillared verandah overlooking Lake Manalapan. These additions turned the simple dwelling into a beautiful, spacious mansion suitable for Bucklew's position in the community.

Notable Collections on Exhibit

Buckelew's coach, used to convey President Lincoln from the Trenton depot to the State House in 1861, is on display in the former conservatory.

Additional Information

A complete blacksmithy is housed in an outbuilding on the property as well as a large brick smokehouse.

Whitman-Stafford Farmhouse

315 Maple Avenue
Laurel Springs, NJ 08021
(609) 784-1105

Contact: Whitman-Stafford Committee, Inc.
Open: By appointment only
Admission: Free. Guided tours, mid-winter craft shows, summer concerts on the Green.
Suggested Time to View House: 45–60 minutes
Facilities on Premises: Small gift shop

Description of Grounds: The grounds are a public park complete with a band shell used for summer concerts.
Best Season to View House: Spring and summer
Number of Yearly Visitors: 5,000
Year House Built: c. 1785
Style of Architecture: Georgian
Number of Rooms: 8
On-Site Parking: Yes **Wheelchair Access:** Yes

Description of House

This lovely farmhouse provided many restful summers for noted poet Walt Whitman during his later years. During 1874 and 1875, Whitman was living in poor health in a small home in Camden after suffering the death of his mother. While in Camden, during the spring of 1876, Whitman had the good fortune to meet Harry Stafford, who worked in a Camden print shop. Harry was the son of George Stafford, who invited Whitman to a weekend at the farm. Whitman liked the farm so much that he stayed all summer and returned each summer until 1882. He regained his health while visiting here, and spent a considerable amount of time revising his masterwork, *Leaves of Grass*.

The structure is a three-story Georgian-style tenant farmhouse, with an addition made in 1865. The first floor features a simply-framed central doorway flanked by two large windows. The facade as a whole is framed horizontally by cornice and foundation, and vertically by cornerboards. In typical Georgian fashion, every element of the house is meant to convey symmetry and balance including the chimneys rising from from the two gable ends of the main structure. Some of the furnishings are from the original residents and some are collected, all are from the same period as the house.

Additional Information

Visitors with an interest in literary history should try and combine a visit to the farmhouse with one to the Walt Whitman House, his home in nearby Camden.

Longstreet Farmhouse

Newman Springs Road
Lincroft, NJ 07738
(908) 946-3758

Contact: Monmouth County Park System's Longstreet Farm

Open: Memorial Day-Labor Day, 10 a.m.–4 p.m.; winter, Sat.-Sun. 9 a.m.–5 p.m.; weekends and holidays, 12–4 p.m.; or by reservation

Admission: Free. Guided tours by reservation; weekend programs focusing on farm and home skills of the 1890s.

Suggested Time to View House: 1 hour

Facilities on Premises: Shelter building in adjacent park

Description of Grounds: Longstreet Farm is an historic living history farm with 18 buildings and 9 acres of land.

Best Season to View House: Each season presents a new overview

Number of Yearly Visitors: 160,000 plus

Year House Built: Original sections dates from the late 1700s

Style of Architecture: Dutch with 1800 Georgian addition

Number of Rooms: 14

On-Site Parking: Yes **Wheelchair Access:** No

Description of House

The Longstreet family lived on this farm from 1806 to 1977. They have been described as well educated, upper-middle class and business oriented. During the 1890s the farm was owned by Mary Ann Longstreet, who was in her seventies, and managed by her great-nephew, Jonathan I. Holmes. Jonathon Holmes inherited the farm upon his aunt's death, and it was from his daughter that Monmouth County purchased Longstreet Farm and the adjoining Holmdel Park.

The original two-room Dutch cottage was substantially expanded in 1800 with a two-and-a-half story three bay side-hall in the Georgian style. In 1840, a one-and-a-half story kitchen wing was added along with a Greek Revival porch. Longstreet Farm was among the largest and most prosperous farms in Holmdel. The house's furnishings reflect the 1890s time period conveyed by the rest of the living history complex. Approximately two-thirds of the collection belonged to the Longstreet's and would have been found in the home during that time.

Notable Collections on Exhibit

Several paintings are of noteworthy interest in the house: two Micah Williams portraits of family members (c. 1815) and three S.B. Waugh portraits (c. 1850). There is also a family owned Eli Terry clock.

Additional Information

The entire farm complex illustrates 19th-century life on a farmed as portrayed by costumed interpreters. The plowing, planting and cleaning is done as it would have been done during the 1890s. The breeds of animals on the site are the same ones found here during that era.

Smith-Cadbury Mansion

12 High Street
Moorestown, NJ 08057
(609) 235-0353

Contact: Historical Society of Moorestown
Open: Tues. 1–3 p.m.
Admission: $2. Guided Tours, occasional special programs and open houses.
Suggested Time to View House: 1 hour
Facilities on Premises: Gift shop, library
Description of Grounds: Small garden areas surrounding house
Best Season to View House: Spring and summer
Number of Yearly Visitors: 500
Year House Built: Earliest portion 1738
Style of Architecture: Federal
Number of Rooms: 9

On-Site Parking: No **Wheelchair Access:** No

Description of House

This attractive mansion was owned from 1766 to 1798 by the Smith family. At that time, the property functioned as a working farm of 160 acres. Samuel Smith was a historian and his son, Richard, was a Freeholder and township committee member for several terms. The Smith Home was considered the largest and most gracious in town and many well-known people were entertained here, including Lafayette, during the Revolution. Later the house passed to the Harris family, recently arrived immigrants from England. The son, Edward Harris Jr., inherited the house in 1822 and lived the life of a scholar and gentlemen. He was also a natural scientist and included among his colleagues the naturalist John Audubon who visited the house on several occasions. The last occupants before the historical society acquired the house were John and Rachel Cadbury.

The Smith-Cadbury Mansion provides a good example of yeoman style frame architecture. The center portion consists of a two-and-a-half story dwelling with a pent eve. The eastern and western wings added several floors in the late 1760s. Despite having been lived in continuously for 232 years, the interior has been very well-preserved. The house has much of its original paneling, fireplaces, wide floor boards and old window glass. All of the furnishings have been collected and, in general, are appropriate to the mid 19th century (c. 1840).

Notable Collections on Exhibit

The mansion houses an extensive costume collection which changes on a regular basis.

Macculloch Hall Historical Museum

45 Macculloch Avenue
Morristown, NJ 07960
(201) 538-2404

Contact: Macculloch Hall Historical Museum
Open: April-Nov., Sun. and Thur. (except holidays) 1–4 p.m.
Admission: Adults $3; seniors $2; students $1. Guided tours, three special exhibits each year in the schoolroom gallery, special garden events.
Suggested Time to View House: 45–60 minutes
Facilities on Premises: Small gift shop

Description of Grounds: Approximately 2½ acres with gardens, trellised and cultivated with plants of seasonal bloom, including 45 old-fashioned shrub roses and wisteria from Japan
Best Season to View House: Spring-early fall
Number of Yearly Visitors: 4,500
Year House Built: 1810, 1812, 1814 in three sections
Style of Architecture: Federal
Number of Rooms: 12 open to the public
On-Site Parking: No

Description of House

The founder of Macculloch Hall was George Perot Macculloch, a Scotsman born in Bombay and educated in Edinburgh. He came to this country with his wife and two children in 1806 and purchased twenty five acres from General John Doughty. George was an adventurer, a scholar, and a dreamer. He is best remembered for his conception of the Morris Canal and for his leadership in planning and building what was then an engineering marvel. The canal's great benefit lay in bringing Pennsylvania coal to local iron mines which was accomplished by means of inclined planes and 23 lift locks. The Macculloch's only daughter, Mary Louisa, married Jacob Welch Miller, the last Whig Senator from New Jersey, and bore nine children. The last Miller to live in the house, Dorothy, married James Otis Post, a prominent architect at the turn of the century.

The house was originally stuccoed or painted, a common practice intended to protect the soft brick of the early 19th century. Macculloch uses a vernacular example of the Federal style, probably designed by the Macculloch themselves in conjunction with a local carpenter. The house was built on the foundation of a pre-Revolutionary farm house and was constructed of bricks at a time when bricks were only used for important public buildings. The center wing was completed in 1812; its pedimented wooden portico carried on four huge square pillars is a later addition, probably dating from 1840. The west wing, added in the year 1814, completes the house, which is nowhere more than two rooms deep, a fact that explains its light-filled interior. The furnishings are Queen Anne, Chippendale, Empire and Federal and are appropriate to the time period that the family was in residence. Only a few pieces in the collection had Macculloch family ownership. The majority is from the collection of W. Parsons Todd who purchased the house to preserve it.

Notable Collections on Exhibit

Macculloch Hall houses a major collection of Thomas Nast drawings and prints, Oriental rugs, china (examples of European, Oriental, and White House china), and W. Parsons Todd memorabilia.

Additional Information

The house was purchased in 1949 by W. Parsons Todd, to preserve it as a museum. Todd was a businessman, philanthropist and humanitarian. He Was active in civic affairs in Morristown, and was a past mayor. He was a direct descendent of John Todd, the first husband of Dolley Madison. In addition to preserving the home of a prominent family, the museum also served to house his collection of antique furniture and decorative arts, a collection so large that his own home could no longer contain it.

The Ballantine House

43 Washington Street
Newark, NJ 07101
(201) 596-6550

Contact: The Newark Museum
Open: Wed.-Sun. 12–4:45 p.m.
Admission: Free. Special programs for children, volunteer docent tours at scheduled times.
Suggested Time to View House: 30 minutes
Facilities on Premises: Gift shop, cafe
Description of Grounds: A museum garden (open until 5 p.m.)
Number of Yearly Visitors: 350,000
Year House Built: 1885
Style of Architecture: Neo-Renaissance with Colonial Revival detailing
Number of Rooms: 21, 6 open to public
On-Site Parking: Yes **Wheelchair Access:** Yes

Description of House

The Ballantine House, built for Newark's premier beer-brewing family, was designed by architect George Edward Harney in 1885. When John Holme Ballantine became president of the brewery started by his father, he wanted a house that would be consistent with his new position. This magnificent mansion on Newark's Washington Park was the result.

Constructed of Philadelphia pressed red brick and grey Wyoming sandstone, the three-story Ballantine House comprises approximately 10,000 square feet in twenty-two rooms. The house features a classic blend of the Renaissance and Romanesque Revival styles. The panels around the top of the porch and the front bay window are carved with floral and foliate designs. The interior is equally impressive with its quartered oak parquet flooring, carved mantelpieces and paneling, unusual leather wallpaper, and stained glass windows. Several of these elegant rooms—the reception room, the drawing room, and the dining room—are currently open to the public. The billiard room and four second floor spaces—the upper hall, master bedroom, boudoir and Alice's room—will be restored and furnished as they would have appeared between 1885 and 1900. A special gallery will be created on the first floor to display the museum's silver collection. Many of the furnishings are family pieces, while the rest is of the period (or older) and part of a decorative arts collection held by the museum.

Notable Collections on Exhibit

The Ballantine House has long been the centerpiece of the Newark Museum's extensive collection of decorative arts, which includes examples of household objects from the Renaissance to the present day. Well known strengths are 19th and 20th-century furniture, silver, ceramics, and glass, as well as objects of New Jersey interest. The music room gallery features changing exhibitions.

Risley Homestead

8 Virginia Avenue
Northfield, NJ 08225
(609) 927-5218

Contact: Atlantic County Historical Society

Open: May-Oct., Wed. 10 a.m.–4 p.m.; Sun. 1–5 p.m.; closed all holidays including Mother's and Father's Day

Admission: Free. Interpretative guided tours limited to six persons per tour.

Suggested Time to View House: 30 minutes

Description of Grounds: Small garden of flowering shrubs, perennials, small trees and some exotic specimens

Best Season to View House: May-June

Number of Yearly Visitors: 200

Year House Built: c. 1790

Style of Architecture: Vernacular

Number of Rooms: 2

On-Site Parking: No **Wheelchair Access:** No

Description of House

The homestead was home to many generations of oystermen, and is the only one of its kind listed on New Jersey's Register of Historic Places. The society received the homestead and all its furnishings by bequest from Virginia Risley Stout in 1989. She was the last of of the Risley family to occupy the dwelling. The land is part of the 100 acre plantation purchased in 1724 by her great-great-great-grandfather. Virginia was forced to move back to the decrepit homestead because of the Great Depression. She and her architect husband made modest improvements to the house to make it livable and to prevent it from being destroyed.

This small cottage is a combination of 18th and 19th-century construction. The original structure is a two-room farmhouse with a sleeping loft. Modest additions were added in the 1930s and 1940s. However, the early ceilings, wood paneling, cupboards, fireplace, a window, and an enclosed stairway were carefully preserved. The original furnishings are on display.

Additional Information

In addition to the Risley Homestead, the society also maintains the nearby Somers Mansion, built in 1714. They also have a museum with major collections of decorative arts and 19th-century household utensils and unusual displays of weaponry, maritime, and Amerind artifacts.

Centennial Cottage

McClintock Street at Central Ave
Ocean Grove, NJ 07756
(201) 774-1869

Contact: Historical Society of Ocean Grove

Open: July-Aug., Mon.-Sat. 11 a.m.–3 p.m;
weekends only, June and Sept.

Admission: Adults $1; children $.25; group
rates. Guided tours.

Suggested Time to View House:
30–60 minutes

Facilities on Premises: Sales desk

Description of Grounds: Beautiful,
authentic Victorian garden, herb garden,
fountain

Best Season to View House: Summer

Number of Yearly Visitors: 1,000

Year House Built: 1874

Style of Architecture: Victorian
Carpenter's Gothic

Number of Rooms: 7

On-Site Parking: No

Wheelchair Access: No

Description of House

This impressive Victorian Gothic cottage was built for Samuel Fels, a leading soap manufacturer (Fels Naptha Soap). He and his family used to summer here in this picturesque seaside resort. Later, the cottage was purchased by Mr. and Mrs. Robert Skold and moved to its present site in 1969, the year of Ocean Grove's centennial. The community has been designated a National Historic Site because of the many historic buildings which supported the 10,000 member camp meetings of former years.

This two-story, white, clapboard cottage has two lovely porches from which the family once viewed the ocean. The original restoration of the interior and exterior was supervised by the historical society. The furnishing was done with the enthusiastic support of community members and all items on display are appropriate for the late 19th century.

Notable Collections on Exhibit

The cottage displays a fine collection of Victorian furniture, red glass, many costumes, and wonderful Victorian toys.

Additional Information

Visitors to the cottage will be impressed by the authentic period garden which includes trees, shrubs, and flowers popular in the late 19th century. The herb garden was designed around a religious theme. Centennial Cottage is a delightful stop along New Jersey's Coastal Heritage Trail which includes many other historic houses and museums.

Lambert Castle

Valley Road
Paterson, NJ 07503
(201) 881-2761

Contact: Passaic County Historical Society
Open: Wed.-Sun. 1–4 p.m.; closed holidays
Admission: Adults $1.50; seniors $1; children (under 15) free. Guided tours; period rooms; changing exhibitions on local history; local history library; special events.
Suggested Time to View House: 45 minutes
Facilities on Premises: Gift shop

Description of Grounds: Castle is set in a public park
Best Season to View House: Spring
Number of Yearly Visitors: 20,000
Year House Built: 1892
Style of Architecture: Eclectic interpretation of English castles (largely Norman)
Number of Rooms: 7
On-Site Parking: Yes **Wheelchair Access:** Yes

Description of House

The Lambert Castle stands out as one of the most unusual historic homes in New Jersey. Catholina Lambert was born in the village of Goose Eye, England, in 1834. The son of working-class parents, Lambert came to America at the age of seventeen to seek his fortune. He found that fortune in silk, starting first as a bookkeeper earning four dollars a week, and by 1890 he had become one of the largest mill owners in Paterson, the Silk City of the New World.

In 1892, Lambert built his dream house, then known as "Belle Vista," on Garret Mountain overlooking Paterson. Mounting debts forced Lambert to mortgage his estate in 1914 and to sell a considerable portions of his vast art holdings in 1916. Despite this, Lambert managed to live comfortably at the castle until his death in 1923. After his death his son, Walter, sold the castle to the city of Paterson.

Lambert Castle is a three-story, sandstone and granite structure. The estate reflects the prosperity and taste of the silk elite in the late Victorian era. The main house is believed to have been designed by Lambert with the help of his brother-in-law. Not an exact copy of an English, the castle instead is a combination of architectural features—battlements and unsusual square and round towers—which appealed to Lambert. The buildings interior functioned with a dual purpose of a wealthy home and a gallery for Lambert's large and fine art collection. Public rooms on the ground floor were built around a larger central space which was once an open three-story atrium with a skylight. The exterior facade reflects the original period construction, while the extant outbuildings (observatory tower and carriage/stable building) reflect the opulence of the original grounds which consisted of over fifty acres.

The furnished period rooms include a formal parlor and music room filled with decorative arts of varying styles. The other rooms are furnished largely in objects collected from other Passaic County homes of the same period and economic status. Some original items have been collected including dining room furniture, chairs and some works of art.

Notable Collections on Exhibit

Collections include formal dining furniture owned by the Lamberts in the Baroque Revival style; important fine art such as paintings by artists Micah Williams and Julian Rik, and marble sculpture by Chauncy Ives, Hiram Powers and Gaetang Geberici. Changing local history related exhibits reflect a rich collection of silk, decorative and fine arts, folk art, material culture, photographs and documents. The Passaic County Historical collection consists of over 100,000 pieces.

Bainbridge House

158 Nassau Street
Princeton, NJ 08542
(609) 921-6748

Contact: Historical Society of Princeton

Open: Tues.-Sat. 12 p.m.–4 p.m.; Jan.-Feb., weekends only; June-Aug., also open Mon.

Admission: $3. Sun. walking tours of the town at 2 p.m.; video on history of Princeton; exhibitions; lectures; workshops

Suggested Time to View House: 30 minutes

Facilities on Premises: Museum shop; library; photo archives

Number of Yearly Visitors: 15,000

Year House Built: c. 1766

Style of Architecture: Georgian

Number of Rooms: 10

On-Site Parking: Yes **Wheelchair Access:** Yes

Description of House

The house was built around 1766 by Job Stockton, a tanner. After his death and the death of his wife, the house passed to his brother, Robert Stockton. Robert rented the home to Dr. Absalom Bainbridge. The doctor's son was born in the house now bearing his name. William Bainbridge is best known as the commander of the frigate Constitution, "Old Ironsides," in the War of 1812. A commodore in the U.S. Navy, he became a national hero for his well-publicized exploits in dealing with the Barbary pirates.

This well-preserved Georgian house has a handsome facade laid in Flemish bond, but the back and sides are covered with beaded clapboards, probably to economize. The house reflects the solid, balanced Georgian style of mid-18th century Philadelphia. In 1814, the front parlor was refurbished with windows cut in the side walls flanking the fireplace. The fireplace itself received a new mantel decorated with the then-current style of Robert Adams with delicate, shallow-cut, oval fan motifs. Over seventy percent of the original woodwork remains in the house.

There are three period rooms on display on the first floor—a dining room and parlor (c. 1820) and an early doctor's office with appropriate medical equipment. The furnishings and artwork related to the original residents and the period of the house are collected and on long-term loan.

Notable Collections on Exhibit

The house displays the most extensive and significant holdings of historic photographs and manuscripts related to history of Princeton.

Thomas Clarke House

500 Mercer Road
Princeton, NJ 08540
(609) 921-0074

Contact: Princeton Battlefield State Park
Open: Wed.-Fri., 9 a.m.–12 p.m. and
1–6 p.m.; Sat. 10 a.m.–12 p.m. and
1–6 p.m.; Sun. 1–6 p.m.
Admission: Free. Guided tours, battlefield
talks, special events, battle reenactments
Suggested Time to View House: 1 hour

Description of Grounds: 85 acre park for
functions and weddings, no indoor shelter
Best Season to View House: All seasons
Number of Yearly Visitors: House-5500;
Park-55,000
Year House Built: c. 1770
Style of Architecture: Georgian (partial)
Number of Rooms: 9
On-Site Parking: Yes **Wheelchair Access:** Yes

Description of House

This simple home witnessed many historic events during the course of
the American Revolution. The dwelling was built by a Quaker farmer,
Thomas Clark, a few years prior to the Revolution. His family lived here
until 1863. The Battle of Princeton was waged around the house which later
served as a hospital. The American general Hugh Mercer was wounded and
lay within the house, dying. Later occupants include the Hale family (1863-
1944) and the Smith family (1944-1960s).

The Clarke House is furnished in the 18th-century style with the 1840
wing area used to house a Revolutionary War exhibit. The collection of
furnishings has been continuously refined to reflect the later 18th century;
some pieces are from the family though none of the pieces can be documented to the house during this period.

Notable Collections on Exhibit

The Carroll collection of Revolutionary War firearms and weapons is on
display on the first floor. There is also a 600 volume library for teachers and
students on the Revolution, furnishings, and various aspects of 18th-century
life and New Jersey history.

Additional Information

A 600 acre forest and wetlands leading to the Delaware-Raritan Canal
is adjacent to the site and open to the public.

Ringwood Manor

1304 Sloatsburg Rd.
Ridgewood, NJ 07456
(201) 962-7031

Contact: State of New Jersey, Dept. of
Environmental Protection & Energy

Open: May 1-Oct. 31, weekdays 10–4 p.m.;
weekends 10 a.m.–5 p.m.; closed Mon.

Activities: Guided tours

Suggested Time to View House:
45–60 minutes

Facilities on Premises: Gift shop, book store

Description of Grounds: Grounds are
accessible, also picnic areas and ball field

Best Season to View House: Spring,
summer, fall

Number of Yearly Visitors: 35,000 in season

Year House Built: 1807, 1864, 1875 (sections)

Style of Architecture: Eclectic-Gothic
Revival

Number of Rooms: 51 (25 open to the
public)

On-Site Parking: Yes **Wheelchair Access:** Yes

Description of House

Ringwood Manor, completed in 1879, was known as the "second White house" during the late 19th century. The manor was also the country home of Abram S. Hewitt, one of the foremost ironmasters of the 19th century in America. Many important politicians and diplomats were entertained within its elegant walls. In addition, Ringwood was the home of several prominent and influential ironmasters prior to and following the American Revolution.

The imposing, but delightfully detailed, facade of Ringwood Manor, has remained unchanged for over one hundred years. A magnificent stone lion has guarded the entrance to the manor since the mid 19th century. The building features many exquisite details which reflect its former residents taste and style including a Corinthian column for the portcochere designed by the legendary Stanford White late in the Classical Revival period. The interior showcases authentic Victorian woodwork adorning many of the distinctive window bays.

Notable Collections on Exhibit

The Ringwood Manor houses a unique collection of furniture, porcelain, china, and a fine collection of Hudson River School paintings.

The Steuben House

1209 Main Street
River Edge, NJ
(201) 487-1739

Contact: Bergen County Historical Society
Open: Wed.-Sat. 10 a.m.–5 p.m.;
Sun. 2–5 p.m.
Activities: Guided tours, living history
demonstrations
Suggested Time to View House: 1 hour
Facilities on Premises: Small gift/book
shop
Best Season to View House: Late
spring-summer
Number of Yearly Visitors: 12,000
Year House Built: 1713
Style of Architecture: "Jersey Dutch" Colonial
Number of Rooms: 13

On-Site Parking: Yes **Wheelchair Access:** Yes

Description of House

Located on the Hackensack River, the Steuben House takes its name from one of its most famous residents, the Prussian Inspector-General of the Continental troops, Baron Von Steuben. The original house is located on land purchased in 1682 by Cornelius Matheus. His son, Matheus Cornelius-son, deeded the property to David Ackerman, who erected the first gristmill on the estate sometime prior to 1710. The house has gone through a series of owners including Jan Zabriskie and his son. Jan Zabrinskie, Jr. inherited the homestead upon his father's death in 1774. He was appointed a Lieutenant-Colonel in the county militia after the battles at Lexington and Concord, and resigned his commission in June of 1776 after being accused of passing military secrets to the British. His property was later confiscated after his arrest. The estate was presented to Major General Von Steuben in gratitude for his service to the Continental troops. Another notable resident, William Randolph Hearst, owned the house from 1911 to 1928.

This large mansion house has undergone several enlargements under its various owners. Jan Zabriskie doubled the size of the house in 1752 and covered the entire dwelling with a gambrel roof. Visitors today will see thirteen rooms with outbuildings consisting of a bake house, smoke house, coach house and two large barns, and a garden.

Notable Collections on Exhibit

There are several unusual collections on display including a group of slip-decorated redware pie dishes, a collection of antique dolls and toys, a textile collection, an Indian dug-out canoe, antique ceramics, metalwork, paintings, needlecraft, and folk art.

Additional Information

The forty acre site includes two other historic houses—the Demarest House and The Campbell-Christie House—an iron bridge, a meadow, and two orchards.

Campbell-Christie House

1201 Main Street
River Edge, NJ
(201) 343-9492

Contact: Bergen County Historical Society
Open: By appointment only
Activities: Guided tours, living history
demonstrations
Suggested Time to View House: 30 minutes
Facilities on Premises: Gift shop
Best Season to View House: Late
spring-summer
Year House Built: 1774
Style of Architecture: Gambrel roof
Number of Rooms: 5

On-Site Parking: Yes **Wheelchair Access:** Yes

Description of House

The Campbell-Christie House was originally erected in New Milford by Joseph Campbell, a member of the county militia during the Revolution. He maintained this modest stone house as a store and tavern. In 1795, John D. Christie, a blacksmith, purchased the property. His grandson, John Walter, was probably the most distinguished resident of the house. He was a prominent engineer who developed forms of automobile driving systems which are still used today. After a variety of owners, the house was in danger of being destroyed. In 1977, the 200-ton house was moved across the river to its present site in the New Bridge Landing Historic Park.

This one-and-a-half story sandstone house features a gambrel roof with a sweeping overhang, features which were prominent in 18th and 19th-century Bergen county domestic architecture. There are two rooms on either side of a central hallway; their windows form a symmetrical composition on the front facade. The structure also demonstrates a variety of stonework on the exterior with well-dressed sandstone set in contrast to the rough coarse and rubble stone on the sides and rear of the house.

Additional Information

Visitors to the house should also plan a stop at the nearby Steuben House, the Demarest House and kitchen, and the New Bridge, the oldest metal truss bridge in the country.

Johnson Ferry House

355 Washington Crossing Penn Road
Titusville, NJ 03560-1517
(609) 737-2515

Contact: Washington Crossing State Park
Open: Wed.-Sat. 9 a.m.–4:30 p.m.; Sun.
1:30–4:30 p.m.; closed Christmas,
Thanksgiving and New Years Day
Activities: Tours, foodways, 18th-century
domestic activities demonstrations,
special events including annual
Washington's Birthday celebration
Suggested Time to View House: 30 minutes
Description of Grounds: Located in a
public park, gardens
Best Season to View House: Spring-fall
Number of Yearly Visitors: 15,000
Year House Built: 1740
Number of Rooms: 9

Style of Architecture: Dutch farmhouse
On-Site Parking: Yes **Wheelchair Access:** Yes

Description of House

This distinguished Dutch farmhouse served as a ferry house during the tumultous days of the American Revolution. It is even rumored that General Washington and his top officers stopped at the house to keep warm and dry while waiting to cross the river. The house's original owner, Garrett Johnson, came to New Jersey from Staten Island in the early 18th century. The son of Rutger Janse, Garrett anglicized the family name from Janse to Johnson, took over the Delaware River Plantation, and established a ferry boat service, tavern and farmstead. The ferry and the tavern were the primary sources of income for his family. Garrett eventually had a fieldstone tavern built, sometime between 1748 and 1766, on the riverfront at the ferry landing. In the 1930s, the Works Progress Administration (WPA) unfortunately tore down the original ferry tavern and restored the farmhouse as a New England-style tavern.

The ferry house is a unique example of an early 18th-century Dutch farmhouse. The characteristic gambrel roof and scallop shingles mark the Dutch origins of the original residents. The house still has the original oak timbers, stone foundation, and a large central chimey and hearth where cooking demonstrations are often given. The period furnishings are collected and are from the area; there are also a few pieces from the original residents.

Notable Collections on Exhibit

The Johnson Ferry House exhibits a fine collection of period country furnishings, household utensils, and tools.

Dey Mansion–
Washington's Headquarters Museum

199 Totowa Road
Wayne, NJ 07470
(201) 696-1776

Contact: Passaic County Parks Department

Open: Wed.-Fri. 1–4:30 p.m.; Sat.-Sun., 10 a.m.–12 p.m. and 1–4:30 p.m.; closed on major holidays, group tours by appointment

Admission: Adults $1; children (under 10) free. Guided tours, special monthly programs.

Suggested Time to View House: 30–45 minutes

Description of Grounds: 2 acres of grounds with garden and picnic area

Best Season to View House: Summer and fall

Number of Yearly Visitors: 5,000

Year House Built: 1740

Number of Rooms: 11

Style of Architecture: Georgian

On-Site Parking: Yes

Description of House

Dirck Dey, a carpenter and builder, constructed this fine Georgian manor houe in the 1740s. His grandfather had come to America during the Dutch colonization of New Amsterdam (New York City). Dirck's son, Theunis, was a prominent farmer and citizen. Theunis was also colonel of the local militia during the Revolutionary War, a position which brought him constant communication with General George Washington. The Dey Mansion served as Washington's headquarters for three months in 1780. In addition, many other famous men passed through this impressive house including Alexander Hamilton, the Marquis de Lafayette, Lord Stirling and Anthony Wayne.

This large stone house has a brick face front and a gambrel-style roof. The Dutch influence can be seen in the combination of materials—huge oak timbers pegged with wooden pins, and the mix of brick and brownstone on the exterior. The interior has been restored to its original appearance and features white plaster walls with colored woodwork and polished wood floors. All of the furnishings were collected after the house became a museum in 1934 and date from the late 1600s to the late 1700s.

Notable Collections on Exhibit

The Dey House displays many historic and decorative items including five of the ten pewter plates given to Gen. Washington by Theunis Dey. There is also an eagle pattern China trade porcelain set once owned by Mrs. Deyon displayed as well as a large cherrywood kas in the bedroom where Washington once slept. Other notable items include leather upholstered bow-back Windsor chairs, Meissen pistol-handled knives; a portrait painted on leather, and a set of Chippendale chairs.

Miller-Cory House Museum

614 Mountain Ave
Westfield, NJ 07090
(908) 232-1776

Contact: Miller-Cory House Association

Open: Mid Sept.-mid June, Sun. 2–5 p.m.
(except holidays; Jan.-Feb., Sun. 2–4 p.m.

Admission: Adults $1; children $.50.
Guided tours and demonstrations of
seasonal activities.

Suggested Time to View House: 1 hour

Facilities on Premises: Gift shop

Description of Grounds: There is an herb
garden, a small sample vegetable
garden, wildflower garden, and fruit
trees all of which date from the period

Best Season to View House: Spring-fall

Number of Yearly Visitors: 4000-5000

Year House Built: 1740

Number of Rooms: 4 open to the public,
plus education center and cookhouse

Style of Architecture: Colonial farmhouse

On-Site Parking: No **Wheelchair Access:** Yes

Description of House

This attractive dwelling was built by Samuel Miller at the time of his marriage in 1740. His three sons were born in the house all of whom served in the Revolution. Several generations of the Cory family next occupied the farmhouse beginning in 1780 with Joseph Cory and continuing on with his son, Levi, and their adopted daughter Theresa. After restoration by the Jones family in the 1960s, the historical society acquired the clapboard farmhouse for their activities in 1972.

The Miller-Cory House is a wonderful example of a living history museum where visitors may learn about colonial lifestyles and traditions. Depending on the season, visitors may see demonstrations of cider making, spinning and weaving, flower arranging and open hearth cooking.

New York

1. **Albany**
    Historic Cherry Hill
    Schuyler Mansion-The Pastures
    1848 Shaker Meeting House

2. **Almond**
    Hagadorn House Museum

3. **Amagansett**
    Miss Amelia's Cottage

4. **Arcade**
    Gibby House

5. **Auburn**
    The Seward House

6. **Belmont**
    Whitney-Halsey Museum

7. **Brockport**
    Morgan-Manning House

8. **Bronx**
    Bartow-Pell Mansion Museum
    Van Cortlandt House
    Poe Cottage
    Valentine-Varian House

9. **Brooklyn**
   Lefferts Homestead
   Pieter Claeson Wyckoff House
10. **Canandaigua**
    Granger Homestead
    Sonnenberg Gardens Mansion
11. **Canton**
    Silas Wright House Museum
12. **Castile**
    Castile Historic House
13. **Cherry Valley**
    Cherry Valley Museum
14. **Constableville**
    Constable Hall
15. **Cortland**
    *1890 House Museum and
    Center for the Victorian Arts*
16. **Cutchogue**
    *The Old House on Cutchogue
    Village Green*
17. **East Meredith**
    John Hanford House
18. **Floral Park**
    Queens County Farm Museum
19. **Flushing**
    Kingsland Homestead
    Bowne House
20. **Fort Edward**
    Old Fort House Museum
21. **Fulton**
    Pratt House
22. **Gardiner**
    Locust Lawn
23. **Garrison**
    Boscobel
24. **Geneva**
    Prouty-Chew Museum
    Rose Hill Mansion
25. **Germantown**
    Clermont
26. **Glen Falls**
    DeLong House
27. **Horseheads**
    Zim House
28. **Hudson**
    Olana
    The Robert Jenkins House
29. **Huntington**
    Dr. Daniel Kissam House
    David Conklin Farmhouse
30. **Huntington Station**
    Walt Whitman House
31. **Jamaica**
    King Manor Museum
32. **Johnstown**
    Johnson Hall
33. **Katonah**
    John Jay Homestead
34. **Kinderhook**
    James Vanderpoel House
    Luykas Van Alen House
    Lindenwald
35. **Kings Park**
    Obadiah Smith House
36. **Le Roy**
    Le Roy House
37. **Lyons Falls**
    Gould Mansion
38. **Mastic Beach**
    William Floyd Estate
39. **Mount Morris**
    The Mills Mansion
40. **Mumford**
    Genesee Country Museum
41. **New City**
    The Jacob Blauvelt House
42. **New Lebanon**
    Mount Lebanon Shaker Village
43. **New Paltz**
    Huguenot Street
44. **New Rochelle**
    Thomas Paine Cottage

45. New York
Morris-Jumel Mansion
Abigail Adams Smith Museum
Dyckman House Museum
Fraunces Tavern
Gracie Mansion
Lower East Side Tenement
Museum
Theodore Roosevelt Birthplace
Old Merchant's House

46. Newburgh
Jonathan Hasbrouck House

47. Newtonville
The Pruyn House

48. Oneida
Cottage Lawn
The Mansion House

49. Orient
Oysterponds

50. Oswego
Richardson-Bates House Museum

51. Oyster Bay
Coe Hall at Planting Fields
Raynham Hall Museum

52. Palmyra
William Phelps Store Museum

53. Parishville
Parishville Museum

54. Pawling
The John Kane House

55. Penn Yan
Oliver House Museum

56. Plattsburgh
Kent-Delord House Museum

57. Poughkeepsie
The Glebe House

58. Ridgewood
Vander Ende-Onderdonk
Farmhouse Museum

59. Riverhead
Hallock Homestead

60. Rochester
Stone-Tolan House
Woodside
Susan B. Anthony House
Campbell-Whittlesey House

61. Rosyln
Van Nostrand-Starkins House

62. Rye
Square House

63. Salisbury Center
1805 Frisbie House

64. Schoharie
1743 Palatine House

65. Seneca Falls
Mynderse-Partridge-Becker
House

66. Smith's Point
The Manor of St. George

67. Smithtown
Caleb Smith House
Judge J. Lawrence Smith
Homestead
Franklin O. Arthur House
Epenetus Smith Tavern

68. Staatsburg
Mills Mansion

69. Staten Island
Alice Austen House Museum
Seguine House
Conference House
Garibaldi Meucci Museum
Historic Richmond Town

70. Stillwater
Philip Schuyler House

71. Tonawanda
Benjamin Long Homestead

72. Troy
Hart-Cluett Mansion

73. Westfield
McClurg Museum

74. Youngston
French Castle

Schuyler Mansion—The Pastures

32 Catherine Street
Albany, NY 12202
(518) 434-0834

Contact: Schuyler Mansion State Historic Site
Open: April-Oct., Wed.-Sat. 10 a.m.–5 p.m., Sun. 1–5 p.m.; Nov.-March, tours by appointment. Groups by reservation only.
Admission: Modest admission fee may be implemented. Guided tours, orientation exhibit; annual Christmas open house and Springfest.
Suggested Time to View House: 1 hour
Facilities on Premises: Small gift area

Description of Grounds: Park-like setting with raised display gardens
Best Season to View House: Spring and summer
Number of Yearly Visitors: 12,000
Year House Built: 1761
Style of Architecture: Georgian
Number of Rooms: 10
On-Site Parking: Yes **Wheelchair Access:** Yes

Description of House

Philip Schuyler was a major general in the Revolutionary War. A descendent of Albany's earliest settlers, he carried on his family's talent for land speculation, trading, politics, and negotiations with the Indians. After the Revolution, Schuyler was in the New York senate for several terms, and in 1789 was appointed one of New York's first two Senators.

The house is a Georgian brick structure, once the center of an eighty acre estate. As part of the original property there were three wings off the back of the mansion, a large Dutch barn and a dozen separate outbuildings. The central mansion structure is all that remains today. In 1777, "Gentleman Johnny" Burgoyne stayed here as a prisoner-guest after burning Philip Schuyler's Saratoga home to the ground during the battle of Saratoga. George Washington, Ben Franklin and dozens of other prominent figures were entertained here during the Revolution.

The mansion contains an 1818 vestibule thought to be designed by noted Albany architect Philip Hooker. Following the results of an historic paint analysis, the rooms are painted in the late 18th-century colors of Schuyler's choice. Historic reproduction wallpapers are being installed where appropriate. Furnishings are appropriate to the period of the house; some are pieces owned by General Philip Schuyler, none are reproductions.

Notable Collections on Exhibit

The mansion houses a substantial collection of fine New York and New England furniture of the Colonial and Federal periods; there are also excellent examples of Chinese export porcelain and English glassware. Notable artifacts on display include a pair of rhinestone boot buckles given by General Burgoyne to a Schuyler daughter after his stay at the mansion, and a diamond and pearl brooch with a lock of George Washington's hair, given by Washington to his goddaughter Catherine Schuyler.

Historic Cherry Hill

523½ South Pearl Street
Albany, NY 12202
(518) 434-4791

Contact: Historic Cherry Hill
Open: Feb.-Dec., Tues.-Sat. 10 a.m.–3 p.m., Sun. 1–3 p.m.
Admission: Adults $3.50; seniors $3; students $2; children (6-17) $1; under 6 free. Guided tours on the hour; special events include spring and Christmas open houses.
Suggested Time to View House: 1 hour
Facilities on Premises: Gift shop

Description of Grounds: 5 acres of land and formal gardens featuring peonies
Best Season to View House: May-Sept.
Number of Yearly Visitors: 5,000
Year House Built: 1787
Style of Architecture: Georgian
Number of Rooms: 10 open to public
On-Site Parking: Yes **Wheelchair Access:** Yes

Description of House

This stately house was built for merchant-farmers Philip and Maria Van Rensselaer, and was lived in continuously by five generations of the family. Philip and Maria were descendants of prominent Dutch and English families. Solomon Van Rensselaer, a national military and political figure, and his wife Harriet were the second generation owners. Subsequent generations who lived at Cherry Hill included Dr. Peter and Harriet Maria Van Rensselaer Elmendorf and Catherine Rankin and her husband, lawyer Edward Rankin. Two of their children, Edward, a lawyer in his father's firm, and Emily, were the last family owners.

Cherry Hill is a 20th-century home, reflecting the lives of successive generations; it has not been restored to an earlier period. Visitors will be able to trace the impact of the different owners on the house. The museum is considered a "preservation" site, exhibiting structural changes made with each successive generation, as well as technological alterations (in plumbing heating and cooking modernization), and varying decorative styles. The house most strongly reflects the Colonial Revival movement as a result of changes made by the fourth and fifth generation owners, the Rankins. Furnishings are original to all five generations, and are arranged as they were left and used by the last owner, Emily Rankin, who lived at Cherry Hill until her death in 1963.

Notable Collections on Exhibit

A large collection of Oriental decorative arts, including Canton and Rose Medallion, brought back by a family member from her time as a missionary in China is on display. Also on exhibit are paintings by local artist Walter Palmer and Hudson River School artist Edward Nichols, furniture reflecting several styles and periods, including Chippendale, Federal and Empire, and a large textile collection, showcasing needlework, clothing, bed coverings, and rugs.

1848 Shaker Meeting House

Albany Shaker Road
Albany, NY 12211
(518)456-7890

Contact: Shaker Heritage Society
Open: Mon.-Fri. 9 a.m.–4 p.m., and by appointment. Closed Easter, July 4, Thanksgiving, Christmas, New Years Day and Eve.
Admission: $2 per person. Guided tours, audiovisual presentations, special programs.
Suggested Time to View House: 45 minutes
Facilities on Premises: Gift shop/book store

Description of Grounds: 770 acre historic district containing more than 20 structures.
Best Season to View House: May-Oct.
Number of Yearly Visitors: 15,000
Year House Built: 1848
Style of Architecture: Shaker
Number of Rooms: 10 rooms—6 are open to the public
On-Site Parking: Yes **Wheelchair Access:** Yes

Description of House

The Shakers were once a thriving community with hundreds of members in the United States from 1776 to 1938. Although the Shaker community has but a few members remaining today, the 1848 Meeting House, the largest in existence, stands as a testament to thier fascinating past. An enormous meeting room, where the community gathered to work and meet, comprises the first floor, along with a weaving room and gift shop. The second floor living quarters, where men and women lived separately, further evokes the Shaker lifestyle. And although work was a major component of Shaker life, the third-story visitors apartment is proof that the Shakers also encouraged socializing and traveled to visit neighboring communities.

A great deal of the original woodwork still remains in the Meeting House as well as the triple-hung windows with their thumb screws. A tremendous walnut truss system in the attic allows the Meeting Room to be over 4,000 square feet with no columns or obstructions.

Notable Collections on Exhibit

This unusually large Meeting House features a collection of over 500 pieces of Shaker furnishings known as "smalls" from the mid-19th century. Simple and functional, yet beautiful in its own way, the furniture, like the Shakers' lifestyle, has been wonderfully preserved here.

Hagadorn House Museum

11 N. Main Street
Almond, NY 14804
(607) 276-6166

Contact: Almond Historical Society, Inc.

Open: Sun. "open house" 2–5 p.m.

Activities: Member meetings, open house program, speakers, exhibits (in "the little gallery")

Suggested Time to View House: Variable, as long as questions are asked

Facilities on Premises: Sales desk

Best Season to View House: All

Number of Yearly Visitors: 1,600

Year House Built: 1800 (first part)

Style of Architecture: Frame with Greek Revival porch

Number of Rooms: 8

On-Site Parking: Yes **Wheelchair Access:** No

Description of House

This charming house was home to a number of families including the Lockharts and the Weatherbys, but was named after a local physician who was an early resident, Dr. Hagadorn. The most famous person to have spent the night here, Teddy Roosevelt, stayed while on an early campaign trip.

The house has changed over the years, depending on the occupant's tastes. Dr. Hagadorn's granddaughter, Marie Kenneth Hagadorn, dropped the ceiling and added a picture window in 1940. The four downstairs rooms are furnished to show how times have changed. The Hagadorn's inherited family furniture is displayed on the front porch. The middle room (known as the Victorian room) includes Oriental rugs and furniture from the Lockhart family. The little gallery was Dr. Hagadorn's office and his grandchildren, Ken and Marie, used it as their bedroom. The front hall and stairway were restored in the 1970s, and 1826 era reproduction wallpaper was installed.

Notable Collections on Exhibit

There is an eclectic group of objects on display in this handsome house: framed oil paintings done mainly by women in the family (1890s), clothing and quilt collections, and a small group of toys and schoolbooks. China, glass, bottles, and stoneware jugs are displayed in an original built-in cupboard.

Miss Amelia's Cottage

Main Street and Windmill Lane
P.O. Box 7077
Amagansett, NY 11930
(516) 267-3020

Contact: Amagansett Historical Association
Open: June-Labor Day, Fri.-Sun. 1–5 p.m.
Admission: $2; children $1. Self-guided
  tour; exhibits change annually.
Suggested Time to View House: 45 minutes
Number of Yearly Visitors: 1,500
Year House Built: 1725
Style of Architecture: Cape Cod
Number of Rooms: 5 plus large
  unfurnished attic
On-Site Parking: Yes
Wheelchair Access: No

Description of House

This small cottage was built in 1725 by Jacob Schellinger, son of a Dutch immigrant. The dwelling was owned and used continually by the Schellinger family until 1930. The last member of family to own the house was Mary Amelia Schellinger, known locally as Miss Amelia. The early Schellingers engaged in the whaling business; later generations were carpenters, millwrights, and farmers.

Miss Amelia's Cottage has unusual vertical plank frame construction which divides the front stairs; this is unique for the Long Island area. A scale model of house is on display, and shows details relating to the construction of the cottage.

The 18th and 19th-century furnishings are appropriate to the period and style of house; they include both original and collected pieces.

Notable Collections on Exhibit

Several noteworthy collections are on exhibit here: a group of Dominy furniture and clocks manufactured between 1760 and 1840, and collections of blue flow-ware and early pearlware (Staffordshire china).

Gibby House

331 W. Main Street
Arcade, NY 14009
(716) 492-4466

Contact: Arcade Historical Society
Open: Tues.-Wed. 10 a.m.–4 p.m.;
weekends by appointment
Admission: Donation. Guided tours.
Suggested Time to View House:
45-60 minutes
Facilities on Premises: Gift shop, book store
Number of Yearly Visitors: 1,000 plus
Year House Built: 1902
Style of Architecture: Queen Anne
Victorian
Number of Rooms: 13 (not all open to the
public)
On-Site Parking: Yes
Wheelchair Access: No

Description of House

This lovely Queen Anne-style dwelling was home to several generations of the Gibby family. John Gibby was a cheese manufacturer who owned several small factories in the area. John and Mary Peet Gibby moved into the House in 1903 with their only child, H. Vernon Gibby. Vernon lived in the house with his wife, Marjorie, following their marriage in 1920. Vernon operated an appliance business from the house, but he was better known for his woodworking ability and his photography (some of which is on display in the house). The couple occupied the house until 1983, when it was left to the Arcade Historical Society to use as a museum.

The house was designed by Buffalo architect Frederick Mohr and is the only known example of his residential architecture to survive. The house has changed little from the time it was built, although Vernon Gibby added a new kitchen and porch enclosures. The house's exterior features a textured wall surface (fish scale and board siding), a turret, a projecting pavilion, porches, and colored glass panels in the windows. The interior is equally lovely with its solid oak woodwork, sliding pocket doors dividing formal rooms, an impressive stairway, and crystal chandeliers.

The living room features unusual painted plaster walls done in the 1930s. They used a technique of dipping a piece of crumpled paper in paint and blotting it in a random pattern on the walls to give the impression of light coming through the windows. There is also an elevator that appears to have been installed in 1905.

Notable Collections on Exhibit

Some of Vernon Gibby's woodwork is on display: a solid cherry Governor's Winthrop desk, a gun cabinet made from one his father's old oak desks, a highboy, grandfather and grandmother clocks, and numerous smaller pieces.

The Seward House

33 South Street
Auburn, NY 13021
(315) 252-1283

Contact: Foundation Historical Society
Assoc. Inc.

Open: April-Dec., Tues.-Sat. 1–4 p.m.

Admission: Adults $3; children (under 12)
$2.50; seniors $2.50. All tours are
personally guided.

Suggested Time to View House: 90 minutes

Facilities on Premises: Sales desk

Description of Grounds: Extensive
grounds with fountain, gazebo and
summer house

Best Season to View House: Spring,
summer and fall

Number of Yearly Visitors: 8,000

Year House Built: 1816 with additions in
1840, 1847 and 1868

Style of Architecture: Originally Federal

Number of Rooms: 30

On-Site Parking: No **Wheelchair Access:** No

Description of House

Five generations of the Seward family lived here including William
Henry Seward, the American politcal figure and statesmen. Perhaps best
known for his involvement in the purchase of Alaska(a.k.a. "Sewards
Folly"), he also served as state senator, governor, and Secretary of State
under Presidents Lincoln and Andrew Johnson).

The structure has had a number of alterations over the years from its
construction in 1816 until 1951 when the last occupant, William Henry
Seward III, died and left the house to a local foundation with all of the
original furnishings intact. Many visitors have remarked that the house
appears as if the family had just stepped out.

The Seward House was opened to the public in 1955 and became a
National Historic Landmark in 1964.

Notable Collections on Exhibit

There are many noteworthy paintings on exhibit including an early
collection by artists Thomas Cole, Emmanuel Leutze, Henry Inman and
Chester Harding. The furniture features pieces of early Sheraton and Hepplewhite, Empire, and Victorian, and many decorative arts. There is a large
collection of clothing (1820 to 1920) including Civil War uniforms (two of
Seward's sons served in the Civil War). Collections of early Alaskan artifacts,
and memorabilia collected by Secretary of State Seward on his trip around
the world from 1870 to 1871 complete this eclectic exhibit.

Whitney-Halsey Museum

Contact: The Americana Manse
Open: June–mid Nov., 10 a.m.–4:30 p.m.
Admission: Adults $3; children, $1; groups (over 15, 10 percent discount). Guided tours, candlelight tours (by appointment)
Suggested Time to View House: 45 minutes
Description of Grounds: 3 acres of landscaped grounds with seasonal flowers
Best Season to View House: Summer-fall
Number of Yearly Visitors: Varies
Year House Built: 1870
Style of Architecture: Italianate
Number of Rooms: 17
On-Site Parking: Yes
Wheelchair Access: No

Description of House

This elegant structure has housed a variety of businesses as well as served as a private residential dwelling. The Whitney Halsey house has been a private school, a tea room, and a local doctor's office since it was first constructed in 1870. The original builder of the house, Charles Smith Whitney, owned the house from 1870 to 1900; his wife continued to live here until 1924. The house was opened to the public in 1964.

This typically Italianate Victorian building features two "Romeo and Juliet" style balconies on the exterior. Inside, a black walnut spiral staircase leads to a cherrywood cupola. The interior was constructed with great attention paid to fine detail. In addition to a fanlight over the entry door, there are two bay windows in the dining room and library. Visitors entering the house will see a beautiful nine foot stained glass window in the foyer and a wedding cake ceiling. The house also features six fireplaces, including four made of marble. There are two large (eight feet in length) mirrors over two of the fireplaces; one is a duplicate of a mirror found in the Treaty Room of the White House. A copper chandelier in the dining room is further evidence of the house's wealthy occupants. All of the furnishings on display were collected and appropriate to the period.

Notable Collections on Exhibit

The Victorian furnishings are a special attraction of the house and include a magnificent eight-foot grand Chickering piano made of rosewood, a cherry bench, a mahogany couch with green velvet upholstery, two painted globe lamps, and a black walnut Victrola case.

Morgan-Manning House

151 Main Street
Brockport, NY 14420
(716) 637-3645

Contact: Western Monroe Historical Society
Open: Easter-Christmas, Sun. 2–4 p.m.; or by appointment
Admission: Free. Tours, monthly programs, 4th of July celebration on lawn, craft sale in Sept.
Suggested Time to View House: 1 hour

Number of Yearly Visitors: 3,000
Year House Built: 1854
Style of Architecture: Italianate Villa
Number of Rooms: 20
On-Site Parking: Yes **Wheelchair Access:** Yes

Description of House

The original owner of this Italianate villa, John Ostrom, constructed the dwelling in 1854. The next owner, Dayton Samuel Morgan (1819-1890), a local businessman, purchased it in 1867 and it remained in the Morgan family for nearly 100 years. The seven Morgan children were born and raised in the house. The last Morgan child, Sara Morgan Manning died as a result of a fire in the house in 1964 at the age of 96. The Western Monroe Historical Society restored and redecorated the house after the fire and opened it to the public.

Constructed of red brick, the Morgan-Manning house has two stories plus an attic. The house's elegant exterior is further distinguished by a circular driveway in the front. The lower staircase in the front hall is of golden oak and was installed shortly before the turn of the century. The original upper staircase is of an earlier period and matches the front gold parlor with its heavy ornate cornice and ceiling plasterwork. The house also features eight fireplaces which were once the main source of heat for this twenty room home. The reception room fireplace is especially noteworthy for its decorative metal lining and magnificent cherry mantle.

A few of the furnishings were once owned by the Morgan family. The other pieces are of the same era; everything is appropriate for a Victorian home.

Notable Collections on Exhibit

A guest bedroom contains the original walnut furniture purchased by the Morgans. The set has been used in exhibitions as a classic example of high Victorian furniture. Another bedroom is used for exhibits which change two or three times a year.

Additional Information

An extensive local history collection is available for research by appointment.

Bartow-Pell Mansion Museum

**Shore Road
Pelham Bay Park
Bronx, NY 10464
(212) 885-1461**

Contact: International Garden Club, Inc.

Open: Wed., Sat.-Sun. 12–4 p.m.; closed in Aug.; gardens open Tues.-Sun. 8:30 a.m.–4:30 p.m.

Admission: Adults $2; seniors $1; children free.

Description of Grounds: Formal terraces, herb and perennial gardens which are maintained by the International Garden Club.

Year House Built: 1654 to 1670

Style of Architecture: Grey stone mansion with Greek Revival interiors

Description of House

Thomas Pell, an English doctor bought the land that today forms Pelham Bay Park from the Siwanoy Indians as part of a nearly 50,000-acre tract in 1654. In 1666, King Charles II chartered the Manor of Pelham, encompassing Pelham and the borough of Westchester. Pell was consigned the land grant, and built a house on the banks of the Long Island Sound. The house was completed in 1670 by Thomas Pell's nephew, Sir John Pell. The home served four generations of Pells before it met an incendiary fate during the American Revolution. In 1836, the estate was bought by publisher and Pell descendant Robert Bartow. Bartow built the present mansion and moved into the house with his wife and children in 1842. The family remained until 1888, when the estate was acquired by the city. In the summer of 1936, Mayor Fiorello La Guardia used this mansion as his summer office.

The Bartow-Pell Mansion Museum is a rare example of county elegance in New York City. Inside the entrance to the mansion, an unusual free-standing staircase rises in a grand spiral. Decorative plaster graces the high-ceilinged double parlor. On the second floor, floor-to-ceiling windows open onto black wrought-iron balconies. The conservatory, rebuilt in the 1914 restoration by architects Delano and Aldrich, shelters fruit trees and a statue of Venus.

The two main floors have been decorated with Empire furniture, including pieces loaned by New York City museums. One bedroom features a crowned mahogany sleigh bed hung in crimson silk.

Additional Information

The house and grounds, which include formal terraces, a fountain, and herb and perennial gardens, have been maintained by the International Garden Club, Inc. since 1914. An unusual 1840s stone carriage house is currently under restoration to serve as an interpretation and education center for the museum.

Van Cortlandt House

**Van Cortlandt Park
Broadway and 246th St
Bronx, NY 10471
(212) 543-3344**

Contact: National Society of Colonial Dames in New York

Open: Tue.-Fri., 11 a.m.–3 p.m., Sun. 1–5 p.m.; call to confirm.

Admission: Adults $2; students and seniors $1.50; children (under 14) free. Converted cellar serves as an education center for school groups and local organizations.

Description of Grounds: Colonial-style garden created in the early 1900s. The grounds also include an herb garden and magnificent shade trees.

Year House Built: 1748-49

Style of Architecture: 18th-century vernacular Georgian home

Description of House

In 1694, Jacobus Van Cortlandt, a merchant and mayor of New York (1710-11, 1719-1720), purchased the land that was formerly the hunting grounds of the Mohican Indians. His son, Frederick, built the current house, the oldest in the Bronx. During the American Revolution the house was the scene of military maneuvers and intrigue. George Washington stayed at the Van Cortlandt House on at least two occasions at the beginning and the end of the war and other military commanders, both American and British, used the house as a headquarters. The National Society of Colonial Dames in New York has operated the house as a museum since 1896.

The Van Cortlandt House is set in a wide valley in the third largest park in New York City. This two-and-one-half story field house has a classic exterior; the windows are accented with brick while those on the front facade, have carved brownstone "grotesques" for keystones. Inside the L-shaped house, large windows and eleven-foot ceilings create light and airy spaces.

The interior houses a distinguished collection of period furniture including a neo-classical bed, typical of the early 19th century, with a crewel work coverlet (c.1700).

Poe Cottage

Contact: The Bronx County Historical
  Society

Open: Wed.-Fri. 9 a.m.–5 p.m.;
  Sat. 10 a.m.–4 p.m.; Sun. 1–5 p.m.

Admission: $2. An audiovisual show
  details Poe's life in Fordham and his
  creative genius.

Facilities on Premises: Gift shop

Description of Grounds: Set in a small
  park on the Grand Concourse with a
  garden

Year House Built: 1812

Style of Architecture: Frame Cottage

Description of House

The Poe Cottage was the last home of Edgar Allan Poe (1809-1849), the great American poet and author of early mystery stories. Thirty-four years after the house was built, Poe and his wife Virginia leased the house for $100 a year. Despite Poe's literary success, he was penniless due to his investment in a magazine venture that went bankrupt. His wife's mother, who lived with them, had to forage in neighboring fields to feed the family. In spite of his hardships, Poe wrote many poems in Fordham, including "The Bells," "Eureka" and "Annabel Lee." Visitors to their meager home today will receive valuable insights into New York's literary heritage.

This tiny, one-and-a-half-story cottage, built in 1812 by John Wheeler, is typical of the workman's houses that once dotted the Bronx. It is set in a small park and is the only house left from the old village of Fordham. The house is painted white with green trim. A narrow staircase winds up to the attic bedroom, whose ceiling is barely six feet high.

The main floor is sparsely furnishd with a 19th-century cast-iron stove, a desk, and a rocking chair, straw bed and mirror that might have been used by Poe. The kitchen includes a locally produced cast-iron stove similar to the one that Poe might have used.

Notable Collections on Exhibit

Painted and sculpted portraits of Poe, as well as early photographs and drawings of the cottage, are displayed.

Valentine-Varian House

3266 Bainbridge Avenue
(at E. 208th Street)
Bronx, NY 10467
(212) 881-8900

Contact: The Bronx County Historical Society
Open: Sat. 10 a.m.–4 p.m., Sun. 1–5 p.m.; call to confirm. Tours by appointment Mon.-Fri.
Admission: $2. Cultural programs.
Facilities on Premises: Gift shop

Description of Grounds: Period plantings, an herb garden, an outdoor seating area, and the Bronx River Soldier monument embellish the surrounding gardens
Year House Built: 1758
Style of Architecture: Georgian Vernacular

Description of House

The house was built by Isaac Valentine, a blacksmith and farmer who bought the parcel of land from the Dutch Reformed Church. During the Revolutionary War, the Valentine family had to abandon their home, which was occupied by British, Hessian and American troops. The Valentines returned after the war, but sold the home and 260-acre property to Isaac Varian, a successful butcher and farmer, in 1792. The Varians kept the house for three generations; one of Isaac's sons (also named Isaac) mayor of New York City from 1839 to 1841. The building was sold at auction to William F. Beller in 1905. In 1965, his son donated the house to the Bronx County Historical Society.

The Valentine-Varian House is the second oldest house in the borough of the Bronx. It stands today inside a wrought-iron fence in a small park in the Norwood neighborhood of north-central Bronx. The two-story fieldstone home utilizes the symmetrical style known as "Georgian Vernacular," with evenly placed windows and identical chimneys at either end. Inside, rooms mirror each other across a central hallway. Deep-set splayed windows throughout the house were designed to let light in and keep cold out. Sections of the house retain the original floorboards, hand-forged nails, and homemade mortar.

Notable Collections on Exhibit

Two rooms contain changing exhibits, while the front parlor has a permanent display about the development of the area, from the Indian and Dutch periods through the Revolution.

Pieter Claeson Wyckoff House

Contact: Wyckoff House & Association Inc.
Open: Fri.-Sun. 12–5 p.m.; winter hours (Dec.-March), 12–4 p.m.
Admission: Adults $2; children and seniors $1. Guided tours, lectures, craft workshops, children's reading hours, special group visits by appointment.

Description of Grounds: There are several gardens on the site, including an 18th-century kitchen garden.
Best Season to View House: Spring and fall
Number of Yearly Visitors: 5,000
Year House Built: 1652
Style of Architecture: Colonial Dutch-American
On-Site Parking: No **Wheelchair Access:** Yes

Description of House

Constructed in 1652, this simple frame house is probably the oldest home in New York City and became the city's first landmark in 1965. Pieter Claesen Wyckoff's life exemplifies the American success story. In 1637, he arrived in America, an illiterate indentured servant. He eventually became a magistrate, a successful farmer, and the wealthiest citizen of New Amersfoort, which later became the town of Flatlands. With his wife Grietje Van Ness, he had ten children. Wyckoff's descendants lived in the house until 1902 at which time it became a stopping place for travelers on nearby Canarsie Lane. The house was repurchased in the 1960s by the Wyckoff House and Association and subsequently donated to the City of New York.

The Wyckoff home is one of the oldest wooden frame houses in the U.S. and a prime example of Colonial Dutch-American architecture. This modest house, with its wide pine floorboards, shingled walls and a gable roof with flaired "spring" eves, is typical for the period. Special care has been taken with the restoration of the house: new beams have been handcrafted; nails were forged on site; old glass has replaced broken window panes; original fireplace tiles were replicated and the paint was analyzed so that the colors are the same as those originally used. Of particular interest are the jamless fireplace, and the more than 300 year old mud and wattle insulation in the earliest part of the house.

Each room has a mixture of objects similar to those accumulated by any family spanning several centuries. The rooms are decorated with objects original to the house, and with objects from other Kings County Wyckoff Houses and include a large wooden "kas" or cupboard, a spinning wheel, and old cooking utensils. Many are on loan from the Society for the Preservation of Long Island Antiques.

Notable Collections on Exhibit

The Wyckoff House Museum's collection includes several hundred pieces of Colonial and early-American furnishings, most dating to the period prior to 1819. The museum's small exhibition area features two changing exhibits on the Pieter Claesen Wyckoff House and local history. Past exhibits include "Restoring a Landmark", a photographic essay on the 1980s restoration of the house. Photographs of the farmhouse as it appeared circa 1890 and immediately before restoration work began are also on display to emphasize the importance of historic preservation. The museum also maintains a collection of original documents dating from the period 1670 to 1866 which include papers related to slave sales and land sales, wills, and several documents written in Dutch. A small library with rare historical resources is available for research.

Additional Information

The museum regularly conducts demonstrations of American crafts (e.g. spinning and outdoor cooking) which recall daily life in Brooklyn's early farming community.

Lefferts Homestead

Prospect Park
Flatbush Ave. at Empire Bl
Brooklyn, NY 11215
(718)965-6505

Contact: Prospect Park Admin. Office and Park Allianc

Open: Sat.-Sun. 12–4 p.m., closed winter months, call for information

Activities: Demonstrations of early American crafts, hands-on family workshops, special events, and a number of other adult educational programs offered by the Prospect Park Alliance

Description of Grounds: Herb and vegetable gardens

Year House Built: 1777-1783

Style of Architecture: Dutch Colonial farmhouse

Description of House

The house was home to at least four generations of the Lefferts family. The homestead was built between 1777 and 1783 by Peter Lefferts, a prominent 18th-century Flatbush landowner who had 240 acres in his possession. Lefferts was one of the wealthiest men in Kings County and headed a large household that included eight family members and twelve slaves. Lefferts served as a lieutenant in the Colonial army and became a judge on the county court of sessions and common pleas. In 1788, he was a delegate to the state convention in Poughkeepsie when New York ratified the Constitution. Lefferts left the house to his six-year old son, John. John Lefferts served at a member of the New York State Senate (1821-1826). Descendants of the family presented the house to the city of New York in 1918.

The Lefferts Homestead is one of the few surviving Dutch Colonial farmhouses in Brooklyn. The structure combines Dutch Colonial architecture with Federal details. A bell-shaped gambrel roof create sloping eaves that hang over front and back porches with slender columns. Carved woodwork and circle-and-diamond pattern transom windows adorn the Dutch-style split front door. The rooms are furnished to reflect daily life in the 1820s.

Notable Collections on Exhibit

The house displays many original pieces belonging to the Lefferts family including a large "kas", or Dutch cupboard, a four-poster bed, Bibles and a grandfather clock.

Granger Homestead

295 North Main Street
Canandaigua, NY 14424
(716) 394-1472

Contact: Granger Homestead Society Inc.

Open: Early May-late Oct., Tues.-Sat. 10 a.m.–5 p.m.

Admission: Adults $3; children $1. Guided tours, 30 minute video on the life of Gideon Granger.

Suggested Time to View House: 90 minutes

Description of Grounds: 12 acre site

Year House Built: 1816

Style of Architecture: Federal

Number of Rooms: 10

On-Site Parking: Yes

Description of House

Born in Suffield, Connecticut, Gideon Granger (1767-1822) was active in state politics during the years of the American Revolution and the Constitutional convention. A supporter of Thomas Jefferson, he was named Postmaster General when Jefferson took office as President in 1800, and continued to serve under President Madison until 1813. After resigning from office, Granger moved to Canandaigua and resolved to build a homestead that would be "unrivalled in all the nation," from which he could administer the many land tracts he had acquired further to the west. After his arrival, Granger became influential in local affairs. Although he died in 1822, succeeding generations of the Granger family played an equally important part in the development of the Canandaigua area.

This Federal-style house features beautifully detailed carved moldings and mantelpieces in its restored period rooms. Granger Homestead was constructed over a two year period by local builders and craftsman at a total cost of $13,000. The furnishings on display include many original pieces owned by four generations of the Granger family.

Notable Collections on Exhibit

An exhibit in the upstairs gallery, "The Statesman from Canandaigua", includes a 30 minute documentary about Gideon Granger. In the Granger Homestead's Carriage Museum, a remarkable collection of fifty horse-drawn vehicles documents the history of 19th-century transportation in western New York.

Sonnenberg Gardens Mansion

151 Charlotte
Canandaigua, NY 14424
(716) 394-4922

Contact: Sonnnenberg Gardens

Open: Mid May-mid Oct.,
9:30 a.m.–5:30 p.m.

Admission: Adults $5; seniors $4; children
(6-16) $2; under 6 free. Tours of mansion
and grounds, special seasonal events.

Suggested Time to View House:
30–45 minutes

Facilities on Premises: 2 gift/book shops,
restaurant (lunches only)

Description of Grounds: 50 acres with
9 gardens of different styles and sizes

Best Season to View House: Mid June to
end of September

Number of Yearly Visitors: 70,000 plus

Year House Built: 1885 to 1887

Style of Architecture: Various–Queen Anne
with Tudor and Richardsonian influences

Number of Rooms: 40 with 2 floors
open to public

Description of House

This beautiful mansion and surrounding gardens provided a summer retreat for Frederick Ferris Thompson and his wife, Mary. Mary was a native of the Canandaigua area and enjoyed returning to her home town during the hot summer months. Frederick worked as a banker in New York and the couple's main residence was on Madison Avenue. The Thompson's philanthropies were many and varied and included colleges, hospitals, libraries, and museums. Because they had no children, the house was left to a nephew in 1923. He maintained the mansion until 1930 when it was sold to the state for use as a veterans' home. This resulted in the mansion's conversion into nurse's quarters. In the 1960s, a group of citizens interested in restoring the mansion's elaborate gardens worked to re-open the estate.

This forty-room structure was designed by Francis Allen of Boston and utilizes an eclectic mix of architectural styles. Today, visitors may experience a fine example of a Victorian summer house built for the wealthy. The interior features a unique use of skylights with colored glass used to defuse the light. The house was built to accomodate visitors and offer them the best in comfort and relaxation. The many balconies and verandas provided spots for enjoying the out-of-doors, for eating, visiting or any quiet activity.

Furnishings are from the same period as the house; some are fromthe original family including Mary's sampler collection and others collected and appropriate to period.

Notable Collections on Exhibit

In addition to the furnishings, Sonnenberg houses an illustrative group of samplers which were a part of a much larger collection owned by Mary Thompson.

Additional Information

The mansion's main attraction are the beautiful and varied gardens open to the public. Close to 200 volunteers maintain the Italian Renaissance garden, the Japanese garden, and a world-famous rose garden.

Silas Wright House Museum

3 East Main Street
P.O. Box 8
Canton, NY 13617
(315) 386-8133

Contact: St. Lawrence County Historical Association

Open: Tues.-Sat. 10 a.m.–4 p.m. , closed holidays

Admission: Free. 2-3 major exhibitions each year; special programming done in conjunction with these exhibits.

Suggested Time to View House: 1 hour

Facilities on Premises: Archives open Tues.-Sat. 12–4 p.m.

Number of Yearly Visitors: 9,800

Year House Built: 1832-33

Style of Architecture: Greek Revival

Number of Rooms: 5 plus 3 county museum rooms

On-Site Parking: Yes **Wheelchair Access:** Yes

Description of House

Silas Wright had a long and varied political career, during which he lived in this lovely home with his wife, Clarissa. Silas was a postmaster and county surrogate in Canton, and then went on to become a state senator. He was Canton's first lawyer. From 1827 to 1829 he was a representative in Congress and later became governor of New York from 1844 to 1847 and a U.S. Senator from 1833 to 1844.

The house was restored and renovated during the 1970s when the historical society obtained ownership. Five rooms on the first floor of this two-story structure have been restored to the period of 1830 to 1850. The deor reflects a number of of styles that were popular during that era. There are only a few furnishings which remain from the Wright family; most are collected and appropriate to the period.

Notable Collections on Exhibit

The archives contain a noteworthy manuscript collection. The manuscripts include the personal and professional papers of Silas Wright, a collection of papers and artifacts of boatbuilder J. H. Rushton, and manuscripts and ephemera from composer and writer Walter H. Leonard.

Castile Historic House

17 Park Road East
P.O. Box 256
Castile, NY 14427
(716) 493-5370

Contact: Castile Historical Society

Open: Tues. 9 a.m.–12 p.m., 1–3 p.m.; other times by appointment-call (716) 493-2894

Admission: Free, donations accepted. Guided tours.

Suggested Time to View House: 30 minutes

Facilities on Premises: Regional books are sold

Best Season to View House: Spring, summer and fall

Number of Yearly Visitors: 2,500

Year House Built: 1860

Number of Rooms: 8

On-Site Parking: No **Wheelchair Access:** No

Description of House

The Castile Historic House was donated to the historical society in 1956 and today houses the society's collection of artifacts, records, and pictures covering more than a century. The furnishings and artifacts represent more than the life of a single resident, instead provide a vast amount of information about the life of this rural community.

All of the items in the house have been donated by area residents with an interest in local history. Seven of the rooms are furnished with Victorian era furniture. There is also a barn on the grounds which houses an exhibit of Colonial farm equipment.

Notable Collections on Exhibit

Visitors to the Castile Historic house will find extensive genealogical records, large picture files of houses, businesses and public builldings in the area, cemetery and census records, scrapbooks and clipping files, newspapers on microfilm, files on surrounding villages and townships, a large collection of clothing, a barn full of colonial farm equipment and war records and memorabilia from the Revolutionary War, the Civil War, and World Wars I and II.

Cherry Valley Museum (Phelan Sutliff House)

49 Main Street, P.O. Box 115
Cherry Valley, NY 13320
(607) 264-3303

Contact: Cherry Valley Historical Association
Open: Memorial Day-Oct.15, 10 a.m.–5 p.m.
Admission: Adults $2; seniors $1.50; groups (10 or more), $1; children with an adult, free. Taped account of history of founding of the village up to 1840; hostess available for information.

Suggested Time to View House: 1 hour
Number of Yearly Visitors: 1,000 plus
Year House Built: 1832
Style of Architecture: Federal
Number of Rooms: 15
On-Site Parking: Yes **Wheelchair Access:** Yes

Description of House

Originally built by Joseph Phelan in 1832, this grand Federal building was given to the historical society for use as a museum by one of its occupants, Grace Sutliff, in memory of her husband, Walter.

The fifteen-room house is located in the Historic Cherry Valley and its collections represent a wide span of historical events ranging from early Colonial history through the industrial revolution to the early 20th century. Only the parlor and bedroom are furnished as period rooms.

Notable Collections on Exhibit

Cherry Valley Museum houses an eclectic collection of artifacts and memorabilia including an extensive display of women's clothing dating from the mid-1800s, children's outfits, and accessories. There are also many household items on display including a dining room ice box, kitchen equipment, spinning wheels, farm tools, toys, and quilts and coverlets.

Additional Information

At the museum, visitors may also obtain directions for a walking tour to see other sites of local interest: the Massacre Monument, the Civil War Monument, the James Morse House, the former Judd Foundry, the Clyde House and other examples of early architecture.

Constable Hall

Box 36-John Street
Constableville, NY 13325
(315) 397-2323

Contact: Constable Hall Association, Inc.

Open: June 1-Oct. 15, Tues.-Sat.,
10 a.m.–4:30 p.m.; Sun., 1–4:30 p.m.

Admission: Adults $2; children (6-13 yrs.)
$.50; groups (notified in advance) $1.50.
Guided tours.

Suggested Time to View House: 75 minutes

Facilities on Premises: Gift shop

Description of Grounds: Historically
restored garden

Best Season to View House: Summer

Number of Yearly Visitors: 2,200

Year House Built: 1819

Number of Rooms: 13

Style of Architecture: Georgian/Federal

On-Site Parking: Yes **Wheelchair Access:** Yes

Description of House

William Constable Jr. spent over nine years building this majestic home which is fashioned after the Constable family's county seat of 17th century Ireland. Constable's father was instrumental in the development of northern New York, and he served as an aide to Lafayette during the Revolution. Five generations of the Constable family lived in the hall. In 1946, the last resident sold the family home to philanthropists who restored the structure and turned it into a historic house museum.

Begun in 1810, Constable Hall was constructed from limestone brought to this remote location by ox cart. Artisans, from as far away as Schenectedy and the Hudson Valley, were employed to create the interior woodwork. Handblown glass was used in the window panes, and window shutters and a shallow fireplace designed by Thomas Jefferson were incorporated. The sixteen rooms have many unique features including a fireproof office, a chapel, and two wine cellars, which even today remain at a constant temperature all year round.

The majority of the furnishings (75 percent) were owned by the Constable family and include noteworthy examples of Chippendale, Hepplewhite, and Sheraton styles.

Notable Collections on Exhibit

Many artifacts that belonged to the Constable family are on display including correspondence with Lafayette, Robert Morris, and Baron von Steuben. There is also a collection of guns and pistols. On the walls hang two Rembrandt Peale paintings and family portraits. The Constable family library (800 volumes) features some rare first editions.

Additional Information

To the east of the hall is a unique formal flower garden in the shape of the Irish flag. Many of the roses, Oriental poppies, and lemon lilies are survivors of the original 1800s plantings.

1890 House Museum and Center for the Victorian Arts

37 Tompkins Street
Cortland, NY 13045-2555
(607) 756-7551

Open: Tues.-Sun. 1–4 p.m.; closed holidays

Admission: Adults $3.50; students and seniors $2.50; children (under 12) free; group rates available. Orientation Center with film; tours of mansion; exhibition of Victorian interiors as well as rotating special interest exhibitions.

Suggested Time to View House: 1 hour

Facilities on Premises: Small gift shop

Description of Grounds: Rose garden and lawn accessible

Best Season to View House: Spring-summer

Number of Yearly Visitors: 15,000-20,000

Year House Built: 1889-1890

Style of Architecture: Chateauesque-Romanesque

Number of Rooms: 30

On-Site Parking: No **Wheelchair Access:** Yes

Description of House

The 1890 House was once the residence of 19th-century industrialist Chester Franklin Wickwire (1843-1910). Chester grew up on the family farm east of Cortland in McGraw. As a young man, he moved to the city and opened a grocery store on Main Street. Gradually, the groceries gave way to a more popular line of hardware and Chester's brother, Theodore, joined him in the business. In 1873, the Wickwire brothers received a carpet loom in payment for a bad debt. Adapting the loom to weave wire screening, Chester transformed the simple hardware store into a major wire manufacturing firm. Secure with the success of the business, Chester turned his attention to the construction of a new family residence, the 1890 House.

This four story limestone mansion was designed by architect Samuel Burrage Reed and duplicated the design of a structure built for Anthony Baily, of Barnum and Baily, in New York. The lavish interior of the thirty-room mansion features ornate stencil designs, parquet floors, stained glass windows, oak and cherry woodwork, and silk wall coverings. Other elegant touches representative of the era may be seen in the mercury mosaic stained glass windows installed in 1890 and manufactured by the Belcher Mosaic Glass Company of New Jersey. There is also a stained glass skylight installed in the 1920s designed by Keck Studios of Syracuse. The furnishings are appropriate to the period with some original pieces. 19th-century photographs of each room indicate the arrangement of the original pieces.

Additional Information

This massive limestone castle is the highlight of Cortland's Historic District, and is listed on the National Register of Historic Places.

The Old House on Cutchogue Village Green

Route 25 and Case's Lane
Cutchogue, NY 11935
(516) 734-7122

Contact: Cutchogue-New Suffolk Historical Council
Open: June-Sept., Sat.and Sun. 2–5 p.m.
Admission: Adults $2; children $.50. Guided tours.
Suggested Time to View House: 30 minutes to 1 hour
Facilities on Premises: Gift shop

Description of Grounds: This building plus two other historic buildings are on the Cutchogue Village Green.
Number of Yearly Visitors: 1,000-1,500
Year House Built: 1649
Style of Architecture: English Domestic
Number of Rooms: 6
On-Site Parking: Yes **Wheelchair Access:** No

Description of House

John Budd, a great-grandson of the Earl of Warwick, built this fine example of English architecture in 1649. The house was originally located in Southold but was moved to Cutchogue after Budd gave it to his daughter as a wedding present. Later the house passed into the hands of the Wickham family and then to several other local families before it became the property of the Cutchogue historical council.

The Old House is one of the finest structures of English domestic origin still standing today. This two-story house has two rooms on each floor with a staircase porch and a great chimney stack, of English origin, to the left of the center of the building. The porch walls are covered with ship-lapped, shadow moulded verticle pine boarding of random width. There are several unusual staircases in the house. The house also features unusually fine examples of three-part casement windows. Despite having been neglected for a period of years, the Old House preserves many of the features of its original construction. All of the furnishings are collected and appropriate to the period.

Additional Information

This house is located on the Cutchogue Village Green along with two other historic buildings, the Wickham Farm House and the Old Schoolhouse. Visitors are encouraged to make a combined visit to all three.

John Hanford House

PO Box 111
East Meredith, NY 13757
(607) 278-5744

Contact: Hanford Mills Museum

Open: May-Oct. 10 a.m.–5 p.m.

Admission: Adults $3; children (6-12) $1.50; children (under 6) and members free. House restoration not yet completed. Ice Harvest 1st Sun. in Feb. (parlor games and slides show). Members holiday party in Feb.

Facilities on Premises: Gift/book shop

Description of Grounds: 1920s vegtable garden, wagon house, chicken coop, smoke house, garage, and buildings associated with Hanford mill business.

Best Season to View House: May-Oct.

Number of Yearly Visitors: 11,000

Year House Built: 1909

Number of Rooms: 12 rooms plus basement and attic

Style of Architecture: Farmhouse

On-Site Parking: Yes **Wheelchair Access:** No

Description of House

John Hanford took over this farm in 1899 after his father's death. At the same time, his brothers, Will and Horace, took over the mill. In 1909, John moved his father's original house and built the house which visitors will see today. He and his wife, Elizabeth, had two sons (one died at an early age), and a daughter. John died in 1938, and his widow sold the house in 1945. The house was used as a summer residence until the museum acquired it in 1988.

The son constructed a plain farmhouse, similar in floor plan to those offered through the Sears catalog. The different areas of the house reflect the different periods of ownership. The one-story kitchen wing was originally a separate milk house built in 1891 for the father's home. Because of the dairy farm operation, the basement houses a 1920s Hercules gas engine used to run milk pumps and other machinery. When the kitchen wing was a milk house, before the rest of the building was built, separators and butter-making machinery were run by a turbine situated behind the house. The living room features a window with farm scene decoration.

Furnishings are from the period of 1909 through the 1920s. To date, most furnishings are original Hanford pieces, though gaps in the furnishing plan will be filled in with appropriate 1920s and pre-1920s pieces.

Queens County Farm Museum

73-59 Little Neck Parkway
Floral Park, NY 11004
(718) 347-FARM

Contact: Colonial Farmhouse Restoration

Open: Sat.-Sun. 12–5 p.m., May-Sept., Thur. 12–5 p.m.; call to confirm

Activities: Educational tours and workshops covering horticulture technology, farm life history and food preparation; an old fashioned country fair, a Native American pow-wow and antique car show.

Facilities on Premises: Gift shop

Description of Grounds: The museum is a working farm surrounding the restored Jacob Adriance Farmhouse. Geese, ducks, cows and sheep roam the grounds.

Year House Built: 1772

Style of Architecture: Dutch-style farmhouse

Description of House

Jacob Adriance built this modest farmhouse in 1772, however, records show that the Adriance family had owned the property since 1697. The house and farmland were bought and sold several times during the 19th century. From 1890 to 1926, two generations of the Stattel family operated a truck farm on the site. The Creedmoor State Hospital acquired the Jacob Adriance property in 1927. For decades the area remained agricultural and was tilled by hospital patients; the house was used by hospital staff until 1973. Two years later the Colonial Farmhouse Restoration Society of Bellrose opened the Queens Country Farm Museum.

The Dutch-style farmhouse was constructed with a steeply pitched roof, four-foot overhanging eaves, and hand-split shingles on the exterior. A greenhouse and other farm buildings were added in the 1930s. The house has two unusual features in the English-style central chimney and the northern orientation of the house. This allowed a nearby hill to protect the structure from winter winds. The home was doubled in size by owner Peter Cox between 1833 and 1840.

Additional Information

The Jacob Adriance Farmhouse was partially restored in the mid-1980s. Today the farm's seven and one-half acres of croplands and orchard are being reclaimed to demonstrate the history of agriculture in New York. The museum staff and volunteers harvest apples and grow herbs, squash, tomatoes and other standard market vegetables, which are sold from a roadside farm stand.

Bowne House

37-01 Bowne Street
Flushing, NY 11354
(718) 359-0528

Contact: Bowne House Historical
Society, Inc.

Open: Tues., Sat., Sun. 2:30–4:30 p.m.;
July 5-Labor Day, Wed.-Thurs.
11 a.m.–3 p.m. (summer hours
subject to change)

Admission: Adults $2; children $.50;
members free. School program daily
10 a.m.–12 p.m.

Suggested Time to View House: 1 hour

Facilities on Premises: Gift shop

Description of Grounds: Herb garden, rare
shrubs and trees

Best Season to View House: Spring,
summer, fall

Number of Yearly Visitors: 5000 plus

Year House Built: 1661

Style of Architecture: Vernacular
Dutch-English

Number of Rooms: 9 open to public

On-Site Parking: No **Wheelchair Access:** Yes

Description of House

In this simple home, John Bowne secured freedom of conscience for inhabitants of New Netherlands in 1662. Bowne, a Flushing merchant and landowner, took his stand against the outlawing of the Quaker sect by Peter Stuyvesant, governor of New Netherlands. Bowne continued to hold religious gatherings in the house and was eventually arrested and sent to Europe. He returned in 1664 and was vindicated; his actions led to the adoption of the First Amendment to the Constitution over 100 years later.

Built in 1661, the Bowne house is considered one of the finest examples of vernacular Dutch-English architecture in the country. The original house consisted of a kitchen, two adjoining rear rooms and an upstairs bed chamber. The kitchen contains an unusually oversized fireplace and beehive ovens. There is also a parlor along side the kitchen, built in 1680. Today called the dining room, this addition retains 17th-century hand-hewn beams and pegged floors.

The building houses a notable collection of 17th, 18th, and 19th-century furniture, portraits, and household objects, all of which belonged to the Bowne family.

The Bowne House is recognized as one of the oldest structures in New York State, and is listed on the National Register of Historic Places.

Kingsland Homestead

143-35 37th Avenue
Flushing, NY 11354
(718) 939-0647

Contact: Queens Historical Society

Open: Tues., Sat. and Sun. 2:30–4:30 p.m. Call to confirm.

Activities: Tours by appointment. The Society offers a regular series of lectures and programs.

Description of Grounds: The 2 acre Weeping Beech Park surrounds the house

Year House Built: 1785 (approx.)

Facilities on Premises: Library and archive

Style of Architecture: Gambrel roof

Description of House

Charles Doughty built this handsome house around 1785. He was the son of Benjamin Doughty, a wealthy Quaker who purchased land on the old turnpike in Flushing. The name "Kingsland" derived from Doughty's son-in-law, British sea captain Joseph King, who bought the home in 1801.

The two-story homestead has a gambrel roof, a cresent-shaped window in a side gamble, and a Dutch-style front door. The original shingles laid over the exterior in 1805 by the owner, Captain King, remain on all but the west side of the house. The only furnished period room is a second-floor parlor decorated as if it belonged to a middle-class Victorian family.

The Kingsland Homestead stands in the shade of the Weeping Beech tree, a designated New York City landmark planted in 1847. The tree has an fascinating history beginning with its origins in Belgium. The parent tree was saved from destruction by the gardener on the estate of Baron de Mann in Beirsal, Belgium who order the tree uprooted. In 1847, Samuel Parsons brought a budded shoot of the parent tree to America with him. To this, every Weeping Beech grown in this country owes its genetic root.

Notable Collections on Exhibit

The first floor is used for local history exhibitions that draw on the collections of the Queens Historical Society and community residents.

Additional Information

The society offers a regular series of lectures and programs and makes accessible to the public a library of source materials covering the 300-year history of Queens.

Old Fort House Museum

22 and 29 Broadway
P.O. Box 106
Fort Edward, NY 12828
(518) 747-9600

Contact: Fort Edward Historical Association
Open: Mid June to mid Sept., daily 1–5 p.m.; Christmas display, Dec. 1-18 1–4 p.m.
Admission: Free. Guided tours and educational tours, programs for school groups
Suggested Time to View House: 1 hour
Facilities on Premises: Gift shop (with local historical books)

Description of Grounds: Groomed lawn with picnic tables. Barn gallery/gift shop is the only building accessible to wheelchairs at this time.
Best Season to View House: Summer
Number of Yearly Visitors: 5,000
Year House Built: 1772-1773
Style of Architecture: Georgian
Number of Rooms: 11
On-Site Parking: Yes **Wheelchair Access:** Yes

Description of House

This historic fort has been home to a distinguished group of residents beginning with Patrick Smyth, a Colonial official, postmaster, and assistant judge. Smyth also made history when he was taken prisoner in the summer of 1777 and put under house arrest by General Benedict Arnold. Another occupant, Dr. John Cochran, was George Washington's personal surgeon. The house served as a tavern and inn during the Revolutionary War (George Washington stopped here on his way to Crown Point). Solomon Northrup took up residence in the house on his wedding day in 1829 and lived here until 1832. A free black man, Northrup is best known as the author of *Twelve Years a Slave* based on his experience of being kidnapped in Saratoga, New York and sold into slavery. Later occupants remodeled the house in the Greek Revival style. In 1900, the house was purchased by J. Henry and Ella Baldwin who operated a produce business from the structure. The Baldwin family remained in the house until 1952, and in 1953 the house was opened to the public as a museum.

The two-and-a-half story Old Fort House is the oldest frame building in Washington County. Early 19th-century residents remodeled the house in the Greek Revival style and added a large cupola. In 1943, a fire completely destroyed the roof and the cupola, and local historians were able convince county officials to return the house to its original 18th-century form by restoring the gambrel roof. The house has recently undergone further renovation to replace the original foundation and other structural elements. The Old Fort House is the center of a six building complex which also contains a restored law office (c. 1853) and a toll house (c. 1840).

The rooms are furnished with local period furnishings and decorative arts appropriate for the period 1780 to 1850. Some belonged to the original occupants and others were collected to reflect their various roles in the community.

Notable Collections on Exhibit
The house contains a large collection of paintings which includes portraits of local historical figures, as well as glassware and locally produced stoneware.

Additional Information
The Old Fort House Museum property is adjacent to the Little Wood Creek archeological site.

Pratt House

177 South First Street
P.O. Box 157
Fulton, NY 13069
(315) 598-4616

Contact: Historical Society of Fulton
Open: Mon. and Wed. 9 a.m.–12:30 p.m.;
Tues. 12:30–3:30 p.m., and by
appointment
Admission: Free. Guided tours, programs
for special groups.
Suggested Time to View House: 1 hour
Number of Yearly Visitors: 2,400
Year House Built: 1863
Number of Rooms: 16
On-Site Parking: Yes
Wheelchair Access: Yes

Description of House

This stately brick house was built for John Wells Pratt and his wife, Harriet, in a prominent location on what was then the leading residential street in Fulton. Timothy and Hanna Pratt, the parents of John, were among the earliest settlers of Fulton. In 1840, Timothy built a stone grist mill on the Oswego River where he milled the grain from surrounding farms as well as linseed and lumber. The house remained in the Pratt family through John's son, George, and his wife, Helen, and his grandson, John. In 1979, through the efforts of the community, the house was saved from demolition and acquired by the historical society to use as its headquarters and museum.

This Italianate dwelling is one of the few large houses in Fulton which maintains most of its original structure. The house features a cupola, typical for this architectural style, elaborate window caps, and large paired brackets under the eaves. The rooms are furnished with collected pieces of furniture which span the period of the different occupants. The downstairs rooms are devoted to changing historical exhibits while the upstairs houses permanent exhibits on local history and industry. The kitchen and out-house are currently under renovation to restore them to their original turn-of-the-century appearance.

Notable Collections on Exhibit

The house exhibits photographs and artifacts from Fulton's current and prior industries, canals, and residents. There is also an area for genealogical research.

Locust Lawn

Route 32
Gardiner, NY
(914) 255-1660

Contact: Huguenot Historical Society
Open: Memorial Day weekend-Sept.,
  Wed.-Sun. 10 a.m.–4 p.m.
Admission: Adults $3; children (under 14)
  $1.50. Tours, special events.
Suggested Time to View House: 90 minutes
Description of Grounds: Estate grounds
  and adjacent wildlife sanctuary
Best Season to View House: May-Sept.
Number of Yearly Visitors: 3,500
Year House Built: 1814

Style of Architecture: Vernacular Federal
Number of Rooms: 10   **On-Site Parking:** Yes **Wheelchair Access:** No

Description of House

Colonel Josiah Hasbrouck, the builder of the house, was a lieutenant in the Revolutionary War and served in the house of representatives during the terms of Presidents Adams and Jefferson. He acquired and inherited extensive properties in New York during his lifetime and became one of the wealthiest men in the country.

The proportions of the building, its pilasters, arches and wide moldings are characteristic of the fine Federal style. One of the outstanding features of the house are the marbleized plaster walls in the central hall. This treatment of plaster was a specialty of the architect Cromwell. The first floor includes three rooms in the main part of the house, the dining room, the parlor, and a schoolroom. The two room kitchen comprises the rear wing. The south end of the second floor, the children's room, was partitioned off from the hall in later years. The stairway which leads to the third story from the hall was given over to the great attic and servant's quarters. Locust Lawn is furnished with pieces from the original residents.

The house is surrounded by a group of outbuildings with displays on exhibit. These include a slaughter-house, a smoke-house, and a carriage barn.

Notable Collections on Exhibit

Locust Lawn houses important American paintings and furnishings including several Ammi Phillips portraits of family members. The outbuildings exhibit coaches, tools and farm implements of an early day.

Additional Information

A short distance from the Locust Lawn mansion stands the house that Evert Terwilliger and his wife Sarah Freer built in 1738. In the early years the house was an inn and the bedrooms on the north side were utilized in this fashion without inconvenience to the family.

Boscobel

Garrison-on-Hudson
Garrison, NY 10524
(914) 265-3638

Contact: Boscobel Restoration, Inc.

Open: April 1-Oct. 31, 9:30 a.m.–4 p.m.; March, Nov.and Dec., 9:30 a.m.–3 p.m.; closed every Tues., Thanksgiving, and Christmas

Admission: Adults $4; children (6-14) and student groups $1. Guided tours (group tours by appointment), special musical or dramatic programs.

Suggested Time to View House: 45 minutes

Facilities on Premises: Museum shop with books

Description of Grounds: Herb garden, formal garden, apple trees, pond, view of Hudson River and West Point

Best Season to View House: Spring-fall

Number of Yearly Visitors: 30,000

Year House Built: 1808

Style of Architecture: Federal

Number of Rooms: 13

On-Site Parking: Yes

Description of House

Boscobel was begun as the planned home of States Morris Dyckman (b. New York, 1755), a descendant of early Dutch settlers. A loyalist, Dyckman acquired a fortune by remaining employed by the retiring British quartermaster general following the American Revolution. He made two long trips to London between 1779 and 1801, and there began to acquire symbols of financial success: silver, crystal, maps, prints, elegantly bounded books. Returning from his last trip to London in 1804, he assumed the lifestyle of a country gentleman and began to work on an elegant new home, named after the forest of Boscobel, using design elements made fashionable by the English architect Robert Adam on his farm on the Hudson River. His widow, Elizabeth Corne Dyckman, completed Boscobel during the two years after Morris's death (1806).

This mansion has been acclaimed as an outstanding example of Federal architecture, a style popular in America subsequent to the Revolution. The home offers an amalgam of the Greek and Roman design motifs which dominated British and American taste in the early 19th century. Boscobel was almost destroyed during the 1950s when the original site was needed for new construction, but was then moved piece by piece and rebuilt at its present location. The mansion is located in the heart of the Hudson highlands and offers visitors an impressive view of the valley below.

Notable Collections on Exhibit

Boscobel's collection of furnishings and decorative arts provide further outstanding examples of the neo-classical period. The interior furnishings of some 1700 objects include 150 major examples comprising one of the country's finest exhibits of three prominent New York cabinetmakers: Duncan Phyfe, Michael Allison, and C. Honore Lannuier. Over 100 pieces of artwork are on display featuring paintings by Bengamin West, Thomas Doughty, and Ammi Phillips. The collections of smaller furniture and accessories include clocks, looking glasses, crystal, lighting devices, porcelain and pottery of the period.

Additional Information

Boscobel's surrounding property enables visitors to learn about Constitution Marsh, one of the few preserved marshlands of the Hudson River. The marsh is maintained by the Audobon Society.

Prouty-Chew Museum

543 South Main Street
Geneva, NY 14456
(315) 789-5151

Contact: Geneva Historical Society

Open: Year round, Tues.-Fri.
10 a.m.–12 p.m. and 1–5 p.m.; Sat.
1:30–4:30 p.m.

Admission: Free, donations accepted.
Guided tours, self guided walking tours
of neighborhood, lectures, changing
exhibits, special workshops and
programs.

Suggested Time to View House: 45 minutes

Number of Yearly Visitors: 14,000

Year House Built: 1829

Style of Architecture: Federal, remodeled
1850s and 1870s

Number of Rooms: 5 period rooms,
3 changing exhibits galleries

Description of House

The original owner of the house was Charles Butler, an attorney who worked in the law office of Martin Van Buren before moving to Geneva. He later became a railroad magnate in Chicago. Later residents, the Prouty family, were involved in banking and local hardware, utility, and preserving companies, and were prominent in local civic affairs. The Chew family, owners of a prominent local optical company, married into Prouty family. The house was donated to the historical society in 1960.

The Prouty-Chew Museum is a Federal-style house which was modified in the 1850s and 1870s. The house has a hipped roof and cresting, a two-story wing, with two bay additions. The modern gallery addition to the back of the building was made in the 1960s. The house has several marble fireplaces and an early patented radiator.

Four of the five period rooms are furnished in Federal style. There are two pieces from the original owner, Charles Butler, and many pieces from the Prouty family; the others were collected from the community. There is also one Victorian parlor furnished in a later style.

Notable Collections on Exhibit

The house displays objects of local interest, as well as a small case of objects crafted by a local silversmith (c. 1810-1830). The house also features one of the most extensive costume collections in western New York state.

Additional Information

A reading room and archives are available for researchers.

Rose Hill Mansion

Box 464
Geneva, NY 14456
(315) 789-3848

Contact: Geneva Historical Society
Open: May 1-Oct. 31, Mon.-Sat.
10 a.m.–4 p.m.; Sun. 1–5 p.m.
Admission: Adults $2; children (under 12)
$1; groups (10 or more) $1.50 with
reservation. Guided tours, audiovisual
program.
Suggested Time to View House: 60–90
minutes
Facilities on Premises: Gift shop, antique
shop
Description of Grounds: Restored
boxwood gardens typical of the
mid-1800s
Best Season to View House: Early summer
Number of Yearly Visitors: 10,000
Year House Built: 1839
Number of Rooms: 24

Style of Architecture: Greek Revival
On-Site Parking: Yes **Wheelchair Access:** Yes

Description of House

The property was named for Robert Rose, a Virginian who emigrated to New York in 1802. He erected a simple frame house in 1809 which later served as the carriage house. William Strong, a New York City wool broker, built the 1839 Greek Revival structure. Robert Swan received Rose Hill as a wedding present and lived here from 1850 to1890. Swan became a master farmer while living here and turned Rose Hill into one of the state's most innovative farms. He installed the first large scale tile drainage system here in the early 1850s.

Rose Hill is a fine example of Greek Revival architecture. A row of six Ionic pillars supports the central portico, and a beautiful cupola rises above the central section. There are two pillared wings on either side of the house and a two-story gallery across the entire back of the main wing. The grounds also feature a carriage house (Rose's original house), a carpenter's shop, and a barn. Listed on the National Register of Historic Places, Rose Hill is located in a picturesque setting overlooking Seneca Lake.

The house is furnished with percent original furnishings, with the remainder from the same period of the house and earlier. Paint colors, wallpaper and textiles in Rose Hill are typical of the period as is the extensive use of wall-to-wall carpeting.

Notable Collections on Exhibit

The house contains many family portraits of the Swans and a collection of silver by New York silversmiths. A distinctive arrangement of 1830s lighting fixtures decorates the house as well as a a sizable collection of Empire furnishings and china which belonged to the Swan family.

Clermont

One Clermont Avenue
Germantown, NY 12526
(518) 537-4240

Contact: Clermont State Historic Site
Open: April 15-Oct. 31, Wed.-Sun. and Mon. holidays; call for seasonal hours
Admission: Free, donations accepted. Guided tours, garden tours, visitor center, special interpretive events and lecture series.
Suggested Time to View House: 1 hour
Facilities on Premises: Museum store, formal gardens

Description of Grounds: 500 acre grounds are accessible, picnic facilities available
Best Season to View House: April-June
Number of Yearly Visitors: 223,000
Year House Built: 1730 (burned 1777, rebuilt 1779-1782), enlarged 1814, 1831, 1874, 1893
Style of Architecture: Georgian (with Victorian additions)
Number of Rooms: 46
On-Site Parking: Yes **Wheelchair Access:** Yes

Description of House

Robert of Clermont (1688-1775), a descendant of Robert Livingston, the founder of the Livingston family in America, built this handsome brick Georgian-style mansion in 1730 as the seat of his estate overlooking the Hudson. A later descendant, Chancellor Robert R. Livingston (1746-1813) lived here during the American Revolution when the British set fire to the estate and burned it to the ground. The family and servants escaped, and within a few years Clermont was rebuilt and refurnished. Among his many accomplishments, Livingston was the negotiator of the Louisiana Purchase and co-inventor of America's first practical steamboat. Clermont remained in the ownership of the Livingston family until 1962 when it was acquired by the state of New York. Later residents include Edward Livingston (1764-1836), who served as Secretary of State, minister to France and mayor of New York City, and Montgomery Livingston (1816-1855), a Hudson River School artist.

The historic house and surrounding 430 acres of formal gardens, planned landscape and vistas, meadowland and forest are restored today to their circa 1930 appearance to reflect the continuum of Livingston family stewardship over three centuries. Preservation of the estate is ongoing. recently completed projects include the adaption of the 19th-century carriage house as a visitor center and the restoration of the 20th-century cutting garden. Clermont is the oldest of the great Hudson River estates in the recently designated "Hudson River National Historic Landmark District", the largest landmark district of this type in the nation. The furnishings on display were acquired by all seven generations of the Livingston family, and rooms are furnished as they were when Clermont was the home of the last two generations. The furniture is American-made (much of it in New York) and features a variety of styles from the 1780 to 1850 period.

Notable Collections on Exhibit

The house displays an impressive arrangement of family portraits by Gilbert Stuart, John Wollaston, Rembrandt Peale, Thomas Sully and William Sidney Mount. The 3200 volume Livingston family library, including over 400 18th-century volumes owned by Chancellor Livingston, is also on display.

Chapman Historical Museum (DeLong House)

348 Glen Street
Glen Falls, NY 12801
(518) 793-2826

Contact: Glen Falls-Queensbury Historical Society

Open: Please call for hours

Admission: Adults $2; seniors $1; children (12-15) $.50; under 11 free. Guided tours, films, demonstrations.

Suggested Time to View House: 1 hour

Facilities on Premises: Gift shop/book store

Description of Grounds: Victorian garden

Best Season to View House: Late spring and summer

Number of Yearly Visitors: 10,000

Year House Built: 1865

Style of Architecture: Victorian-Second Empire

Number of Rooms: 8

On-Site Parking: Yes **Wheelchair Access:** Yes

Description of House

Zopher Isaac DeLong and Catherine Lewis Scott DeLong were born, raised and married in Luzerne where they ran a successful hardware store. In 1858, DeLongs decided to move to Glen Falls and Zopher once again opened a hardware business which prospered. They purchased the property now known as the museum grounds and, it is surmised, built a huge brick addition onto an existing structure. They moved into their new home in 1860. Several generations of the DeLong family continued to live in the home until Mabel DeLong Chapman, a granddaughter of Zopher DeLong, died in the late 1930s. The house was given to the historical museum in her honor.

This Victorian home has been restored to its original turn-of-the-century elegance. Period rooms are furnished to the 1865 to 1910 period of the DeLong family's residence and reflect the dramatic changes in the lives of American families. There are a few furnishings from the family but most were collected from the appropriate period.

Notable Collections on Exhibit

The museum exhibits a nationally significant collection of 7,000 photographs by American luminist, artist and guide-book writer Seneca Ray Stoddard (1844-1917).

Zim House

601 Pine Street
Horseheads, NY 14845
(607) 739-1926

Contact: Horseheads Historical Society
Open: Late June-Labor Day, Thur. 2–4 p.m.,
by appointment year round.
Admission: Free. Guided tours.
Suggested Time to View House: 45 minutes
Number of Yearly Visitors: 175 (average)
Year House Built: 1888
Style of Architecture: Queen Ann
On-Site Parking: Yes
Wheelchair Access: No

Description of House

This lovely Victorian house was home to Eugene Zimmerman (1862-1935), the political cartoonist and caricaturist. He was born in Basile, Switzerland in 1862 and came to America at the age of seven. He lived in New York City and New Jersey before coming to Elmira, New York to work as an apprentice sign painter. He was hired by *Puck* in 1883 to work as an illustrator and later joined *Judge Magazine* to work as a political cartoonist. He built this home in Horseheads in 1886 after marrying Mabel Bear, a local resident. He worked from his home for *Judge* until 1912, and wrote and produced a large volume of his art until his death March 26, 1935. His only daughter, Laura, lived here her entire life (1888-1980).

Typical of Queen Anne houses, the structure is constructed of different materials, clapboards, shingles, many gables, boxed decorated cornice boards, and a variety of differently shaped windows and several porches and balconies. The floor plan features a layout in which the rooms flow into each other rather than separated by walls. The entrance foyer has an inlaid "ZIM" in the flooring. Fine carpentry throughout the house appears in the ornate staircase, and oak and cherry woodwork. In addition, the interior has been restored with wallpapering and stenciling.

Zim House has been maintained in its original state with all of the Zimmerman's original furnishings and appears just as it did in the days that Eugene Zimmerman lived and worked here.

Notable Collections on Exhibit

The walls of the house are covered with example of Zim's work, including his caricature of Mark Twain, as well as sketches by his contemporaries. Of particular interest is a caricature of Zim done by his good friend the opera singer, Enrico Caruso. Zim's two-story studio features Indian artifacts, bayonets, Japanese samurai swords, and other objects related to his interests.

The Robert Jenkins House

**113 Warren Street
Hudson, NY 12534
(518) 828-9764**

Contact: Daughters of the American
Revolution, Hendrick Hudson Chapter
Open: July and Aug., Wed. 1–4 p.m., Sun.
1–3 p.m.; or by appointment
Admission: Adults $1; seniors $.75; under
12 free. Guided tours, special programs
monthly and/or seasonal.
Suggested Time to View House:
60–90 minutes
Year House Built: 1811
Style of Architecture: English
On-Site Parking: No
Wheelchair Access: No

Description of House

The house was given to the Daughters of the American Revolution for use as a museum by the granddaughter of Robert Jenkins, the former mayor of Hudson. Jenkins lived in the house for two years until his death aboard a whaling ship. The house now holds a genealogy library, as well as various local history, military and whaling artifact collections.

The interior has been rebuilt to accommodate a museum, library and a meeting room. The antique furniture is from the original residents and collected to represent the period.

Notable Collections on Exhibit

The exhibits include many works by Hudson School artists: Ernest and Arthur Parton, Henry Ary, Burt Phillips and Victor Dawling. In addition to the 19th-century furniture, there is also a display of quilts and Oriental memorabilia as well as some unusual examples of hair jewelry and a wreath. Historical exhibits feature a personal table of General Grant, a discharge signed by George Washington; the original seal of Hudson; an original Zouave uniform from the Civil War; and a display of military weapons from the Civil War. In honor of Jenkins, there are a number of whaling artifacts including a whale jawbone, and a captain's log.

Olana

RD 2
Hudson, NY 12534
(518) 828-0135

Contact: Olana State Historic Site

Open: April 15-Oct.31; Wed.-Sun.
10 a.m.–4 p.m. (grounds open at 8 a.m.)

Admission: Adults $3; children $1; special group rates for tours arranged in advance. Visitor Center, guided tours.

Suggested Time to View House: 1 hour

Facilities on Premises: Visitor Center

Description of Grounds: Grounds were landscaped by the artist Frederic Church as part of this total "work of art".

Best Season to View House: All

Number of Yearly Visitors: 280,000

Year House Built: 1870 plus 1891 addition

Style of Architecture: Persian-style villa

Number of Rooms: 10 open to the public

On-Site Parking: Yes **Wheelchair Access:** Yes

Description of House

This unusual stone and brick villa was designed and was built by Frederic Edwin Church (1826-1900), a noted landscape artist and leading member of the Hudson River School. Olana remained in the family until 1966 when it was purchased with all of its furnishings intact.

Church's design for his family residence was influenced by his travels throughout the Middle East. While there, he was fascinated by the contrast of subtle stone colors with elaborate decorative details. Returning to America, he embarked on realizing his vision of building a home for his family. Church created Olana in the same way that he planned a work of art: pencil sketches followed by more finished color sketches. He also chose and mixed the colors for every room and designed the interior and exterior stencils. His influence extended to the placement of the furniture, decorative objects, and paintings. The Arabic influences can be seen in the painted arches, balconies, and painted tiles. Church's contemporaries regarded Olana as one of his major works of art–a work against which his family could live out their lives surrounded by beauty and culture.

In addition to the house, Church also designed the landscaping for the surrounding grounds to complete his "masterwork". Using a Romantic design, the grounds feature a magnificent view of the Catskill mountains and the Hudson river below.

Notable Collections on Exhibit

Visitors will see many of Church's exotic and artistic furnishings from the late 19th-century on display as well as an extensive collection of mementoes from the artist's travels abroad. In addition to the unusual furnishings, the house also displays paintings by Church and other Hudson River School artists.

David Conklin Farmhouse

2 High Street
Huntington, NY
(516) 427-7045

Contact: Huntington Historical Society
Open: Tues.-Fri. and Sun. 1–4 p.m.; closed
holidays; groups by appointment
Admission: Adults $2; children and seniors
$1. Guided tours.
Suggested Time to View House: 45 minutes
Facilities on Premises: Museum shop,
antique shop
Best Season to View House: Summer
Number of Yearly Visitors: 6,000-10,000
Year House Built: 1750
Style of Architecture: Federal/Victorian
Number of Rooms: 9

On-Site Parking: Yes **Wheelchair Access:** No

Description of House

This charming farmhouse was occupied by the Conklin family for over 150 years. The original rooms of the house were constructed around 1750, and although the setting appears tranquil today, the former occupants witnessed a great deal of turmoil. Sybil Conklin and her children lived and worked here while her husband, David, was held prisoner by the British in 1777.

The Conklin Farmhouse is representative of a unique style of Colonial architecture found on Long Island which is often referred to as a "half-house" or three-quarter plan. The house has a large side with a smaller wing. One of the earliest museums on Long Island, this home was given to the historical society by Ella Conklin Hurd in 1911, and is listed on the National Register of Historic Places. The rooms are furnished with items from local sources and are appropriate to the period.

Notable Collections on Exhibit

The collections feature 19th-century redware and stoneware made in Huntington. There are also paintings by James Long Scudder, an artist noted for his animal and hunting scenes, which were also exhibited at the Academy of Design in New York in the 1870s. A table and chair used by George Washington during his tour of Long Island in 1790 is on display as are decorative arts from the 18th and 19th centuries, many made in Long Island The study collections by appointment and feature quilts, blue and white coverlets, watercolors by Edward Lange, and 18th and 19th-century clothing.

Additional Information

The society also administers the nearby Kissam House and barn.

Dr. Daniel Kissam House

434 Park Avenue
Huntington, NY
(516) 427-7045

Contact: Huntington Historical Society
Open: Tues.-Fri. and Sun. 1–4 p.m.; closed
holidays; groups by appointment
Admission: Adults $2; children and seniors
$1. Guided tours.
Suggested Time to View House: 45 minutes
Facilities on Premises: Museum shop,
antique shop
Best Season to View House: Summer
Number of Yearly Visitors: 6,000-10,000
Year House Built: 1795
Style of Architecture: Long Island Colonial
Number of Rooms: 8

On-Site Parking: Yes **Wheelchair Access:** No

Description of House

The house now standing on this historic site, one of the original home lots that faced the old town green, was built in 1795 by Timothy Jarvis, a housewright. The house was first occupied by Dr. Daniel Whitehead Kissam, a physician from Oyster Bay. In 1840, Dr. Charles Sturges, the son-in-law of Dr. Kissam, added a modern kitchen wing and converted the old kitchen wing to a formal dining room.

The Kissam House is considered one of the most outstanding three-quarter plan houses on Long Island, and is noted for its fine architectural details. The interior features Egyptian revival woodwork inspired by America's interest in archeological expeditions to Egypt during the period. The furnishings are collected and appropriate to the period.

Additional Information

The English style barn standing on the Kissam House property was reconstructed by the society in 1973. It is now used for school programs and special events.

Walt Whitman House

246 Old Walt Whitman Road
Huntington Station, NY 11746
(516) 427-5240

Contact: Walt Whitman Birthplace
Association

Open: Wed.-Fri. 1–4 p.m.; Sat. and Sun.
10 a.m.–4 p.m.; closed holidays

Admission: Free; group and school tours
by a fee. Guided tours, audiovisual
presentations, poetry readings, lectures
and festivals.

Suggested Time to View House: 90 minutes

Facilities on Premises: Museum shop

Best Season to View House: Spring

Number of Yearly Visitors: 8,200

Year House Built: c. 1819

Style of Architecture: Farmhouse with
Federal features

Number of Rooms: 6

On-Site Parking: Yes **Wheelchair Access:** Yes

Description of House

This simple farmhouse has historic importance because of its most famous resident, poet Walt Whitman. Although the Whitmans lived in the building for only four years after Walt was born in 1819, the poet spent many formative years as a young adult in and about the West Hills area while working as a schoolmaster, carpenter, and printer. The Whitman family had inhabited West Hills since the 17th century. The poet left Long Island in 1862, but always treasured his West Hill associations. After the Whitmans sold the property to Carlton Jarvis in 1823, it was maintained by Jarvis and Watson families until purchased by the Walt Whitman Birthplace Association and given to the state of New York in 1957.

The house is a two-story farm dwelling with a one story kitchen wing. The house also has three bays and a side hall. The house is similar to others built in the area by the poet's father, Walter Whitman, Sr. One notable feature is the corbelling of two separate fireplace chimney flues into a single one within the attic of the building.

The home is furnished to represent a typical mid 19th-century Long Island dwelling. The dwelling contains furniture, utilitarian objects, and decorative items from the colonial period of Long Island through the Civil War era. The second floor contains an exhibit room, museum shop and staff offices.

Notable Collections on Exhibit

In addition to the historic furnishings on the first floor, the Birthplace Association maintains collections of objects that were once owned by Whitman or his family including sculpture, original and file photographs, music, framed art works, facsimiles of documents, and a library of works by and about Walt Whitman.

King Manor Museum

King Park, 150th St. and Jamaica Ave.
Jamaica, NY 11432
(718) 291-0282

Contact: King Manor Association
Open: Call forcurrent hours
Activities: Exhibitions, educational and cultural programs

Description of Grounds: Period landscaping and native plant and wildflowers are being reintroduced along with park benches and fences.
Year House Built:1800
Style of Architecture: Dutch-style with an attached Long Island "half-house."

Description of House

The house takes its name from Rufus King, a signer of the Constitution of the United States, who bought the house in 1805. King was born in 1755, the eldest son of a prosperous merchant from Maine. He studied law at Harvard before serving in the American Revolution. After the war, King embarked on a career in public service. He was a member of the Constitutional Congress, a framer and signer of the Constitution, one of the first Senators from New York and the first ambassador to Great Britain, under Presidents Washington, Adams and Jefferson. King made an unsuccessful bid for the presidency, the last Federalist to run, losing to James Monroe in 1816. King lived in the manor with his wife, Mary, and five children, and kept the estate as a working farm.

King Manor is the centerpiece of an eleven-acre historic park in Jamaica, Queens. In 1805, Rufus King bought an existing farm that included an 18th-century Dutch-style farmhouse with an attached Long Island-style "half-house." A year after moving in, King added a kitchen to the rear of the house. Four years later, he further expanded the house to its stylish Georgian grandeur by adding a Federal dining room and two bedrooms. In 1827, King's son John added the Greek Revival exterior details, such as the classical portico and entranceway.

Several period rooms are furnished to highlight the life of Rufus King and his contributions to American politics.

Johnson Hall

**Hall Avenue
Johnstown, NY 12095
(518) 762-8712**

Contact: Johnson Hall State Historic Site
Open: May 15-Oct. 31, Wed.-Sat.
10 a.m.–5 p.m.; Sun. 1–5 p.m.
Admission: Free. Guided tours, Market
Fair (2nd weekend in June) and Holiday
Open House (Sun. following Christmas
day) held annually; special programs.
Suggested Time to View House: 1 hour
Facilities on Premises: Small gift shop
Description of Grounds: 20 acres of
park-picnic tables
Best Season to View House: All seasons
Number of Yearly Visitors: 15,000 in house
Year House Built: 1763
Number of Rooms: 4

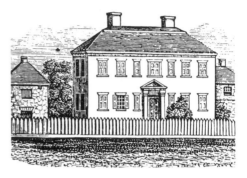

Style of Architecture: Georgian
On-Site Parking: Yes **Wheelchair Access:** Yes

Description of House

Born in Ireland in 1715, William Johnson arrived in America at age twenty two to oversee the development of his uncle's lands in the Mohawk Valley. At the same time, he began a prosperous trade with the Mohawk Indians on his own behalf. Johnson served successfully in the French and Indian Wars and rose from the rank of colonel to major general. In 1756, Johnson was appointed superintendent of Indian Affairs north of the Ohio River, and soon after began to build this considerable house which would reflect his new position. Johnson Hall was confiscated in 1779 by the state of New York as Loyalist property and was subsequently sold at an auction. The house remained a private residence until 1906, when New York state acquired it as a historic site.

The noted Boston-trained carpenter Samuel Wood designed this Georgian house of wood made to look like stone. Johnson Hall became the nucleus of a working estate designed to encourage settlement and further Johnson's contol of his lands. Sir William ordered the latest books, acquired fine furnishings, and established formal gardens. A mill, blacksmith shop, Indian store, barns, and other necessary buildings were added, as well as housing for servants. Johnson Hall contains some period furnishings, a few original pieces, and some reproductions.

John Jay Homestead

**P.O. Box AH, 400 Rt. 22
Katonah, NY 10536
(914) 232-5651**

Contact: John Jay Homestead State
Historic Site

Open: April 15-Labor Day, Wed.-Sat.
10 a.m.–4 p.m., Sun. 12–4 p.m.; then
until Oct. 31, Wed.-Sun. 12–4 p.m.

Activities: Guided tours, special lectures,
concerts, children's programs, Dec.
holiday programs

Suggested Time to View House: 1 hour

Facilities on Premises: Sales desk

Description of Grounds: 60 acres of
meadow, woodland with stream and
pond, formal gardens, new herb garden
and lawns with picnic tables.

Best Season to View House: Early summer

Number of Yearly Visitors: 55,000

Year House Built: Main structure 1801

Number of Rooms: 10 of 60 on display

Style of Architecture: Georgian/Federal

On-Site Parking: Yes **Wheelchair Access:** No

Description of House

John Jay began his public career in 1774 with his election to the Continental Congress. In the years of the Revolution, he represented the people of New York and the nation as a legislator, jurist and diplomat, notably as president of the Congress, minister to Spain and co-author of the Treaty of Paris with Adams and Franklin. He continued to serve the people after the war as secretary of foreign affairs, and as the first Chief Justice of the Supreme Court. Jay left the court in 1794 at President Washington's bidding to be chief negotiator and author of the controversial and unpopular "Jay Treaty." Although it is said that the treaty cost Jay the chance to succeed Washington, it delayed open conflict with Great Britain until 1812 and enabled the US to grow and solidify.

During his twenty-seven years of public service, John Jay looked forward to the day when he would retire with his wife and family to "the house on my farm in the country." The house John Jay designed and built here, set high against a pine covered hilltop on his 900 acre tract, became home to five generations of the family. The original twenty-four room Georgian/Federal style building, with its sweeping veranda, and two set back wings, was added onto several times, creating more living space, entertaining areas and work rooms for the growing family. The house, however, retains its original family-oriented, quiet elegance.

Most of the furnishings displayed are family pieces. The family rooms of the first and second floors are fitted with John and Sarah Jay's belongings and augmented with items from the succeeding generations and some objects collected and appropriate to the period.

The family decendants of John Jay took their role of preserving the legacy of their forefather seriously. Each generation was entrusted with retaining the traditions of the past even as they welcomed the innovations of the day. The homestead has survived to the present, with much of its integrity intact due to their loyalty.

Notable Collections on Exhibit

Jay's roll top desk, personal game table and chess set, astral globe and extensive collection of books fill the family library. A portion of John and Sally's wedding china is on view in the dining room, highlighted as it is displayed on the family dining table by silver candlesticks and cutlery both brought to the house in 1801 and purchased under the watchful eye of John by his daughters after their mother's death. The visitor can see the many portraits of the original occupants. Artists such as Gilbert Stuart, Jonathon Trumbell, Benjamin West, Daniel Huntington and John Singer Sergent painted the faces of the Jay family.

Additional Information

Continued efforts to reconstruct the past in and around the Homestead through on-going study of the building, the family and the lifestyle of the early 19th century is carried out today at this State Historic Site by professional museum employees and a devoted group of volunteers.

Luykas Van Alen House

Rte. 9H
Kinderhook, NY 12106
(518) 758-9265

Contact: Columbia County Historic Society

Open: Memorial Day weekend-Labor Day weekend, Wed.-Sat. 11 a.m.–5 p.m.; Sun. 1–5 p.m.

Admission: Adults $3; seniors and students $2; children (under 12) free. Guided tours, antiques festival in June, 18th-century fair in Oct.

Suggested Time to View House: 30 minutes–1 hour

Description of Grounds: Grounds open at all times

Best Season to View House: Spring-fall

Number of Yearly Visitors: 3,000 plus

Year House Built: 1737

Number of Rooms: 5

Style of Architecture: Dutch

On-Site Parking: Yes **Wheelchair Access:** Yes

Description of House

Luykas Van Alen, the original owner, was a farmer, a merchant, and one of the largest landowners in the area. Eight generations of the Van Alen family owned the home until 1964 when it was donated to the Society.

The Van Alen House is one of less than a dozen of its type that has survived intact from the days when hundreds of these parapet gable Dutch houses (having gable or end walls extending above the roof) dotted the farms of the Hudson River Valley. The interior features a first floor with three large rooms with jambless fireplaces. There are also two rooms in the garret.

Characteristics of Dutch culture are preserved in the furnishings which have been collected for exhibit in the house including a "kas" used as a linen cupboard, delft tiles for the hearth, and Hudson Valley-made scripture paintings which closely imitate paintings made in the Netherlands.

Notable Collections on Exhibit

Period furnishings include ironware, pottery, tables, chairs, a Dutch Bible, spinning wheels, looms, a linen press, and delftware.

James Vanderpoel House

**Broad Street
Kinderhook, NY 12106
(518) 758-9265**

Contact: Columbia County Historical Society

Open: Memorial Day weekend-Labor Day weekend, Wed.-Sat. 11 a.m.–5 p.m.; Sun. 1–5 p.m.

Admission: Adults $3; seniors and students $2; children (under 12) free. Guided tours, Kindercrafters Craft show in June.

Suggested Time to View House: 30–60 minutes

Description of Grounds: Grounds open at all times

Best Season to View House: Spring-fall

Number of Yearly Visitors: 3,000 plus

Year House Built: c. 1820

Number of Rooms: 8

Style of Architecture: Federal style

On-Site Parking: Yes **Wheelchair Access:** No

Description of House

James Vanderpoel, a prominent lawyer and politician, built this home for his wife and children. He served as a county surrogate, state assemblyman, and worked closely with the young politician, Martin Van Buren. After 1832, the house changed hands several times until the society purchased it in 1925.

This brick, two-story Federal home was built around 1819 by Barnabus Waterman, a talented New England builder residing in Hudson. The structure has remained virtually unchanged for 170 years. This elegant home features delicate architectural ornamentation, plastered high ceilings, and large windows. The house is a prime example of Federal architecture with a Palladian window, ellyptical stairway and perfect symmetry. From formal public rooms to informal private bedrooms, the Vanderpoel House represents the lives of a prosperous, rural family in the early 19th century.

The furnishings are of the period and have been collected since the 1920s when the home was purchased by the society.

Notable Collections on Exhibit

The collection in the house features Duncan Rhyle style tables and chairs, as well as Chippendale, Sheraton, and Hepplewhite furnishings. Paintings of James and Anna Vanderpoel grace the hallway. Examples of period needlework, coverlets and children's furnishings are also displayed.

Lindenwald

Rt. 9H, P.O. Box 545
Kinderhook, NY 12106
(518) 758-9689

Contact: Martin Van Buren National
Historic Site

Open: April 20-Oct. 31, 9 a.m.–5 p.m.

Admission: $1 (age 18-61). Guided tours;
special presentations on weekends.

Suggested Time to View House: 45 minutes

Description of Grounds: The grounds are a
rustic rural setting. Open dawn to dusk.

Best Season to View House: Summer and
fall

Number of Yearly Visitors: 16,500

Year House Built: 1789, remodelled 1849

Style of Architecture: Italianate/eclectic

Number of Rooms: 38

On-Site Parking: Yes **Wheelchair Access:** No

Description of House

Martin Van Buren was born in Kinderhook in 1782, soon after the end of the Civil War. His parents kept a tavern and, like their Dutch predecessors of 150 years, made a moderate living farming in the Hudson Valley. Young Martin possessed a fine mind and a strong ambition, and embarked on a legal career at the age of fourteen with an apprenticeship to a local attorney. In 1804, he joined his half brother's law practice in their home town. Three years later Van Buren married a distant relative and childhood sweetheart, Hannah Hoes. Meanwhile, he was becoming known as more than a country lawyer. His first appointed post, as a county official, set him on an upward course that led to the highest office in the state—and eventually, the nation.

The large two story red brick house was built by the wealthy judge Peter Van Ness using local materials. He followed a simple square plan which emphasized a Palladian window illuminating the second story hallway. The Georgian style carried over to the inside as well; pilasters and entablatures framed six-panel molded doors, and finely carved cornices edged the ceilings. Adorning the entrance is a silver-plated doorknocker inscribed with "1797," the year the house was completed.

All furnishings are associated with Martin Van Buren in Lindenwald for the period 1841 to 1863 and include his painted-grain shaving stand and a ten-piece matching persimmon-colored parlor set.

Notable Collections on Exhibit

Lindenwald houses an excellent collection of original historic wallpapers and wallpaper fragments. Good examples of late-classical furniture manufactured in New York City are on display as well as a large collection of political material dating from 1800 to 1865.

Obadiah Smith House

8 St. Johnland Road
Kings Park, NY 11754
(516) 265-6768

Contact: Smithtown Historical Society
Open: By appointment only
Admission: Donation. Guided tours.
Suggested Time to View House: 1 hour
Best Season to View House: Spring-fall
Year House Built: 1700
Style of Architecture: Dutch and English
Number of Rooms: 9
On-Site Parking: Yes
Wheelchair Access: Yes

Description of House

The original owner of the house was Obadiah Smith (1687-1765), son of Samuel Smith, and grandson of Richard Smith, the patentee (original land grant owner). Obadiah's father, Samuel, owned the property on which the house was built. Obadiah gave the house to his son Obadiah II (1720-1794), who gave it to his son David (1755-1835), who gave it to his son Obadiah III (1788-1852). Obadiah III and his wife Rebecca had eight daughters and no sons. Two of the daughters, Minerva and Louisa, married two Harned brothers, David and James. When Louisa Smith and James B. Harned were married in 1834, Obadiah III transferred the title of the house to his son-in-law. The dwelling remained in the Harned family until 1940.

The floor plan of the structure is typical of certain houses built by grandsons of Richard Smith. The house faces south, and has a hill behind it to protect it from the chilly winter winds. Cleverly contrived bridges give access from the second floor to the hillside. The kitchen fireplace has a lintel over eight feet long. The vaulted arch over the fireplace which supports the hearth of the room above represents a very old style. The furnishings are collected and appropriate to period.

Notable Collections on Exhibit

In addition to the furnishings, the house features changing exhibits of decorative arts.

Le Roy House

23 East Main Street
Le Roy, NY 14482
(716) 768-7433

Contact: Le Roy Historical Society
Open: Tues.-Fri. 10 a.m.–4 p.m.;
  Sun. 2–4 p.m.
Admission: $1. Guided tours, exhibits,
  lectures and hands on activities.
Suggested Time to View House: 1 hour
Year House Built: 1822
Number of Rooms: 9 open to the public
On-Site Parking: Yes
Wheelchair Access: No

Description of House

The original brick dwelling was built by Egbert Benson, Jr. as a land office for the Triangle Tract, an 86,000 acre grant that stretched from Le Roy to Lake Ontario. Benson was related to Herman Le Roy, the founder of the town which bears his name. Jacob Le Roy became the land agent in 1819, and enlarged the structure when he brought his family here in 1823. In later years, the chancellor of Ingham University occupied the house. In addition to being a private residence, the structure also served as a boarding house for students. The house's 19th-century period furniture reflects the various periods of occupancy.

Notable Collections on Exhibit

Fortunatus Gleason, Jr. operated a pottery in nearby Morganville during the 19th century. An impressive exhibit of redware produced by Gleason and successive owners of the Morganville pottery are displayed in Le Roy House's buttery. Also included in the exhibit are fine examples of stoneware and Bennington pottery.

Gould Mansion

Box 277, High Street
Lyons Falls, NY 13368
(315) 348-8089

Contact: Lewis County Historical Society
Open: Late May-Oct., Tues-Sat.
Admission: Adults $1; children $.50.
   Guided tours, special programs, Yankee
   Fair (second Sat. in August).
Suggested Time to View House: 90 minutes

Facilities on Premises: Gift shop
Best Season to View House: Summer
Year House Built: 1902
Style of Architecture: Richardsonian
   Romanesque
Number of Rooms: 13

Description of House

This lovely home was built by Gordias Henry Plumb, a self-made man who built the first paper mill on the nearby Black River. Gould was born in 1848, and began working at the age of sixteen, driving a stagecoach between Lyons Falls and Boonville. In 1869, he acquired his first tract of timber land, and for the next twenty years reserved the woods from these lands. In the 1880s, he formed a partnership with the daughters of Lyman Lyon, after whom the village is named, in order to create the Lyons and Gould Paper Company. In 1892, when Mr. Gould obtained the water power rights in Lyons Falls, the Gould Paper Mill was built. The Gould family retained ownership of the mill until 1945, and it has been under varying ownership since then.

The thirteen-room mansion was planned for the Gould family in 1889 by architects Fuller and Pitcher who were prominent in Albany at that time. The structure is a fine example of Richardsonian Romanesque architecture. The house is built of of Governeur marble, and the walls are made of brick covered with plaster. The entire house is panelled with oak and black walnut, made and brought to Lyons Falls as it was built. The elegant interior is complemented by tapestry-covered ceilings and walls. Although the house was heated by coal, there are several beautiful fireplaces including one made of Italian marble and another of ceramic tile.

Some of the furniture belonged to the Goulds, other items are typical for the period and are on permanent loan to the historical society for display in the house. These lovely Victorian furnishings include an intricately inlaid game table, a solid oak dining room set, and a grandfather clock, made especially for the house. The stairway also exhibits portraits of Lyman Lyon and Mary Lyon painted by Frank Carpenter, the well-known Civil War artist.

Additional Information

The entire complex included this house, the carriage house (now the Lyons Falls Free Library) and the smaller building at the lower level, which was the mill office building.

William Floyd Estate

245 Park Drive
Mastic Beach, NY 11951
(516) 399-2030

Contact: National Park Service

Open: May-Oct., site hours change each season, please call (516) 399-2030 for current times.

Admission: Free. Guided house tours, self-guided ground tours.

Suggested Time to View House: 1 hour

Facilities on Premises: Sales desk

Description of Grounds: Formal gardens, historic outbuildings, and family cemetery

Best Season to View House: Spring and fall

Number of Yearly Visitors: 10,000-12,000

Style of Architecture: Colonial

Year House Built: 1724 (original section)

Number of Rooms: 25

Description of House

Between 1718 and 1976, eight generations of the Floyd family managed this estate on Fire Island and adapted it to meet their changing needs. One of the most prominent members of the family to live here, William Floyd, was a signer of the Declaration of Independence, a state senator, and a U.S. Congressman. He was born at the estate (1734) and lived here (except during the period of British occupation during the Revolution) until 1803 when he moved upstate and left the property to his son, Nicoll Floyd II. Nicoll held several local political offices and built a substantial fortune by the efficient management of the estate. The last member of the family to live here, Cornelia Floyd Nichols, used the estate for her husband's naturalist research before donating the house and grounds to the National Park Service. All furnishings are original to house and span 260 years of varying tastes and styles.

The house has changed considerably over the years. The original two-story, wood-frame structure built in 1724 had only six rooms but was designed for easy expansion. When William Floyd returned to Mastic after the Revolution, he enlarged the house, making it suitable for entertaining national leaders such as his political allies, Thomas Jefferson and James Madison. Later occupants restyled the house, adding a large porch, cornice, and other details in the Greek Revival style. In 1898, a wing was added to accomodate the many guests visiting the family during the summer. In the 1920's Cornelia enlarged the northwest wing to make room for a modern kitchen and dining area.

Notable Collections on Exhibit

There are over 14,000 catalogued objects at the Floyd estate. The furnishings feature many fine examples of Empire furniture (c.1830), a Chippendale sofa and secretary (c. 1780), Windsor chairs, and ceramics. On the walls hang two portraits of Floyd Family members by Sheppard Alonzo (c. 1830).

The Mills Mansion

14 Main Street
Mt. Morris, NY 14510
(716) 658-3292

Contact: Mt. Morris Historical Society
Open: June 1-Sept. 1, Fri.-Sun. 12–4 p.m.;
and by appointment
Admission: $1 donation. Guided tours,
19th-century Holiday dinner
(reservations only), Christmas by
Candlelight—an open house.
Suggested Time to View House:
30–45 minutes
Number of Yearly Visitors: 3,000
Year House Built: 1838
Style of Architecture: Federal with Greek
Revival accents
Number of Rooms: 14

On-Site Parking: Yes **Wheelchair Access:** No

Description of House

William Augustus Mills, known as the founder of Mt. Morris, came to the site of the future town in 1794 as a young man of seventeen. He later became a prosperous grain farmer and also served as the town's first supervisor. Mills also organized the state militia for the surrounding counties to fight in the War of 1812. In 1838, at the age of sixty, Mills built this beautiful brick mansion. He lived here for only six years before his death.

The Mills Mansion is a stately fourteen room Federal-style home. The dwelling features an elegant cantilevered staircase with a double banister, solid cherry pocket doors between the two parlors, and an open hearth and bake oven in the kitchen. The rooms still have their original plaster, floors, and baseboards, and architects have described the mansion's condition as pristine. This is remarkable considering the fact that the house was unattended for a period of fifteen years and its only occupants were pigeons.

Ten of the rooms are restored and partially furnished with authentic Empire pieces. Some of the furnishings were owned by the Mills family, others have been collected for exhibit in the house.

Notable Collections on Exhibit

Mills Mansions displays temporary exhibits which change quarterly. They include men's, women's and children's costumes from 1820-50, various pieces of pink lustre of unusual design and spode, and antique toys. Permanent collection include those on native sons John Wesley Powell, an early explorer of the American west, and Francis Bellamy author of the "Pledge of Allegiance".

Genesee Country Museum

P.O. Box 310, Flint Hill Road
Mumford, NY 14511
(716) 538-6822

Contact: Genesee Country Museum

Open: July-Aug., daily 10 a.m.–5 p.m.; May, June, Sept.and Oct., closed on Mon.; Spring and fall Tues.-Fri., 10 a.m.–4 p.m.

Admission: Adults $9; seniors $8; youths (13-17) $6; children (6-12) $4.50; under 6 free; group rates (20 plus) available. Special events each weekend include Civil War reenactments, 4th of July celebrations, agricultural fairs.

Suggested Time to View House: 5–6 hours for entire complex

Facilities on Premises: 3 gift shops, wildlife art gallery

Description of Grounds: 125 acres with vegetable and flower gardens appropriate for the period

Best Season to View House: May-Oct.

Number of Yearly Visitors: 130,000 plus

Year House Built: 1797

Style of Architecture: Varied

On-Site Parking: Yes **Wheelchair Access:** Yes

Description of House

The Genesse Country Museum recreates a typical 19th-century Genesse Valley village. The village provides a living history of the area with demonstrations showcasing the art of cabinetmakers, weavers, and potters. There are over forty historic structures in the village ranging from a cooper's shop, brewery, and land office to more than a dozen historic homes. All of the buildings were moved from different parts of the Genesse valley to create this special village. Visitors to the village will see the dramatic changes that occured during the first seventy-five years of the 19th century.

The architecture and history of each of the historic houses is extremely varied. Perhaps one of the most unusual is the Octagon House, originally built for Corporal Hyde and his wife Julia in 1870. Based on a plan by Orson Fowler, a progressive thinker from the mid-19th century who called this architectural style "a home for all", this eight sided dwelling combines Gothic Revival and Italianate features. The house has an unique combination of verandas, a bracketed roof, and a cupola with pointed arch windows in the Gothic style.

The Jones Farm, built in 1820, reflects the improved lot of the Genessee farmer as he moved from a log house to one of post and beam construction. This typical farmhouse features stenciling on the interior walls to imitate more expensive wallpaper.

The George Eastman birthplace complements many other noteworthy houses in the village. This simple home was moved from nearby Waterville and shows the lifestyle of the father of modern photography. The MacArthur House represents a typical saltbox style house from 1833 while the Hamilton House was built using the Italianate villa style in 1870 by John Hamilton.

The furnishings come from various sources. Some belonged to the original owners, but most have been collected; all of the furnishings are fromthe same period as the first use of the building.

Notable Collections on Exhibit

Each building is filled with period antiques which are representative of the different lifestyles found in the village life. These include furniture and accessories which vary from primitives in the log cabin to hair wreaths in the Victorian buildings. The Gallery of Sporting Art houses the largest collection of wildlife art in North America. The Carriage Museum displays a large collection of 19th-century horse drawn vehicles.

Additional Information

The two hundred acres occupied by the museum buildings are surrounded by over a thousand acres of grain and corn fields, grasslands, ponds, and wetlands which furnish a rich habitat for game and wildfowl. The Nature Center affords opportunities for the public to observe the undisturbed flora and the unthreatened fauna within the preserve.

The Jacob Blauvelt House

20 Zukor Road
New City, NY 10956
(914) 634-9626

Contact: The Historical Society of Rockland County

Open: Sun. 1–5 p.m.; closed major holidays; special appointments available

Admission: Adults $2; under 12 free; group rates available. Guided tours, food preparation demonstrations.

Suggested Time to View House: 30–60 minutes

Facilities on Premises: Gift shop, book store

Description of Grounds: 4 acres; lawns, picnic tables; herb garden; farm outbuildings

Best Season to View House: Warm weather

Number of Yearly Visitors: 20,000

Year House Built: 1832

Number of Rooms: 6

Style of Architecture: Dutch/Greek Revival

On-Site Parking: Yes   **Wheelchair Access:** No

Description of House

Jacob J. Blauvelt (1796-1858) was a descendant of Gerrit Hendricksen (Blauvelt), who arrived in New Amsterdam in 1638. In 1741, one of Gerrit's grandsons, Jacob A. Blauvelt (1692-1779), purchased 300 acres in the then-frontier area of northern New City. Between 1745 and 1753, his sons began to cultivate and occupy the New City farmland and baptise their children in the Clarkstown Reformed Church.

The Blauvelt House is a fine example of rural Hudson River Valley architecture. Built in 1832, the handsome red brick farmhouse combines stylistic features of colonial Dutch, Federal and Greek Revival architecture. The large west wing with Dutch style gambrel roof, Federal and Greek Revival doorways and fireplace mantles, is accompanied by a small, brick outkitchen. Blauvelt then added a connecting center wing in order to provide his wife with an improved kitchen and dining area.

Notable Collections on Exhibit

Along with the Blauvelt House the property also has a museum which houses an extensive permanent collection of artifacts from all periods of Rockland's history including prehistoric stone tools, Colonial and Federal era furnishings, farm equipment, Victorian clothing, and 19th and 20th-century painting and prints. The house also features an ongoing schedule of temporary exhibitions on varied aspects of regional history and art. Recent exhibits have been devoted to regional dress and dollhouses.

Mount Lebanon Shaker Village

P.O. Box 629
New Lebanon, NY 12125
(518) 794-9500

Contact: Mount Lebanon Shaker Village

Open: Memorial Day-Labor Day, daily
9:30 a.m.–5 p.m.; Oct., Sat. and Sun.
9:30 a.m.–5 p.m.; or call for appointment

Admission: Adults $4; children $2; family
(2 adults and 2 or more children) $10;
groups (20 or more) $3. Guided tours,
slide presentation, workshops and
special events.

Suggested Time to View House: 2 hours

Facilities on Premises: Gift shop,
refreshments

Description of Grounds: 26 buildings,
Shaker gardens, lawns, ponds, herb and
seed gardens

Best Season to View House: Spring,
summer and fall

Number of Yearly Visitors: 2,000

Year House Built: 1785-first house

Style of Architecture: Shaker

On-Site Parking: Yes **Wheelchair Access:** Yes

Description of House

Mount Lebanon was the head ministry of Shakerism from 1787 to 1947, and its members were considered leaders of the Shaker movement. All the doctrine, rules for behavior, design and architectural styling came from Mount Lebanon. The village has been called the "Vatican" of the Shakers.

The village contains more than twenty different structures which reflect the Shaker maxim "hands to work-hearts to God". The structures include several dwelling houses, the brethren's workshop (1829), the sister's workshop and store (1852), the forge (c. 1849), the wash house (c. 1854), an early granary (c. 1838), and a stone barn (1858) which was once considered the largest all-stone barn in the western hemisphere.

The few furnishings in the buildings are of the same period but they are minimal. This site stresses architecture, landscape, and a hydropower system, and other examples of the unique Shaker lifestyle.

Notable Collections on Exhibit

The village displays a small, but important collection of Shaker chairs, household objects and small items of furniture as well as several photographic exhibitions. There is also a collection of machinery, including a steam engine and farm equipment.

Huguenot Street

P.O. Box 339
New Paltz, NY 12561
(914) 255-1660

Contact: Huguenot Historical Society
Open: Memorial Day-Sept., Wed.-Sun. 10 a.m.–4 p.m.
Admission: Complete tour of all houses: adults $6; seniors 5; children (7-12) $3; children (under 7) free. Tours, special events.
Suggested Time to View House: 2½ hours
Facilities on Premises: Gift shop, restaurant, picnic facilities

Description of Grounds: This historic street contains six houses and their gardens, a church, an assembly hall, and a library. There is also a nearby walking trail.
Best Season to View House: May-Sept.
Number of Yearly Visitors: 3,500
Year House Built: Varies: 1692-1712
Style of Architecture: Flemish-Dutch Stone
Number of Rooms: Varies
On-Site Parking: Yes **Wheelchair Access:** No

Description of House

In 1677, the Duzine ("Twelve Men") united by family and religious ties, purchased a large tract of land from the Esopus Indians on generous terms which guaranteed them a peaceful home which they had sought after years of exile from France. By 1692, they began to replace their original log cabins with stone houses which today constitute the oldest street in America with its original houses, Huguenot Street. The first one-room houses were enlarged as the next generation grew and prospered, but for over 250 years, five of the six dwellings remained virtually unchanged and occupied by descendants of the builders.

Located at the north end of the street, the Hugo Freer House was built in two sections by Freer and his son-in-law, Johannes Low beginning in 1694. The original stone structure has a wooden addition, probably made in the late 18th century to use as a shop. Like many of the houses on the street, the house features a jambless fireplace. The dwelling houses a fine collection of period furnishings including an old chest brought to America by Hugo Freer and tables and chairs which belonged to his descendants.

Further down the street stands the Abraham Hasbrouck House, constructed in 1692. Visitors interested in architecture will see a fine example of how additions were made without losing the perfection of the architectural scheme; one can still see the divisions on the exterior walls. The house contains a restored medieval fireplace with no mantel or sides in the "room of seven doors". A great beehive chimney rests directly on the huge beams.

The house's kitchen is probably the finest on the street with its great fireplace, flagstone pavement, period kitchen utensils, and a Dutch oven. In addition, the Abraham Hasbrouck House displays many notable furnishings an original Dutch kas brought from Holland by one of the families and an Elizabethan chest dating from 1609.

The Jean Hasbrouck House has earned a citation as an outstanding American example of Flemish stone architecture. The house was owned continuously by descendants of the Hasbrouck family until 1899 when the society purchased the property. The house features an extremely well-preserved jambless fireplace, the finest of all those found on the street. The continuous ownership has meant that many of the furnishings are original to the house including the Louis DuBois chest and hamper dating from 1660 when Hasbrouck first came to the country. A tavern table, Hudson valley rush chairs, kitchen utensils, a pewter cabinet and a Bible and its box belonging to his wife also decorate the rooms.

The other houses on the street are equally well-preserved and furnished. The Bevier-Elting House, built in 1698, has a side porch and large windows, including a rare thirty-pane window in the front room. The Deyo House is one of the few on the street to have completely altered its appearance from the original Dutch stone to the late 19th-century alterations which gave it a Victorian or Edwardian appearance. The largest stone building on the street, the Dubois Fort, served as a residence for the Dubois family for many generations and was large enough to serve as a meeting place for the early settlers. The structure now houses the restaurant for this historic street.

Additional Information

Visitors to New Paltz are also encouraged to visit the society's other houses, Locust Lawn and the Terwilliger House, located a few miles south of town.

Thomas Paine Cottage

983 North Avenue
New Rochelle, NY 10884
(914) NE2-5376

Contact: Thomas Paine National Historic
Association
Open: Spring-fall, Fri.-Sun. 2–5 p.m.; or by
advance appointment in any season
Admission: Adults $3; children (12 and
under) $1. Guided tours.
Facilities on Premises: Book store
Number of Yearly Visitors: 1,500
Style of Architecture: Early American

Suggested Time to View House:
30–60 minutes
Best Season to View House: Spring-fall
Year House Built: 1794
On-Site Parking: Yes

Description of House

One of the founding fathers of our country, Thomas Paine (1737-1809), lived in this simple cottage. Paine was a key participant in both the American and French Revolutions, and was a seminal thinker whose writing continues to inspire. Among other great works, Paine wrote "Common Sense," "The Rights of Man," and "Age of Reason." These profound works inspired his contemporaries and continue to challenge thinkers today.

In 1784, the New York State legislature granted Paine the cottage and 300 acres of farmland in appreciation of his services during the Revolution. When Paine died in 1809, he was buried on the farm. Thirty years later, the Paine Monument was erected near the gravesite by his friends from New York City and has been a place of reunions ever since. The cottage is an excellent example of early American architecture, and has been designated a National Historic Landmark. The Paine Cottage contains period furniture and artifacts from Paine's life.

Notable Collections on Exhibit

Memorabilia and artificacts related to the American Revolution are on display in the cottage.

Additional Information

In addition to the cottage, the association also maintains the adjacent Thomas Paine Museum and the Sophia Brewster Schoolhouse.

Abigail Adams Smith Museum

421 East 61st Street
New York, NY 10021
(212) 838-6878

Contact: Abigail Adams Smith Museum
Open: Mon.-Fri. 10 a.m.–4 p.m.; groups
  only 10 a.m.–12 p.m.; Sept.-May, Sun.
  1–4 p.m.; June-July, Tues. 5:30–8 p.m.;
  closed Aug.
Admission: Adults $2; seniors $1; children
  under 12 free. Guided tours, lectures,
  workshops, concerts, children's
  programs, walking tours, and craft
  demonstrations.
Suggested Time to View House: 1 hour
Facilities on Premises: Gift shop, rest rooms
Description of Grounds: 18th-century style
  garden surrounds the historic house.
Best Season to View House: Spring
Number of Yearly Visitors: 8,000
Year House Built: 1799
Number of Rooms: 9 open to the public

Style of Architecture: Federal
On-Site Parking: No **Wheelchair Access:** No

Description of House

The property was owned for a short time in the late 18th century by Abigail Adams Smith, daughter of President John Adams, and her husband, William Smith. The building was originally a carriage house and was not converted for human occupancy until 1826, when it was renovated and became the Mount Vernon Hotel. The museum focus is now on the period when the building served as a hotel and day resort for residents of New York City eager to escape the stresses of urban life.

This three-story structure was constructed from Manhattan schist, brick and brownstone. The exterior has Greek Revival detailing in its woodwork which was added to the building along with its Greek Revival interior architectural details, when the structure was converted from a carriage house into a country hotel and day resort in 1826. The building originally had dovecotes on the third floor, no fireplaces, and wide doors to accommodate carriages on the second floor. The building's landscape and situation are unique in New York City, as is the museum's ornamental garden.

The museum has one period room furnished with Colonial Revival pieces in keeping with the time period of the structure's addition. All the other furnishings are contemporary with the building's early 19th-century Greek Revival interior.

Notable Collections on Exhibit

The collection includes early 19th-century New York furniture, silver, English ceramics and glass, French clocks and ceramics, an rare Chinese lacquerware ladies writing desk, Chinese export porcelain and paintings, documents and letters, early kitchen utensils, and American ironware.

Dyckman House Museum

4881 Broadway (at 204th Street)
New York, NY 10034
(212) 304-9422

Contact: City of New York Parks and Recreation

Open: Tues.-Sun. 10 a.m.–4 p.m.; call to confirm

Admission: Adults $2; students and seniors $1; children free. Concerts, lectures, exhibitions, poetry readings and craft demonstrations.

Suggested Time to View House: 25 minutes

Facilities on Premises: Museum shop, library

Description of Grounds: An herb garden and a cutting garden of colonial flowers add local color.

Best Season to View House: Spring-fall

Number of Yearly Visitors: 6,000

Year House Built: 1785

Style of Architecture: Dutch Colonial Farmhouse

Number of Rooms: 7

On-Site Parking: No **Wheelchair Access:** No

Description of House

The area around the house was settled by Jan Dyckman from Westphalia (now a part of Germany) in 1661. His grandson, William Dyckman, inherited the the farm. The house was occupied by Hessian soldiers durinng the American Revolution. After the war, William built the present house. The Dyckman family sold the farm in 1868 and moved to a more fashionable mansion on Broadway. In 1915, two sisters, Mary Alice D. Dean and Fannie Fredericka D. Welsh, descendants of William Dyckman, bought back the house and began extensive reconstruction. They presented the house to the City in 1916 with 18th and 19th-century furniture and objects representative of their family's belongings.

The Dyckman House is the only remaining Dutch colonial farmhouse in the borough. The present house was built in 1785, however its southern wing, known as the "summer kitchen" (currently the caretaker's quarters), is an earlier structure that may date from 1725. The two-story building has wide unvarnished floorboards and a gambrel roof that slopes over front and back porches that were added before 1825. Except for the brick front, its lower walls are of fieldstone and its upper story white clapboard. Visitors arrive at a central hall leading to a parlor, a dining room and a farm office. The stairs descending to the kitchen skirt a large rock outcropping.

The upstairs bedrooms are decorated with period furnishings. The cellar kitchen is filled with old waffle irons and sausage stuffers, wooden bowls and pewter dishes, and a hearth with kettles and a bake oven belonging to the Dyckman family.

Notable Collections on Exhibit

Notable antiques include a Chippendale drop-leaf dining table (c. 1760), Queen Anne's wing back chair (c. 1750), and a portrait of Jacob Dyckman, New York's first health commissioner in 1819. The house also on displays the Reginald Delham Bolton Collection, an exhibit of Revolutionary War artifacts which were discovered in the barn.

Additional Information

The house site includes a re-created smokehouse and a Hessian hut erected from original building materials during the 1915-1917 restoration.

Fraunces Tavern

54 Pearl Street
New York, NY 10004
(212) 425-1778

Contact: Fraunces Tavern Museum

Open: Mon.-Fri. 10 a.m.–4 p.m.; Sun.
12–5 p.m. (Oct.-May only); closed
Nov. 24-25, Dec. 24-25, Dec. 31, Jan. 1

Admission: Adults $2.50; children, students
and seniors $1; free on Thur. Changing
exhibitions, public program series.

Suggested Time to View House: 30 minutes

Facilities on Premises: Gift/book shop

Number of Yearly Visitors: 40,000

Year House Built: Original structure 1719;
restoration in 1905-07

Style of Architecture: Neo-Georgian

On-Site Parking: No **Wheelchair Access:** No

Description of House

It is believed that tavern-keeper Samuel Fraunces was born in the West Indies and came to New York in the 1750s. He operated taverns before opening the one that eventually bore his name. Fraunces was a superb cook and his establishments were known for their fine food, especially desserts, but he was not know to be an especially astute businessman. For a time, he operated the Vauxhall Gardens which he featured elaborate waxwork tableaus of historical and biblical scenes. He was caputured and a prisoner of war during the British occupation of New York during the Revolution. After the war he became George Washington's house steward. He eventually re-located to Philadelphia and opened another tavern.

What is today the Fraunces Tavern Museum was built in 1719 as a residence by Stephen DeLancey, a member of the New York elite. Built on New York City's first landfill, the house was in a fine residential neighborhood. By the mid-18th century, the neighborhood was more commercial, and in 1762 Samuel Fraunces purchased the building and opened a tavern. Known initially as the "Queen's Head Tavern", the building soon achieved a reputation as one of the finest taverns in New York. During the years prior to the revolution, it saw much pro-revolution activity, and the close of the revolution, it was the site of George Washington's farewell to his troops.

Only two rooms are furnished as period rooms. One, the Long Room, has furnishings of the period of Washington's farewell in 1783. The other is furnished as an early 19th-century private dining room. Fraunces Tavern and the adjacent Fraunces Tavern block are some of the few surviving remnants of colonial New York in the canyons of Wall Street.

Notable Collections on Exhibit

The museum features changing exhibits on aspects of Revolutionary history and related topics. The permanent collections are strong in documenting tavern life in the 18th century and also include notable prints and paintings of colonial figures and events, silver, ceramics, furniture and textiles.

Gracie Mansion

Carl Schutz Park
89th St. and East End Ave
New York, NY 10128
(212) 570-4751

Contact: Gracie Mansion Conservancy
Open: Tours on Wed., by reservation only
Admission: Adults $3; seniors $2. Group tours, tea and snacks.
Facilities on Premises: Shop

Description of Grounds: Gracie Mansion stands in Carl Schultz Park above Hell Gate, a roaring stretch of water where the Harlem and East Rivers meet.
Year House Built: 1799
Style of Architecture: Federal-style mansion

Description of House

Archibald Gracie, a Scottish shipping magnate, bought the property in 1798 and the following year built the mansion where the mayor of New York City now lives. Gracie built an addition in 1809, and this lovely mansion remained his country retreat through 1823. As a member of New York society, he staged elegant parties that attracted Louis Phillipe, later King of France, President John Quincy Adams, Washington Irving, and Rufus King, ambassador to Britain. Because of debts due to shipping embargoes, Gracie had to liquidate his assets in 1823. He died six years later. The Foulke and Wheaton families owned the mansion over the next sixty years, during which time urban development destroyed nearby farm land. The property was condemned and seized by the city in 1896. Fiorella La Guardia made it the official mayor's residence six years later.

The Federal-style Mansion is notable for its three-sided porch and for the trellis railing that sweeps around the house at the second-story and attic levels. In the late 1880s, a sea wall and a promenade were built along Hell Gate. At the center of the faux-marble entryway floor, a painted compass recalls ships that built the Gracie fortune. Several of the furnishings on display belonged to the Gracie family.

Early in this century, the house was used for children's carpentry and home economics classes, as well as for an ice-cream parlor. Gracie Mansion opened as the first Museum of the City of New York in 1924.

Notable Collections on Exhibit

The mansion, restored in 1984 through gifts to the Gracie Mansion Conservancy, today presents the main floor to the public and is a showcase for art and antiques created by New York designers, cabinetmakers, painters and sculptors.

Lower East Side Tenement Museum

97 Orchard Street
New York, NY 10002
(212) 431-0233

Contact: Lower East Side Tenement
Museum
Open: Tues.-Fri. 11 a.m.–4 p.m.; living
history programs every Sun.
Facilities on Premises: Gift shop
Description of Grounds: Tenement
building located in the historic and
colorful Lower East Side
Year House Built: 1863
Style of Architecture: Tenement
On-Site Parking: No

Description of House

No one has called 97 Orchard Street
home for over fifty years, but the 1863
tenement was the first address in New York for hundreds of Germans, Turks,
Eastern European Jews, Chinese, and Italians who were part of the great
immigrations of the 19th and early 20th centuries.

The building, untouched since it was sealed in 1935, is now home to a
museum which mounts exhibitions on the urban immigrant experience. In
the spring of 1993, the museum expects to open the upstairs floors which
will display rooms and furnishings of typical tenement apartments of the
late 1800s.

Notable Collections on Exhibit

Living history programs, such as the "Peddlar's Pack Tour," provide
reenactments of aspects of the daily lives of immigrants on the Lower East
Side. Also on display is an oversized dollhouse-style model of 97 Orchard
Street that portrays frenetic activity taking place in each room and on the
sidewalk, which offers a unique and amusing glimpse of an imagined
day-in-the-life of the tenement building.

Morris-Jumel Mansion

Roger Morris Park
1765 Jumel Terrace
New York, NY 10032
(212) 923-8008

Contact: Morris-Jumel Mansion, Inc.

Open: Tues.-Sun. 10 a.m.–4 p.m.; call to confirm

Admission: Adults $2; students and seniors $1. Tours, exhibitions.

Facilities on Premises: Museum shop, library

Description of Grounds: Garden

Year House Built: Approximately 1765

Style of Architecture: Palladian design

Number of Rooms: 9 restored period rooms

Description of House

The house was built in 1765 as a summer retreat for British colonel Roger Morris and his wife. With the outbreak of the Revolutionary War, Morris, a Loyalist, left for England, during which time the home was occupied in turn by George Washington, British lieutenant general Sir Henry Clinton, and Baron Wilhelm von Knyphausen, the Hessian commander. After the war, the mansion was confiscated by the American government and became Calumet Hall, a popular tavern. In 1810, Stephen Jumel, a rich French merchant, and his wife, Eliza, bought the property. The Jumels spent several years in France, where they kept company with the Napoleonic court circle, but settled in the mansion in 1828. One year after Stephen Jumel's death in 1832, his wife married former vice president Aaron Burr.

The Morris-Jumel Mansion, Manhattan's oldest surviving house, is a monument to colonial grandeur. Its distinctive style was very advanced for its time. The Palladian design includes a two-story portico and triangular pediment, classical columns, and a large octagonal room in the rear—the first of its kind in the country. The mansion has nine restored rooms including George Washington's office. The house was redecorated in 1810 in the Empire style.

Notable Collections on Exhibit

The dining room glitters with 19th-century ceramics and glass. Eliza Jumel's chamber, contains a bed that is said to have belonged to Napoleon. The third floor is used for temporary exhibitions and houses an extensive archival collection.

Theodore Roosevelt Birthplace

28 East 20th Street
New York, NY 10003
(212) 260-1616

Contact: National Park Service

Open: Wed.-Sun. 9 a.m.–5 p.m.; closed Thanksgiving, Christmas Day, and New Years Day

Admission: Adults, $1; 16 and under free; 62 or over free. Guided tours, audiovisual presentation, weekend concerts: Sat. 2 p.m.

Suggested Time to View House: 1 hour

Number of Yearly Visitors: 17,000

Year House Built: 1923 Reconstruction

Style of Architecture: Mid-Victorian Brownstone

Number of Rooms: 5 period rooms, 2 museum display rooms

On-Site Parking: No

Wheelchair Access: No

Description of House

The Roosevelt family was one of the most prominent families in 19th century New York City. Theodore Roosevelt Sr. was a great philantropist helping to found the American Museum of Natural History, along with other institutions. Teddy was born on this urban site in 1858, the only American president ever to be born in New York City. Best known as the 26th president of the United States, Roosevelt also served as New York state assemblyman, New York City police commissioner, governor of New York, and was a hero of the Spanish-American War, noted author, explorer, and Nobel prize winner.

This reconstructed five-story Victorian brownstone was restored by the prominent female architect Theodara Pope Riddle. Forty percent of the furniture was donated by the Roosevelt family. The Roosevelt birthroom contains all of the original furniture; the rest has been collected and is appropriate for the period.

Notable Collections on Exhibit

The museum contains the largest collection of Teddy Roosevelt memorablia in the country. Notable objects include Roosevelt's Rough Rider uniform, many hunting trophies, an original "Teddy Bear", the shirt he was wearing during a 1912 assassination attempt, and hundreds of other objects related to his life.

Old Merchant's House

**29 East Fourth Street
New York, NY 10003
(212) 777-1089**

Contact: Old Merchant's House of New York

Open: Sun. 1–4 p.m.; group tours Mon.-Thur. by appointment; closed Aug.

Admission: Adults $3; students and seniors $2.50; members and children (12 and under) free. Guided tours.

Suggested Time to View House: 45–60 minutes

Facilities on Premises: Gift shop

Description of Grounds: A small garden behind house

Number of Yearly Visitors: 10,000

Year House Built: 1832

Style of Architecture: Federal and Greek revival

Number of Rooms: 20, 9 open to public

On-Site Parking: No

Wheelchair Access: No

Description of House

Seabury Tredwell, a merchant of marine hardware, purchased this three-story building in 1835. The Tredwell family can be traced to the 17th century but they lived mainly on Long Island until the 19th century. Seabury raised eight children, six girls and two boys. The youngest, Gertrude, was born in the house in 1840 and died there in 1933.

This was originally one of a row of similar homes, but today the house stands alone. The interior design, almost pure Greek revival, includes extraordinary plaster work. Over ninety percent of the furnishings are original to the Tredwell family; a few are gifts to the house. The furnishings reflect changes in the family's tastes and range from a field bed (c. 1800) to a Belta-style chair.

Notable Collections on Exhibit

The house also exhibits an unusual collection of early 19th-century hairy-paw pieces, bandsaw pieces from the 1840s, and a Nunn and Fisher piano.

Jonathan Hasbrouck House

P.O. Box 1783
Newburgh, NY 12551
(914) 562-1195

Contact: Washington's Headquarters State Historical Site

Open: Mid April-late Oct., Wed.-Sat. 10 a.m.–5 p.m., Sun. 1–5 p.m.; Nov.-early April, groups by advance notice

Admission: Free. Guided tours, videotape program of the site's Revolutionary War history, annual special events.

Suggested Time to View House: 45 minutes

Description of Grounds: 6½ acres with Hudson River Highlands view

Best Season to View House: May-Oct.

Number of Yearly Visitors: 22,000

Year House Built: 1750-1770

Number of Rooms: 8

Style of Architecture: Dutch Vernacular

On-Site Parking: Yes **Wheelchair Access:** Yes

Description of House

Jonathon Hasbrouck began to build this house in 1750, adding more rooms over the next twenty years to accommodate his family and to reflect his increased prosperity. Hasbrouck, a militia colonel who supported American Independence, died in 1780. In 1782, his widow Tryntje and daughters moved out so that George Washington could make his Continental Army headquarters there. Washington remained in the house for more than sixteen months from April 1, 1782 through August 19, 1783. His wife, Martha, lived here for one year. Mrs. Hasbrouck, who received the news of having to vacate her house "in sullen silence," is thought to have lived elsewhere in the Newburgh area.

This Dutch vernacular fieldstone house has survived many changes and still retains many of its original features. There is a Dutch-style jambless fireplace in the dining room with heavy overhead beams supporting the chimney above it. One of Washington's guests in 1782 described the dining room as the room with "seven doors and one window" even though there are eight doors! The house was acquired by the state of New York in 1850, and opened on July 4th of the same year as the first publicly-owned historic site in the nation. Preservation and restoration of the house have been continuous since that time. The furnishings are a mixture of period, reproduction, and just a few items from original residents. The house is furnished to reflect the period when its most famous residents, George and Martha Washington, lived here.

Notable Collections on Exhibit

Exhibits on the first two floors illustrate American Revolutionary and Hudson River themes. Notable objects on display include a tiger maple desk-on-frame once used by General Washington, Hudson Valley-made chairs, and an early gate leg table.

The Pruyn House

207 Old Niskayuna Road
Newtonville, NY 12128
(518)783-1435

Contact: Town of Colonie Cultural Center

Open: Open year round, Mon.-Fri.

Admission: Donations appreciated. Guided tours, Civil War Day, Old-fashioned Sun. art exhibits, concerts. Exhibits: Nat'l Chapter Embroidery Group, Hudson-Mohawk Weavers Guild and Federated Garden ClubsAmerica.

Suggested Time to View House: 1 hour

Description of Grounds: Perennial and herb gardens are in full bloom during the summer. Picnic tables available.

Style of Architecture: Transitional with elements of Federal and Greek Revival

Best Season to View House: Summer-fall

Number of Yearly Visitors: 9,000

Number of Rooms: 10

Year House Built: 1825-1830

On-Site Parking: Yes **Wheelchair Access:** Yes

Description of House

Casparus Francis Pruyn (1792-1846) was the land and business agent for Stephen Van Rensselaer III, one of the last patroons of Van Rensselaer manor. Pruyn worked collecting rents for the estate from 1835 to 1844. He would accept payment in livestock or produce from the tenant farmers. Because almost all of Albany County and other lands were under lease from the patroon, it was an important and responsible position. Pruyn was married to Ann Hewson and had ten children. One son, Robert Hewson Pruyn, was named ambassador to Japan by President Abraham Lincoln. The Pruyn House was actually the family's summer residence. Their main residence was in Rensselaer.

This large two story house is five bay windows wide. The house's end walls rise above a flat roof forming a parapet with four symmetrically placed chimneys. The entrance is recessed with side lights, a transom and a tripart window above containing stone lintels, sills and an adorned, channeled cornice. The interior retains original Greek Revival details including grained doors, authentic moldings, marble mantels, newels and balusters. The house is set back from the road on a small rise and has numerous outbuildings surrounding it creating a well-preserved farm complex. The outbuildings consist of a large barn, a carriage house, a potting shed, a pump house, a smoke house and a woodshed/privy. The furnishings have been collected or donated to reflect time up to the 1850s.

Notable Collections on Exhibit

Furniture on exhibit includes a Butler's desk made by an Albany cabinet maker; a Hepplewhite sideboard; an inlaid, early-style tall clock; two Victorian game tables; a sleigh bed; and a Pine poster rope bed. Also on display are early reverse paintings on glass of George and Martha Washington.

Cottage Lawn

435 Main Street, P.O. Box 415
Oneida, NY 13421
(315) 363-4136

Contact: Madison County Historical Society

Open: Tues.-Sat. 1–5 p.m.

Admission: Adults $2; children and groups arranged in advance $1. Guided tours.

Suggested Time to View House: 1 hour

Facilities on Premises: Gift shop (incl. books)

Description of Grounds: Residential grounds: original trees and shrubs, some flower beds

Best Season to View House: May-July

Number of Yearly Visitors: 12,000

Year House Built: 1849-1850

Number of Rooms: 11

Style of Architecture: Gothic Revival

On-Site Parking: Yes **Wheelchair Access:** No

Description of House

This distinctive cottage was built by Niles Higinbothom, son of the founder of Oneida, Sonds Higinbothom. Niles was the first banker in Oneida and the house even served as the first offices of the bank. Niles and his wife lived here with their three daughters. The house was left to the historical society when the last daughter (none were ever married) died in 1931.

Designed by A.J. Davis, this two-story Gothic "cottage" features brick exterior walls, stuccoed and scored to imitate ashlor blocks of sandstone. The house has an asymmetrical facade with larger and smaller gables, detailed with decorative vergeboards, casement windows with Gothic tracery, and a porch spanning entire front of house. Cottage Lawn has an attached carriage house which currently houses a Tally-ho Concord stage coach. The house also features a cedar-lined gymnasium, and an original bank vault, where Higinbothom started what is now the Oneida Valley National Bank. Cottage Lawn is listed on the National Register of Historic Places.

The furnishings include some originals but most have been collected, and are approximate to period. They include furniture, china, silverware, stoneware, and vases from the second half of the 19th century.

Notable Collections on Exhibit

The collection features paintings of Gerrit Smith (noted abolitionist and friend of John Brown), Polly DeFerrier (Indian "princess" married to a French nobleman), and other important figures in Madison County history. There is also a Powell & Goldstein cigar manufacturers exhibit with a full-size cigar store figure representing Napoleon Bonaparte (used to advertise "Napoleon" cigars).

The Mansion House

170 Kenwood
Oneida, NY 13421
(315) 343-0745

Contact: Oneida Community Mansion House, Inc.

Open: Wed.-Sun. 10 a.m.–4 p.m.

Admission: $5. Guided tours, orientation exhibit, meals available by reservation.

Suggested Time to View House: 3 hours

Facilities on Premises: Book store

Description of Grounds: 14 acres with landscaping showing influences of Downing and Olmstead

Best Season to View House: June-Sept.

Number of Yearly Visitors: 6,000

Year House Built: 1862

Style of Architecture: Italiante, Second Empire

Number of Rooms: Originally 300 rooms

Wheelchair Access: Yes

Description of House

The Oneida Community was a religious and social society founded in 1848 by John Humphrey Noyes and his followers. This small group originally gathered together in the Noyes homestead in Putney Valley, Vermont to put into practice their religious and social theories. They called themselves "Perfectionists" and proceeded to substitute the larger unit of group-family and group family life for the small unit of home and family. The Oneida Community had a fundamental belief in the dignity of work and supported themselves with the manufacture and sale of traps and chains, canned fruits and vegetables, sewing thread and later silverware.

The Oneida Community Mansion House was built to house the 300 members of this utopian community from 1862 to 1877. The exterior of the mansion appears very much as it once did. The interior features significant public spaces which include a decorated Big Hall (1862), the upper sitting room, the court, a nursery kitchen, and a library.

Oysterponds

Contact: Oysterponds Historical Society

Open: June-Sept. 30, Wed., Thur., Sat.-Sun. 2–5 p.m.

Admission: Adults $3; children $1 (includes admission to all 6 buildings). Guided tours, audiovisual orientation, lecture series, country fair and croquet tournament (Aug.), Memorial weekend yard and book sale, June garden studio tour and Christmas house tour.

Suggested Time to View House: 20 minutes per building

Facilities on Premises: Gift/book shop

Description of Grounds: The grounds include 6 acres of lawns and parkland on either side of Village Lane. Poquatuck Park borders the Webb Tavern and overlooks Orient Harbor.

Best Season to View House: June-Aug.

Number of Yearly Visitors: 8,000

Year House Built: Webb House-c. 1770, Village House-1799

Style of Architecture: Webb-Georgian, Village House-Victorian

On-Site Parking: Yes**Wheelchair Access:** No

Description of House

The Oysterponds Historical Society maintains a number of historic structures, including two historic homes, representing 18th-century life in a Long Island seaside village. Typical North Fork architecture is well represented in the buildings of this historic area.

The Village House was built by Augustus Griffin, a local historian. He wrote the first history of Southold in 1855 when he was in his eighties. Griffin spent most of his life in the Village House (his name for it), living here from 1799 to 1866. It was then acquired by the Vail family, who enlarged it and turned it into a summer boardinghouse, and called it the Village Hotel. Mrs. Vail brought Village Hotel to the height of fashion with a croquet court and hammoks in the trees. The Victorian parlor, dining room, and kitchen which visitors see today reflect the periof of her ownership.

The Webb House Tavern was built by Orange Webb about whom very little is recorded, other than he was a prosperous merchant in Greenport, New York. The house was moved in 1820 to the farm of the Youngs Family, where it was extensively remodelled. The Webb Houuse is probably the only surviving structure of its age on Long Island built as an inn and then transformed into a private dwelling.

There are very few furnishings original to any of the buildings, but all of the pieces are from local sources. Extensive photo research was done to restore the rooms to appropriate appearances both for the time and for this locale. The period rooms, costumes, toys, books, account records, day books, and photographs help visitors picture activities and customs of the 18th and 19th centuries.

Notable Collections on Exhibit

The Webb House features an extensive collection of fine 18th and 19th-century furniture, mostly from Long Island, and some locally made chairs and chests. The Village House exhibits local Victorian furniture (c. 1875-1895), exhibits of textiles and decorative arts appropriate to the boardinghouse period. The other buildings in the complex house collections of maritime paintings and folk art (Hallock Building) and changing exhibitions of area artists and traditional craftspeople (Schoolhouse).

Additional Information

In addition to the two houses, the complex contains the Amanda Brown Schoolhouse, the Little Red Barn, and the Hallock Building, originally used as a cookhouse and dormitory.

Richardson-Bates House Museum

135 East Third Street
Oswego, NY 13126
(315) 343-1342

Contact: Oswego County Historical Society
Open: Tues.-Fri. 10 a.m.–5 p.m., Sat. and
Sun. 1–5 p.m., closed all national
holidays
Admission: Adults $2; students and seniors
$1; children (5-12) $.50. All tours
guided, special exhibitions throughout
the year.
Suggested Time to View House: 1–2 hours
Facilities on Premises: Gift shop
Year House Built: House done in two
stages between 1867 and 1890.
Style of Architecture: Italian Villa

Number of Yearly Visitors: 4,000 (1991)
Number of Rooms: 6 period rooms and 4
exhibition galleries
On-Site Parking: Yes **Wheelchair Access:** Yes

Description of House

The house was built for Maxwell Richardson. He was an attorney, a real estate broker, and a two term mayor of Oswego. Max was a bachelor, sharing the residence with his widowed mother, his bachelor brother, and his divorced sister and her son, Norman Bates. Mr. Bates married and moved out in 1900 but returned in 1911 when Max died. Norman's widow died in 1946 and the Bates children gave the house and selected furnishings to the historical society to be used as a museum.

This three-story masonry structure features a four-story central tower. The 1867 wing was designed by Andrew Jackson Warner of Rochester, New York while the 1887 wing features a design by a local architect. The original porches were removed around 1952.

The period rooms are arranged according to photographs taken in the house around 1890. The museum owns about 90 percent of the furnishings shown in the pictures. The original Renaissance Revival furniture and window cornices are from the firm of Pottier and Stymus in New York. The amount of original furnishings coupled with a wealth of documentation (photos, letters, receipts, etc.) make for a unique glimpse into the lives of upper-middle class family from an industrial community in upstate New York at the end of the 19th century.

Notable Collections on Exhibit

Fifty-three original oil paintings and over 200 decorative objects are on exhibit in the first floor period rooms. In addition, Naomi Richardson's bedroom, on the second floor, gives vistors a look at the private side of Victorian lives.

Additional Information

The museum also holds permanent and changing exhibitions on the history of Oswego County. The museum owns about 25,000 objects, documents, and photographs about county people, places, and events. The house was listed on the National Register in 1975.

Coe Hall at Planting Fields

Planting Fields Road
Oyster Bay, NY 11771
(516) 922-9210

Contact: Planting Fields Foundation

Open: April-Sept., open daily except Wed. 12:30–3:30 p.m.; groups by appointment only

Admission: Fee in addition to Park Admission: adults and senior citizens $2; children (over 12) $1. Tours by trained vols; videotape orientation; associates GRP; special self-guided exterior walking tour of the house.

Suggested Time to View House: 45 minutes

Description of Grounds: 409 acres designed by Lowell & Sargant with greenhouses open year-round and outbuildings of former estate

Best Season to View House: Late spring-early summer

Number of Yearly Visitors: 150,000

Year House Built: 1918 to 1921

Style of Architecture: Tudor Revival

Number of Rooms: 65; 10 period rooms on main floor are open to the public

On-Site Parking: Yes **Wheelchair Access:** Yes

Description of House

W.R. Coe moved to the United States from England in 1884 to work as office help in the insurance firm of Johnson-Higgins. By age forty, he was president and chairman of the company. He married Mai Rogers, daughter of H.H. Rogers of Standard Oil. The Coes also owned Lake Irma Lodge in Cody, Wyoming and were a major force in the development of the Buffalo Bill Historical Center. Coe was a major collector of Western Settlement memorabilia and was responsible for funding over sixty chairs in American history throughout the United States.

The house, Coe Hall, is built of Indiana limestone and erected over the foundations of a Queen Anne-style house built by Grosvenor Atterbury which burned to the ground in 1918. The Tudor revival house was designed by Walker and Gillette with interiors appointed by Charles of London, Alavoine et cie, metalwork by Samuel Yellin, and stained glass from Chartres, Rowen, Heiner castle. The surrounding 409 acres were landscaped by James Greenleaf, Lowell and Sargant and the Olmstead Brothers. Respectively the outbuildings include the Camellia Greenhouse, Hibiscus House, Hay Barn, Tea House, Childrens Play House, Garages, Dower House designed by Eric Gugler, a laundry house and a late lodge.

Approximately half of the furnishings are original to the house and the remaining furnishings are appropriate to the documentation of the interiors using period photos from 1924 to 1932 and inventories.

Unique features include plasterwork ceilings, Samuel Yellin metalwork, stained glass, carved woodwork by Lewis and Casson. The exterior consists of carved brick chiminies, decorative stone work, and half timbering and surrounding vistas designed by the Olmstead brothers.

Notable Collections on Exhibit

Period rooms open to the public include a family den furnished with Charles of London pieces, a Louis XVI reception room (Alavoine), dining room, breakfast room totally muraled with scenes of Wyoming by Robert Chandler, a sport room, a telephone room, a gallery, a writing room and a Great Hall. The Tea House has been restored with murals by Ev Shinn. Also on display in various rooms is furniture from the 15th through the 20th century and paintings by Gheerhardts, Gaudi, van Weesop and Ostade.

Additional Information

Planting Fields is one of the few Long Island estates that retains its outbuildings intact. Efforts are underway to restore the historical landscape areas and to change the image of Planting Fields from an arboretum to a historic site. Visitors can get a sense of the self-contained nature of an estate and the idea of the gentleman farmer. The Carshalton gates, the former main entrance to the property, are dated to 1711 and were obtained by Charles Duveen for the Coes.

Raynham Hall Museum

20 West Main Street
Oyster Bay, NY 11771
(516) 922-6808

Contact: Friends of Raynham Hall

Open: Tues.-Sun. and Mon. holidays
1–5 p.m. Closed Christmas,
Thanksgiving and New Years.

Admission: $2; seniors and students $1;
children under 7 free. Guided tours for
school and adult groups upon
reservation; adult and children
workshops, children summer program,
lecture series, and changing exhibits.

Suggested Time to View House: 40 minutes

Facilities on Premises: Gift shop

Description of Grounds: Victorian gardens

Best Season to View House: Spring

Number of Yearly Visitors: 6,000

Year House Built: 1738

Style of Architecture: Colonial Saltbox (5
rooms) and Victorian (5 rooms)

Number of Rooms: 10

On-Site Parking: No

Wheelchair Access: Yes

Description of House

This gracious dwelling was home to five generations of the Townsends family. The house was purchased in 1738 by Samuel Townsend whose accomplishments were many. He was the town clerk, justice of the peace, a successful merchant, and general store owner. His grandson, Solomon Townsend II, transformed the original Colonial structure into a Victorian mansion in 1850, and named it Raynham after an ancestral home in Norfolk, England. The Townsends were an extremely influential family in Oyster Bay: they were instrumental in bringing the railroad to Oyster Bay and owned an early newspaper. They also developed a commercial area named Audrey Avenue after Samuel's daughter. Samuel's son Robert Townsend was a spy for George Washington in the Culper spy ring. The Colonial house served as headquarters for British officers during the American Revolution.

The Colonial rooms have furnishings which belonged to the Samuel Townsend family, and feature original floors and doors. The Victorian rooms have been furnished in 1870 tradition.

Notable Collections on Exhibit

Raynham Hall displays an impressive collection of decorative arts from the period ranging from 1700 to 1900.

William Phelps Store Museum

140 Market Street
Palmyra, NY 14522
(315) 597-5788

Contact: Historic Palmyra
Open: May 30-Sept. 6, Sat. 1–4 p.m.; other
   times by appointment
Activities: Guided tours
Suggested Time to View House: 45 minutes
Best Season to View House: Summer
Year House Built: 1830
Number of Rooms: 9

Description of Grounds: A small yard
Number of Yearly Visitors: 500
Style of Architecture: Federal-Mercantile
On-Site Parking: No **Wheelchair Access:** No

Description of House

This store and home located on the banks of the Erie Canal has changed little since the early 1900s. The store was purchased in 1868 by William Phelps. He ran the small business with his wife, Catherine, and later with his children, Mary Louise and Julius. In 1895, Sybil Eugenia was born to William's son Julius and his wife, Mary. For the next twelve years the entire family worked in the store and lived together in the rooms on the second and third floors of the building. William Phelps died in 1917, after which his son Julius ran the business until the 1940s, when the store closed. His son, Julius, died in 1960 at the ripe old age of 91. His granddaughter, Sybil, who never married, continued to live in the upstairs apartment until her death in 1976. A well known figure in Palmyra, Sybil maintained many of the items on display in the house today.

The William Phelps Store Museum is an outstanding example of a canal town mercantile family home from the turn of the century. The upstairs dwelling rooms are being renovated to overcome the damage created by leaks in the original tin roof throughout the years. The rooms have most of the original home furnishings and articles, some of which date back to the 1940s era.

Notable Collections on Exhibit

The original signs, displays, and barrels are on display as well as an unusual collection of circus posters and memorabilia (a special interest of Sybil Phelps).

Parishville Museum

East Main Street
Parishville, NY 13672
(315) 265-7619

Contact: Parishville Historical Association Inc.

Open: June and Sept. Wed. 12:30–3 p.m.; July-Aug., Mon.-Fri. 12:30–3 p.m.; also by appointment

Admission: Free. Guided tours and special program on Annual Historical Day (always 3rd Sat. of August).

Suggested Time to View House: 2 hours

Description of Grounds: Accessible to public

Best Season to View House: Summer

Number of Yearly Visitors: 250

Year House Built: Around 1850

Number of Rooms: 13 (plus 4 walk-in closets)

On-Site Parking: Yes **Wheelchair Access:** No

Description of House

This comfortable home is beautifully situated at the top of the hill on Main Street and offers a commanding a view of both uptown and downtown. The house was owned by a very "well-to-do" family who owned most of the factories. They were influential during the town's industrial era.

Two white porches with green trim surround this three-story dwelling. The two stained glass windows in entryway elegantly reflect the occupant's social standing. The rooms have been arranged as they were when the original owners lived here with furnishings collected and appropriate for the period. In addition to the house, the museum includes a separate carriage house and blacksmith shop.

Notable Collections on Exhibit

The rear of the house contains a photograph gallery with a comprehensive collection of pictures depicting the buildings and people of our industrial history. The separate carriage house holds some working transportation equipment of the horse-drawn era.

The John Kane House

East Main Street
Pawling, NY 12564
(914) 855-9316

Contact: Historical Society of Quaker Hill & Pawling

Open: May 15-Oct. 15, Sat.-Sun. 2–4 p.m.; special openings for groups available year around; open-house each Dec.

Admission: Free during season; suggested donation for special openings $2. Tours, video available, Christmas open house.

Suggested Time to View House: 1 hour

Facilities on Premises: Gift shop

Description of Grounds: Period herb garden, lawns can be used for walking, picnicing

Best Season to View House: Late spring-early fall

Number of Yearly Visitors: 400-500

Year House Built: 1740

Style of Architecture: Federal

Number of Rooms: 12

On-Site Parking: Yes **Wheelchair Access:** No

Description of House

The house was used as the headquarters of General Washington during the fall of 1778. The 13,000 troops of the Continental Army were stationed on these hillsides waiting and watching the activities of the British army. General Lafayette was in Pawling during that time, for the dinner commemorating the one year anniversary of the defeat of Burgoyne at Saratoga and the would-be courtmartial of General Philip Schuyler.

The John Kane House is comprised of two parts: a large main block an ' an abutting kitchen wing. The main block, five bays long and three bays deep, is of frame construction lined with brick. The house exhibits many distinguishable features of the Federal style. A centered doorway, flanked by sidelights and topped by a rectangular transom window, is embellished with fluted pilasters and a projecting cornice. Similar pilasters on a smaller scale are found on the second story Palladian window placed directly above the doorway. A single-story, Greek Revival portico runs the length of the main block. The interior of the Kane House retains much of its original configuration. The kitchen wing contains a fireplace with a carved wooden mantel. All the rooms in the main block have fireplaces: those in the drawing rooms have carved marble mantels while those in the library and dining room have mantels of hand-carved painted wood. The furnishings were collected and donated by residents of the area and were from area homes and represent various periods.

The Kane House is located in the lovely country village of Pawling. Because the house remained in the hands of a few families, its architectural integrity remains. The lovely porch is the focal point of the south side of the house and is used by the historical society to host summer concerts and puppet shows.

Notable Collections on Exhibit

The collection contains 19th-century coverlets and quilts; men's and women's clothing and shoes from the late 1800s; collectibles, ledgers, records, photos, documents of Pawling's early days; the key to the room George Washington used while in Pawling in 1778; and memorabilia of adventurer, broadcaster, and author Lowell Thomas.

Oliver House Museum

**200 Main Street
Penn Yan, NY 14527
(315) 536-7318**

Contact: Yates County Historical Society

Open: Nov.-May, Tues.-Fri. 10 a.m.–5 p.m.;
June-Oct., Wed.-Sat. 10 a.m.–5 p.m.;
closed major holidays

Admission: $2. Guided tours, slide
presentations, educational programs,
and workshops.

Suggested Time to View House: 20 minutes

Facilities on Premises: Gift shop

Year House Built: 1852

Style of Architecture: Italianate

Number of Rooms: 16

On-Site Parking: Yes

Wheelchair Access: Yes

Description of House

The Oliver House was built in 1852 by Dr. Andrew Oliver for his son William as a wedding gift. Andrew was the first of three consecutive generations of doctors who practiced in Penn Yan and lived at Oliver House. The house was occupied by the family until 1942 when Carrie Oliver, the last surviving family member, willed the home to the village with the stipulation that it remain as a museum and a historical site.

The architectural style is primarily early Victorian Italianate with a brick exterior although some features are Greek Revival. These include the porch columns, interior hallway pilasters, interior molding, and window and door frames. Many of the furnishings belonged to the Oliver family; however, the Yates County Historical Society's collections are also housed here, and date from a number of periods.

Notable Collections on Exhibit

The Oliver collections and the Yates Historical Society collections together contain approximately 30,000 objects. Included within are extensive collections of paintings, prints, photographs, costumes, and household furnishings. In addition, the museum houses numerous artifacts and documents from the pre-Iroquoian and Seneca settlements of Native Americans to the arrival of the religous sect "Publick Universal Friends", led by Jemima Wilkinson.

Kent-Delord House Museum

17 Cumberland Avenue
Plattsburgh, NY 12901
(518) 561-1035

Contact: Kent-Delord House Corporation

Open: Tues.-Sat. 12–3 p.m. (only for guided tours); and by appointment; closed Federal holidays

Admission: Adults $3; seniors and students $2; children (under 12) $1. Guided tours.

Suggested Time to View House: 45–60 minutes

Facilities on Premises: Museum store

Best Season to View House: May-Oct.

Number of Yearly Visitors: 3,500

Year House Built: 1797-1810 (2 phases)

Number of Rooms: 9 open to public

Style of Architecture: Late Georgian/Federal

On-Site Parking: Yes **Wheelchair Access:** No

Description of House

Nathan Averill, Sr. built the original house circa 1797 for William Bailey. The ownership changed hands many times before Henry Delord purchased the house from James Kent in 1810. Born and raised in France, Henry Delord left his home for the French West Indies in 1784. After becoming a successful merchant there, he was forced to flee during an upheaval caused by the French Revolution and made his way to Peru, New York, in 1796. Three years later he married Betsy Ketchum, who came to the North Country with her family from the Dutchess County town of Red Hook, New York. After Henry's death in 1825, Betsy and Frances Henrietta (their daughter) remained in the house. In 1832, Frances Henrietta married Henry Webb, whose Wethersfield, Connecticut family played a prominent role in the American Revolution.

This stately home contains a central hall, two side parlors, and a bedroom and dining room at the rear of the house with a kitchen wing off the dining room. The rooms are restored to their original 1810 colors. Today, as a historic landmark and chartered museum, the house stands as a tribute to the Delords and others who made significant contributions to their community and country.

The house is furnished with a wide variety of furniture acquired by three generations of the DeLords during their 103 years of residency. The furnishings include a notable array of china, implements and artifacts. Every two years the exhibits change to represent a different time period of occupancy.

Notable Collections on Exhibit

The museum houses an impressive collection of American portrait art attributed to such well-known artists as William Johnston, John Singleton Copley, Robert Fulton, Abraham G.D. Tuthill, John Wesley Jarvis, George Freeman, Henry Inman, and others.

The Glebe House

635 Main Street
Poughkeepsie, NY 12602
(914) 471-1630

Contact: Dutchess County Historical Society
Open: By appointment only
Admission: Donation $2; discount for
school groups or seniors. In season
guided tours and seasonal special
programs.
Suggested Time to View House: 45 minutes
Facilities on Premises: Sales desk
Description of Grounds: At the rear of the
house is a modern, landscape yard with
plantings.
Best Season to View House: Spring and fall
Number of Yearly Visitors: 1000 plus
Year House Built: 1767, with later additions
Style of Architecture: Anglo-Dutch
vernacular
Number of Rooms: 7 exhibit rooms

On-Site Parking: No **Wheelchair Access:** Yes

Description of House

The Reverend John Beardsley was an Anglican minister who lived in the house until the Revolutionary War, when his loyalty to the crown drove him into exile. Peter DeReimer, a silversmith occupied the house from 1792 to 1809. His descendants live in the area today.

Built by the members of local churches as a minister's residence, this one-and-a-half story house utilizes a simple hall-parlor plan. The house was enlarged and renovated in the early 19th century and used continuously until 1929 when it was purchased by the city of Poughkeepsie to be used as a historic house museum. Glebe House is noteworthy for being one the few early vernacular houses in the area today which retains many original features.

The furnishings are consistent with the period of the house and with area styles of the time. None of the pieces belonged to the Beardsley family, however, a painting and two pieces of furniture belonged to later residents, the DeReimer family.

Notable Collections on Exhibit

The Dutchess County Historical Society has notable collections of documents and materials as well as photographs, postcards, county materials, and artifacts. There is also an interesting collection of early samplers, county related memorabilia and costumes. These are not on exhibit, but are available to scholars for research purposes.

Vander Ende-Onderdonk Farmhouse Museum

18-20 Flushing Avenue
Ridgewood, NY 11385
(718) 456-1776

Contact: Greater Ridgewood Historical Society

Open: April-1st week of Dec., Sat. 2–4:30 p.m., Wed. by appointment; library open Tues.-Thurs and Sat. 10 a.m.–4:30 p.m.

Admission: Adults $1; seniors and children $.50.

Facilities on Premises: Museum shop

Description of Grounds: Garden

Year House Built: 1709

Style of Architecture: Farmhouse

Description of House

The Onerdonk Farmhouse was originally part of the Hendrick Berentz Smidt plantation, received in a land grant from New Amsterdam governor Pieter Stuyvesant. The Vander Ende family built this charming farmhouse in 1709; members of the family lived here for close to a century. The property passed through a number of hands before the Onderdonk family purchased it in 1821. After 1905, the farmhouse served a number of purposes including housing local businesses and even a speakeasy during Prohibition. The house was abandonned in the 1970s and was almost destroyed. Concerned citizens organized a restoration effort which is still on-going. In addition to museum exhibits, the farmhouse currently has one period room furnished to represent the Victorian era (c. 1860).

Additional Information

Onderdonk Farmhouse serves as a museum for the study of local history, culture, architecture, and archeology from Indian times to the present. The society's library contains more than 5,000 volumes related to local history and genealogy.

Hallock Homestead

163 Sound Avenue.
Riverhead, NY 11901
(516) 298-5292

Contact: Hallockville Museum Farm

Open: Wed. to Sun. 10 a.m.–4 p.m. all year except holidays.

Admission: Adults $2.50; children $1.50; members free. Tours, exhibits, lectures, school programs.

Suggested Time to View House: 45–60 minutes

Description of Grounds: 2½ acres plus barn and other 19th-century farm buildings

Best Season to View House: Summer-fall

Number of Yearly Visitors: 12,000

Year House Built: 1765; continually modified and expanded until 1907

Style of Architecture: Long Island Vernacular

Number of Rooms: 10 open to the public

On-Site Parking: Yes **Wheelchair Access:** Yes

Description of House

This modest home was occupied by five generations of Hallock family from the late 18th century up until 1979. Hallockville is a historic name that refers to the concentration of Hallocks in this particular area of Riverhead, Long Island.

Built in 1765 as a typical one-and-a-half story five bay Cape Cod home, the Hallock Homestead grew throughout the 19th century to accomodate a larger family and reflect the prosperity and success of agriculture on Long Island's north fork. The original 19th century architectural features and elements have been remarkably preserved and a number of stylistic features, including a faux-marbre mantelpiece, and influences are evident. The homestead is furnished for the period 1880 to 1910, and much of the furniture was locally made. All of the 19th-century carpets are original to the house.

The Hallock complex, including the homestead and outbuildings, is listed on the National Register of Historic Places and is located in a New York State designated scenic and historic corridor.

Notable Collections on Exhibit

The barn features an exhibit of agricultural tools and equipment.

Woodside

485 East Avenue
Rochester, NY 14607
(716) 271-2705

Contact: Rochester Historical Society

Open: Mon.-Fri. 10 a.m.–4 p.m.; other times
  by special appointment

Admission: Adults $1.50; seniors and
  students $1.25; children (12-16) $1.
  Guided tours, lectures, entertainment.

Suggested Time to View House: 45 minutes

Description of Grounds: Enclosed
  perennial garden, laid out in parterres

Best Season to View House: June-Oct.

Number of Yearly Visitors: 2,000

Year House Built: 1839-41

Style of Architecture: Greek Revival

Number of Rooms: 19

On-Site Parking: Yes

Description of House

Woodside was owned by two prominent residents of Rochester before it was bequeathed to the historical society in 1940. The house's first occupant owned large amounts of property, including a flour mill on the Genesee River. He also founded two Episcopalian churches and sat on the boards of many local charities. The last owner was a banker, who was also active in church and other civic affairs.

This elegant house features a brick exterior with limestone sills and a cupola, two stone porches with Doric columns, and a semi-circular rear veranda overlooking the garden. The interior is equally lovely; the main rooms have Grecian style marble fireplaces, and the windows and doors on main floor are flanked by pilasters, surmounted by capitals copied from the ruined "Tower of the Winds" in Athens. Opulence is also evident in the great staircase which ascends four floors. Period furnishings donated to the historical society fill the house, and most have Rochester associations.

Notable Collections on Exhibit

Woodside holds a major collection of over 400 oil portraits and landscapes, and watercolors. The house exhibits a lace collection and a large costume collection spanning 130 years (all were owned by Rochester people, though a number were made in Paris).

Additional Information

The society has published twenty-five volumes on Rochester history, and maintains a reference library and extensive archives.

Susan B. Anthony House

17 Madison Street
Rochester, NY 14608
(716) 235-6124

Contact: Susan B. Anthony Memorial, Inc.
Open: Thur.-Sat. 1–4 p.m.; or by special arrangement for groups
Admission: Adults $2; children (under 12) and seniors $1. Guided tours.
Suggested Time to View House: 1 hour
Facilities on Premises: Sales desk

Description of Grounds: Small yard
Best Season to View House: Summer
Year House Built: c. 1850
Style of Architecture: Vernacular Italianate
Number of Rooms: 12
On-Site Parking: No **Wheelchair Access:** Yes

Description of House

Susan B. Anthony (1866-1906) shared this house with her sister Mary for the last forty years of her life. Anthony is best known for her tireless efforts to achieve women's suffrage, or the right to vote. The 19th amendment granting this right named after her. She was also an active abolitionist and a temperance reformer.

Susan B. Anthony was arrested for voting in 1872 in this middle-class Victorian home. She met and made plans with the famous reformers Elizabeth Cady Stanton and Frederick Douglass in the parlor. In the third floor attic workroom, Anthony helped write the monumental *History of Women's Suffrage*. This red brick house, built before the Civil War, is distinguished by an ornamental wood entrance porch and a shingled front gable with an oriel window.

Susan B. Anthony's family, friends and co-suffrage workers sent back many of the original furnishings, including Anthony's desk where she planned the final campaign for the 19th amendment, for display in the house. The dwelling has been designated a National Historic landmark.

Notable Collections on Exhibit

Carrie Chapman's original photo collection of early leaders of women's rights and suffrage is on display. The house also exhibits a marble bust of Anthony by Adalaide Johnson (on loan from the Metropolitan Museum of Art) and a painted lithograph of Abraham Lincoln (one of only two—the other is in Springfield, Illinois at the Lincoln Museum). In addition, there is a unique collection of memorabilia from the women suffrage movement which includes buttons, posters and photos, Anthony's clothing and a quilt made by her.

Campbell-Whittlesey House

123 South Fitzhugh Street
Rochester, NY 14610
(716) 546-7029

Contact: The Landmark Society of Western New York

Open: March-Dec., Tues.-Fri. 10 a.m.–2 p.m., Sat.-Sun. 12–2 p.m.; closed major holidays

Admission: Adults $2; seniors $1; children $.25. Guided tours, self-guided walking tours of neighborhood, audio-visual presentations (video and slide shows), special holiday programs in late Nov.-Dec.

Suggested Time to View House: 60–90 minutes

Facilities on Premises: Museum shop, meeting/education room

Number of Yearly Visitors: 3,700

Year House Built: 1835-36

Style of Architecture: Greek revival

Number of Rooms: 9 restored rooms (first floor only)

On-Site Parking: Yes **Wheelchair Access:** Yes

Description of House

Benjamin Campbell came to Rochester in 1820 as a merchant of drygoods, hardware and crockery. The Erie Canal, completed in 1825, brought success to his merchant enterprise, enabling him to enter the business of flour milling. During this prosperous period, Rochester was known as the "flour City" and the "boomtown" of the nation. Business losses in 1841 forced Campbell to sell his house at public auction to Thomas Rochester, son of city founder Nathaniel Rochester. In 1842, the house was purchased by Frederick Whittlesey, a prominent lawyer, judge and congressman. The house remained in the Whittlesey family until passed to the Landmark Society in 1937.

The house well represents Rochester's period of prosperity. A two-story, brick temple-style house, the structure is considered to be one of America's outstanding restorations of the Greek revival style of architecture. Plans for the house were either inspired or furnished by Minard Lafever, author of *The Beauties of Modern Architecture* (1835), and other builder's guides. The parlors feature twelve color tones, carefully researched and recreated, using pigments and formulas of the 1830s.

The furnishings are generally of the same period of the house (or earlier), but are not original to the house. Many were collected from families who lived in the immediate neighborhood.

Notable Collections on Exhibit

The furnishings include fine examples of New York State pieces in the Sheraton and early Empire styles, with an outstanding ornament collection with gold stenciled decoration. Several pieces closely reflect the designs of Duncan Phyfe and Joseph Meeks, while one piece is labeled "George Miller of New York City". Rochester cabinetmakers are well represented; there is also a notable collection of stenciling on velvet known as "theorem paintings".

Additional Information

The house is part of a complex known as the Landmark Center. Adjacent to the house, and part of the guided tour, is the Hoyt-Potter House, a Greek Revival house built circa 1840. This house showcases the tasteful rehabilitation of a historic structure that was vacant for twenty years. It houses the Landmark Society headquarters, the Landmark shop, the Wenrich Memorial Library, and an education center.

Stone-Tolan House

2370 East Avenue
Rochester, NY 14610
(716) 546-7029

Contact: The Landmark Society of Western New York

Open: March-Dec., Fri.-Sun. 12–4 p.m.; closed major holidays

Admission: Adults $2; seniors $1; children $.25. Guided tours; Stone-Tolan Country Fair, last weekend in Sept.

Suggested Time to View House: 45 minutes

Description of Grounds: Nearly 4 acres with an apple orchard, kitchen garden, smokehouse, and native plants of period

Best Season to View House: May-Oct.

Number of Yearly Visitors: 8,700

Year House Built: c. 1792

Style of Architecture: Federal

Number of Rooms: 5 restored rooms (downstairs only)

On-Site Parking: Yes **Wheelchair Access:** Yes

Description of House

Orringh Stone, the son of a Revolutionary War captain, came here from Lenox, Massachusetts in 1790, settling on a 210 acre tract of land. He married Elizabeth Maybee in 1792; they had eight children. After her death in 1814, he married Sally West and raised two more children. In addition to farming, Stone operated a rural tavern, welcoming travelers, hunters, and settlers. He became an active community and church leader, hosting the founding meetings of the Town of Brighton in 1814, and the First Congregational Church of Brighton in 1817. He died in 1830 at the age of 73. The second primary occupant was John Tolan, who purchased the house and fifty-two acres in 1860. He established a nursery business. His daughter, Ellen, sold the house to the Landmark Society in 1956.

Listed on the National Register of Historic Places, this modest frame house consists of a two-story main-block, with a tavern room and parlor/bedroom, and a one-story kitchen wing, with pantry and small bedroom. Furnishings are generally of the same period of the house (or earlier), but are not original to the house. Reproductions of early 19th-century tavern accessories have been added to provide a more complete setting of the tavern/home scene. These include tableware, artificial food, games, clothing, and bedding.

The present landscape, approximately four-and-a-half acres, has been carefully researched and planted with native trees, shrubs and wildflowers, along with old favorites imported by early settlers from New England. The apple orchard contains approximately fifty trees representing eight varieties that existed in the early 19th century. The kitchen garden is planted with herbs used for culinary and medicinal purposes, and heirloom vegtables that grow alongside modern day varieties.

Notable Collections on Exhibit

Period furnishings include pieces of New York or New England origin from the period of 1790 to 1820 and are generally country style. Notable objects include a Sheraton field canopy bed and a set of painted Windsor side chairs.

Additional Information

The annual Stone-Tolan Country Fair, held on the last weekend in September, is a special family event, featuring craft demonstrations, early 19th-century entertainment, horse and wagon rides, a farm animal display, a military encampment, and a host of children's activities.

Van Nostrand-Starkins House

221 Main Main Street
Rosyln, NY 11576
(516) 621-3040

Contact: Roslyn Landmark Society
Open: May-Oct., Sat. 1–4 p.m.
Admission: $1; groups by negotiation.
  Guided tours, permanent architectural
  and arcgeological exhibits.
Suggested Time to View House: 1 hour
Facilities on Premises: Bookstore

Best Season to View House: May-Oct.
Number of Yearly Visitors: 1,000
Year House Built: c. 1680
Style of Architecture: Medieval English
  Cottage
Number of Rooms: 6
On-Site Parking: No

Description of House

Prior to the end of the 18th century, the history of the Van Nostrand-Starkins House is only conjecture. By the 1790 census, William Van Nostrand, a blacksmith, was the head of the household there. Van Nostrand and his wife, Sarah, sold their their house and land to Joseph Starkins, who was also a blacksmith, in 1795. Through three centuries, from the early days of nearby Hempstead Harbor up until 1970, the house was continually in use as a residence. The house was restored in the early 1970s to its original appearance at the time it was the home of Joseph Starkins and William Van Nostrand.

This 17th-century cottage has undergone numerous alterations over the years, but still remains suprisingly intact. A major part of the original white oak framing has survived. The original structure with its early 18th-century lean-to (circa 1730) remained virtually unchanged for over a half a century. Later occupants made Greek Revival alterations to the facade and added to large windows and a porch.

The furnishings have been donated by local families and are from the period 1680 to 1750. These include a Kirby lowboy and a Kirby kas, and a two-drawer cherry blanket chest made in Long Island. Some furnishings appear to have been from the original Van Nostrand family.

Notable Collections on Exhibit

The house displays a permanent collection of samplers made by Long Island girls, a collection of toolboxes, and samples of fences and other architectural fragments.

Square House

1 Purchase Street
Rye, NY 10580
(914) 967-7588

Contact: Rye Historical Society

Open: Tues.-Sun. 2:30–4:30 p.m. with extended hours on Tues. and Sat. 12:30–4:30 p.m.

Admission: $1 donation. Guided tours, lectures, craft classes and in-service teacher training courses.

Suggested Time to View House: 45 minutes

Facilities on Premises: Gift shop

Description of Grounds: Colonial herb garden adjacent to Rye Village Green

Best Season to View House: Spring-summer

Number of Yearly Visitors: 10,000

Number of Rooms: 7

Year House Built: c. 1730 with additions in 1787 and 1937

Style of Architecture: Dutch Colonial

On-Site Parking: Yes **Wheelchair Access:** Yes

Description of House

In its over 260 year history, the Square House has had twenty six owners. Some of the more notable include Peter Brown, a miller, believed to be the builder of the house. In 1770, Dr. Ebenezer Haviland bought the house. Dr. Haviland's occupations were many including working as a surgeon/barber, a town clerk and a fervent patriot, who was killed during the American Revolution. In 1781, his widow came back to run the tavern after staying with relatives in Connecticut during the war. Widow Haviland made numerous changes to the building, including adding the gambrel roof and the ballroom wing. Daniel Mead bought the house in 1835 and returned it to a private home. David was a justice of the peace, a church trustee and for a time, Rye's postmaster. Listed on the National Register of Historic Places, this house and tavern was visited by George Washington, John Adams, Samuel Adams and General Lafayette.

Architecturally the house is an outstanding example of local styles. The Square House features a white, fishscale shingle and clapboard exterior with a gambrel roof and a covered open porch along the front of the building. The five period rooms are furnished to represent the late 18th century when the building as a popular tavern on the Boston Post Road. One bedroom reflects the period of the late 1830s when the house private home. The last period room is the 1930s Village Council Room. The Square House served as Rye's municipal hall from 1904 to 1964. The 18th-century ballroom is used as a gallery for exhibitions on Rye's history. In spite of its current use, this room retains its 18th-century appearance, including a barrel vaulted ceiling.

Notable Collections on Exhibit

The period rooms contain an assortment of 18th, 19th and 20th-century decorative arts which clearly illustrate the uses of the house. In its changing exhibitions, the society uses its general and archival collections including photographs, costumes, toys and business artifacts.

1805 Frisbie House

Route 29A, P.O. Box 185
Salisbury Center, NY 13454

Contact: Salisbury Historical Society
Open: June-mid Oct. weekends 1–4 p.m.
Activities: Special exhibits in July, Aug. and Dec., historical society meetings held here March-Nov., including programs and speakers
Suggested Time to View House: 30 minutes

Description of Grounds: Large yard, walking distance to 1865 covered bridge
Number of Yearly Visitors: Over 500
Year House Built: 1805
Style of Architecture: Federal
Number of Rooms: 6
On-Site Parking: Yes **Wheelchair Access:** Yes

Description of House

Augustus Frisbie was an early settler and industrialist who owned a local carding mill. Frisbie, a civic minded person, was a founder of the Universalist Church in Salisbury Center.

Built in 1805, the Frisbie House is the oldest frame building in Salisbury Center. The Federal style can be seen in the simple central entrance and the symmetrical windows on the facade. Inside, a large center stairway connects two floors where a large ballroom extends across the entire front of the second story. A large tavern room completes the first floor. Although there are several paintings on display of ancestors of a prominent town family and a complete set of locally produced bedroom set, the house is not furnished as a home but instead displays several collections of objects related to Salisbury history.

Notable Collections on Exhibit

The exhibits include a large collection of artifacts from a Salisbury cheese factory. In addition, there are also artifacts from a local iron mine and a large priest's vestment chest from a local Catholic church.

1743 Palatine House

Box 554
Schoharie, NY 12157
(518) 295-7505

Contact: Schoharie Colonial Heritage
  Association
Open: June-Oct., Sat.-Sun. 1–5 p.m.;
  July-Aug., also open Mon., Thur. and Fri.
  1–5 p.m.; and by appointment
Admission: Adults $2; students $1. Guided
  tour, a living history museum with craft
  demonstrations each weekend.
Suggested Time to View House:
  45–60 minutes
Facilities on Premises: Small shop

Description of Grounds: Small herb garden,
  small vegetable garden, large cemetary,
  and a picnic table
Best Season to View House: June-Sept.
Number of Yearly Visitors: 1,000
Year House Built: 1743
Style of Architecture: Post & Beam
Number of Rooms: 4
On-Site Parking: Yes **Wheelchair Access:** No

Description of House

Also known as the Old Lutheran Parsonage, the 1743 Palatine House
has been designated the oldest existing building in Schorarie county. This
simple German home, typical of the 18th century, was built by the Palatine
colonists (a generic term for German immigrants of the early 18th century)
for their minister, Peter Nicholas Sommers, who had agreed to come from
Hamburg, Germany in 1743.

The building is of post and beam construction in the German style with
a steeply pitched roof. The walls are filled with wattle and daub, the wattle
being quarted saplings or sticks with grooves made in the uprights. A
mixture of straw and mud (daub), is then applied quite thickly with the
inside surface being smoothed and later white washed. The large jambless
fireplaces have been restored and the beaded siding was duplicated and
replaced. The furnishings are all locally made and were collected for display
in the house.

Additional Information

Palatine House is a living history museum and features demonstrations
of wool drying, spinning, and weaving, as well as candle and soap making.

Mynderse-Partridge-Becker House

55 Cayuga Street
Seneca Falls, NY 13148
(315) 568-8412

Contact: Seneca Falls Historical Society

Open: Mon.-Fri. 9 a.m.–5 p.m.; Sat.
12–4 p.m.

Admission: Adults $2; students $1; tours
$1.50; members free. Guided tours, slide
talk for handicapped, local history
programs, Victorian culture programs.

Suggested Time to View House: 1 hour

Facilities on Premises: Museum shop

Description of Grounds: Large yard
surrounding house

Best Season to View House: Summer

Number of Yearly Visitors: 6,000 plus

Number of Rooms: 23

Year House Built: 1855, redesigned in 1880

Style of Architecture: 1885-Italianate,
1880-Queen Anne

Description of House

This picturesque house was built in 1855 in the Italianate style by Edward Mynderse, the son of one of the area's first settlers. In 1880, he sold the house to Mrs. Leroy Partridge, who employed prominent Rochester architect James D. Cutler to enlarge and redesign the house into the current popular Queen Anne style. Stained glass windows, elegant lighting fixtures and carved woodwork were added along with imported wall and floor coverings from France. The house was sold again in 1890 to Norman Becker, a Waterloo banker. The family lived in the house until 1961 when the historical society purchased it and made it their home.

This twenty-three room brick structure has not changed since 1880 and today provides a splendid showcase of Victorian decoration. Visitors will enjoy the carved woodwork, elegant lighting fixtures, brass ornate chandeliers, wonderful stain glass windows, parquet floors, and original wall coverings from 1880. There are nine rooms of Victorian furnishings on display including an original dining room furniture made for house in 1890. There are also fine examples of Roccoco Revival, Empire and Renaissance Revival furnishings in the drawing room, parlor and bedrooms. The house also contains a fine research library and local history exhibits which provide insight into the history of Seneca County and the Victorian era.

Notable Collections on Exhibit

In addition to the Victorian furnishings, the house also exhibits paintings, historical engravings and etchings, local history exhibits, and changing exhibits devoted to Victorian textiles and other regional topics.

Additional Information

Visitors to the property will also see the 1895 town clock and a structure known as "the Bee Hive", a wood frame Gothic Revival building once used as a tool shed.

The Manor of St. George

Off William Floyd Parkway
Smith's Point, NY
(516) 281-5034

Contact: Estate of Eugene A. T. Smith
Open: May-Oct., Wed.-Sun.
Admission: Free. Guided tours.
Suggested Time to View House: 1 hour

Description of Grounds: 100 acres, green lawns on Great South Bay
Year House Built: 1670s
On-Site Parking: Yes

Description of House

Over the last three centuries, the Manor of St. George has had a long and illustrious history. The first owner and Lord of the Manor of St. George was William Smith, an ambitious young man who had started his metoric career in Tangier, Morocco. Known as Colonel William "Tangier" Smith, he married Martha Tunstall and had thirteen children, only six of whom survived. In 1686, Colonel Smith embarked for America with his family to seek his fortune, and arrived in New York harbor early that fall. He bought the lands of the manor on May 16, 1688 and subsequently bought additional tracts of land from a native named John Mayhew. Members of the Smith family lived in the manor until 1954.

The manor also fell into British hands during the Revolutionary War and was later recaptured by Colonial forces led by Colonel Benjamin Tallmadge. Today, the manor often re-enacts this battle along with other skirmishes which took place at the estate.

Notable Collections on Exhibit

The manor houses an extensive collection of rare documents, correspondence, and books including first editions of *Uncle Tom's Cabin* and Thomas Paine's *Common Sense* as well as letters from Governor George Clinton and John Jay.

Caleb Smith House

North Country Road (Rte 25A)
Smithtown, NY
(516) 265-6768

Contact: Smithtown Historical Society
Open: Mon.-Fri. 9 a.m.–4 p.m.; Sat. 12–4 p.m.
Admission: Adults $1; children $.25. Tours
Suggested Time to View House: 30 minutes
Facilities on Premises: Consignment shop
Description of Grounds: Herb garden

Best Season to View House: April-Oct.
Year House Built: 1819
Style of Architecture: Federal
Number of Rooms: 9
On-Site Parking: Yes **Wheelchair Access:** No

Description of House

The house was home to several generations of the Smith family beginning with Caleb Smith II who built the dwelling in 1819. After the death of Caleb II in 1831, the house passed to his son, Caleb III. In 1904, a son of Caleb III, Robert Bailey Smith, sold the house and farm to Carl S. Burr, Jr., an assemblyman and well-known horseman. The sale of the house to Burr marked the first transfer of the lands out of the Smith family in almost 250 years.

Notable Collections on Exhibit

In addition to the period furnishings, the house features changing exhibits devoted to decorative arts, toys, and costumes.

Epenetus Smith Tavern

**211 Middle Country Road
Smithtown, NY 11787
(516) 265-6768**

Contact: Smithtown Historical Society
Open: Mid June-Sept., by appointment only
Admission: Donation
Number of Yearly Visitors: 4,000
Year House Built: 1740
Style of Architecture: Saltbox wing with
  Colonial addition
Number of Rooms: 2 available for school
  programs
On-Site Parking: Yes
Wheelchair Access: Yes

Description of House

Epenetus Smith I (1724-1803), the original owner of the house, was one of the great-grandson's of Richard Smith, the patentee or land grant owner. He was a public-spirited man, devoting over forty years of his life to matters of community welfare. Some of his community activites included election as chosen "Fence Viewer and Prizer of Damage," at the town meeting's of 1753. He held other offices for many years such as overseer of the poor, assessor, town supervisor, and finally served seven years as town clerk.

Built some time before 1750, the building stood on the north side of the Main Street, west of the "protestant Prispiterian dissenting Meeting House." As a tavern, this hostelry was famous for two generations, and was run by both the father and son. The tavern served as a stopping place for stagecoaches traveling between Fulton Ferry and Sag Harbor stage coaches as early as 1772. Later known as the Israel Whitman Tavern, the structure became a part of the David J. Ely estate, and in 1911 was moved to the site where it stands today by Mrs. Charles Duncan Miller, and was used as a residence until 1963. The house and tavern are furnished with reproductions of period furniture.

Franklin O. Arthur House

245 Middle Country Road
Smithtown, NY 11787
(516) 265-6768

Contact: Smithtown Historical Society
Open: Mid June-Sept., by appointment only
Admission: Donation. School programs.
Best Season to View House: Spring-fall
Number of Yearly Visitors: 4,000
Year House Built: 1740
On-Site Parking: Yes
Wheelchair Access: Yes

Description of House

Several generations of the Arthur family, a prominent local family lived in this modest home. The house is said to have been built between 1730 and 1750 on property later owned by William Arthur, but by whom it was built is not known. William Arthur was a great landowner in Smithtown Township and elsewhere in Suffolk county, and had a considerable business in real estate. He was the son of John Arthur, born in Scotland in 1695, who settled in Islip and who died in Smithtown in 1785. His son, William Arthur (1730-1815) settled in Smithtown, where his sons Isaac and Thomas were born. In 1847, the house was owned by a Phineas Baldwin; in 1849 it was acquired by Samuel Arden Smith, a lawyer and town clerk. It was brought back into the Arthur family by Franklin O. Arthur, son of Thomas Arthur, the grandson of William Arthur. Since then, Franklin's descendants have continued to live in the family dwelling.

This simple Colonial structure features a "bee-hive oven" in the original kitchen which is now used as the hall. The fine paneling in the living room and the steep "dancing stairs" are representative of the house's Colonial origins.

Notable Collections on Exhibit

The barn houses an interesting collection of old-time sleighs and buggies, as well as a flock of sheep.

Judge J. Lawrence Smith Homestead

205 Middle Country Road
Smithtown, NY 11787
(516) 265-6768

Contact: Smithtown Historical Society
Open: Mid June-Sept., by appointment only
Admission: Donation
Best Season to View House: Spring-fall
Year House Built: 1768
On-Site Parking: Yes
Wheelchair Access: Yes

Description of House

The Homestead has been owned by members of only two families: William Blydenburgh I and his descendants and by Judge J. Lawrence Smith and his descendants. William Blydenburgh I (1728-1768) left the house to his son William II (1759-1836) who, having no children of his own, left it to his brother Richard III's children, William Floyd and Richard Floyd, who made additions to the house. The homestead was acquired by Judge Smith in 1845. Judge Smith was born in Nissequogue in 1816, a descendant of Richard Smith, the owner of the original land grant. He attended Clinton Academy in East Hampton, Yale College, and graduated from Princeton in 1837. He married Sarah Nicoll Clinch in 1845, daughter of James Clinch of New York, and settled in Nissequogue. They moved soon thereafter into this house.

There is a Victorian air, rather than Colonial, about the ground floor rooms. Black marble mantelpieces replaced the original wooden mantels on the ground floor and the windows, in Victorian style, reach nearly to the floor. The one story addition at the east end,probably built in the 1880s, houses a large ballroom where delightful balls and dances were held. There have been further alterations to the structure in recent years.

Mills Mansion

Old Post Road
Staatsburg, NY 12580
(914) 889-8851

Contact: Mills Mansion State Historic Site

Open: April-Oct., Wed.-Sat. 10 a.m.–5 p.m.,
Sun. 12–5 p.m.; mid Dec.-Dec. 31, for
holiday programs, by appointment

Activities: Guided tours, special events and
activities (car shows, Celtic Day, dog
shows, etc.)

Suggested Time to View House:
45–60 minutes

Description of Grounds:
Turn-of-the-century garden style
landscaping with direct access to the
Hudson River

Best Season to View House: All

Number of Yearly Visitors: 35,000

Year House Built: 1895

Number of Rooms: 79

Style of Architecture: Beaux-Arts

On-Site Parking: Yes **Wheelchair Access:** Yes

Description of House

This grand mansion was occupied by the noted financier and philanthropist Ogden Mills. Mills was born into a family whose wealth derived from the development of the American west. His father, D.O. Mills, was a brilliant businessman who established a great fortune in California in the decades following the Gold Rush. Ogden Mills followed in his father's footsteps, and married Ruth Livingston, who also came from a family prominent in the Hudson Valley. Mrs. Mills's great-grandfather, Morgan Lewis, purchased 1,600 acres at Staatsburg in 1792. Lewis, an important figure in the American Revolution, later served as the third governor of New York, and as quartermaster general of the army during the War of 1812.

The mansion's exterior is embellished with balustrades, pilasters, floral swags, and a massive portico. The interior is lavishly decorated, mostly in the styles of the 17th and 18th-century France. The rooms are furnished with elaborately carved and gilded furniture, fine Oriental rugs, sumptuous silk fabrics, and a collection of rare art objects from Europe, ancient Greece and the Far East. There is also a prominent display of portraits of Ruth Mill's ancestors.

Garibaldi Meucci Museum

420 Tompkins Avenue
Staten Island, NY 10305
(718) 442-1608

Contact: Garibaldi Meucci Museum
Open: Tues.-Fri. 9 a.m.–5 p.m.;
  Sat.-Sun. 1–5 p.m.
Facilities on Premises: Research library
Year House Built: 19th century
Style of Architecture: Gothic

Description of House
This early 19th century country Gothic cottage was home to Antonio Meucci, the Italian-American inventor who developed a working model of the telephone by 1857. He lived and conducted his scientific work here from 1850 to 1889. From 1850 to 1851, Meucci gave refuge to Giuseppe Garbaldi, the charismatic military leader of the unification of Italy.

Additional Information
Maintained by the Order Sons of Italy in America and restored in the 1950s, this national landmark includes exhibits on Meucci and Garibaldi and a library. The museum also offers programs on Italian-American heritage.

Seguine House

441 Seguine Avenue
Staten Island, NY 10307
(718)667-6042

Contact: City of New York Parks and Recreation
Open: Call for information, public tours are
  scheduled four times a year
Year House Built: 1838

Description of Grounds: A broad expanse of
  lawn creates a wide vista to Prince's Bay
Style of Architecture: Greek Revival

Description of House
Joseph Sequine built the elegant two-story house in 1838. A man of diverse pursuits, he also founded Staten Island Oil and Candlemaking, a manufacturing enterprise he built on the property and helped establish the Staten Island Railroad Company. Following Joseph's death in 1856, the house remained in the family until 1868. During the late 19th century the builing served as an inn. The house returned to the Seguine family from 1916 through 1977 and was then sold in an auction to George Burke. Burke stabilized the house in 1989 and donated it to the city of New York.

The Seguine House is located in Lemon Creek Park, along the southern shore of Staten Island. Built in 1838, the house is a physical reminder of the classical architecture and thriving commerce of Staten Island during the mid 19th century. The house is notable for its large portico with paneled piers surmounted by a classical pediment.

Additional Information
Lemon Creek Park also contains a riding academy, and a broad lawn with a wide vista to the water. The natural terrain is home to a large purple martin bird population.

Conference House

7455 Hylan Boulevard
Staten Island, NY 10307
(718) 984-2086

Contact: Conference House Association

Open: Wed.-Sun. 1–4 p.m.; call to confirm

Admission: Adults $2; seniors and children $1. Lectures and classes on herbs, craft workshops, art exhibitions, concerts, talks, lectures.

Facilities on Premises: Museum shop

Description of Grounds: Rose and herb gardens

Year House Built: approximately 1680

Style of Architecture: 17th-century stone manor

Description of House

In 1676, British naval captain Christopher Billop was granted a 932-acre property known as the Manor of Bentley where he built the Conference House. During the American Revolution, the manor was owned by Billop's great-grandson (a Tory colonel), also called Christopher Billop. On September 11, 1776, his house was the site of peace negotiations between British Lord Admiral Richard Howe and Benjamin Franklin, John Adams and Edward Rutledge. The talks occurred just two month after the Declaration of Independence had been signed, with Britain controlling New York City, Long Island and Staten Island. Lord Howe offered to end the conflict if the Colonies would return to British control. The Continental Congress refused and the war continued for seven more years. After the Revolution the house was confiscated by the State of New York, it served as a multi-family dwelling, a 19th-century hotel, and as a rat-poison factory before being deeded to the City of New York in 1926.

The two-story structure of native fieldstone was built in 1680. The home was enlarged in 1720 with a lean-to in the rear. The house includes a large basement kitchen with glazed brick floors and a vaulted root cellar. On the main floor, original hand-hewn beams span the ceiling of the conference room; the second floor has three rooms and there is also a large attic.

The furnishings date primarily from the 18th-century and are simple and functional, though the house was quite luxurious in its day. Today the only remaining object that belonged to the Billops is a 17th-century sea chest.

Notable Collections on Exhibit

Other notable furniture on exhibit includes a double-backed Queen Anne settee and a kas, or Dutch cupboard. The Conference House also features a regular series of demonstrations of life in Colonial times.

Alice Austen House Museum

2 Hyland Boulevard
Staten Island, NY 10305
(718) 816-4506

Contact: Friends of Alice Austen House, Inc.

Open: Thur.-Sun., 12–5 p.m.; call to confirm; gardens open daily until dusk

Admission: $2. Festivals, fairs, teas and other special events.

Facilities on Premises: Gift shop

Description of Grounds: The restored Victorian garden was replanted according to Austen photographs with shrubs (weeping mulberry and flowering quince)

Year House Built: approximately 1690

Style of Architecture: Victorian cottage-style

Description of House

This modest cottage was home to 19th-century photographer Alice Austen. The property was originally bought in 1844 by John H. Austen, Alice's grandfather. Alice was born nearby at Woodbine Cottage in 1866. After her father abandoned the family, she and her mother moved into her grandparent's home. Alice continued to live in the house until 1945. Taught by her uncle, she took up photography with a passion, shooting more than 7,000 pictures that captured a quieter Staten Island, as well as a growing New York City. Austen, who captured images of New York's aristocrats and its working people, experienced both extremes during her lifetime. Alice lost her savings in the stock market crash of 1929. Eventually she entered a poorhouse and became a self-declared pauper. However, Austen had the satisfaction of seeing her work recognized before her death in 1952.

The Austen house is a Victorian-cottage style home, with a magnificent view of New York Harbor. The original house, one of the city's oldest, dates to 1690. Austen expanded the small one-and-a-half-story farmhouse, named it "Clear Comfort" and gave it a romantic Gothic Revival facelift that included steeply peaked dormer windows and of "gingerbread" wood trim. The parlor is restored to look as it did in the 1890s with the arrangement of ornate period furniture, rugs, delft fireplace tiles, and Oriental vases.

Notable Collections on Exhibit

The display features prints from large glass negative collection of Alice Austen's work depicting turn-of-the-century American life.

Additional Information

The Staten Island Historical Society owns Austen's collection of negatives and helps the Friends of Alice Austen House, which operates the museum, present photographic exhibitions.

Historic Richmond Town

441 Clarke Avenue
Staten Island, NY 10306
(718) 351-1617

Contact: Staten Island Historical Society
Open: Mon.-Fri. 10 a.m.–5 p.m.; Sat.-Sun.
1-5 p.m.
Admission: Adults $4; seniors and students
$2.50; children under 6 free. Music
programs; crafts demonstrations;
exhibitions; lectures; fairs; celebrations;
and other special events.

Facilities on Premises: Museum shop;
restaurant; tavern
Description of Grounds: Park and picnic
grounds
Year House Built: Varied-beginning in 1690

Description of House

This historic village began as a hamlet in 1690 and by 1730 became the seat of the county government. Richmondtown has been restored to portray the evolution of a Staten Island settlement over the course of four centuries—from the 1600s to the 1900s. Occupying 100 acres, Richmondtown has more than two dozen historic buildings representing a variety of architectural styles ranging from a Greek Revival courthouse to Dutch vernacular farmhouses to a 19th-century one-room general store. The Voorlezer's House (c. 1695), the oldest surviving schoolhouse in the country, is also located within the complex.

Authentic furnishings, antique toys, vehicles, costumes, and memorabilia fill the school, general store, farmhouses, barn, churches, trade shops, and even the jail of the village.

Additional Information

Richmondtown is a living history museum where visitors will see reenactments of daily trades and customs including spinning, carpentry, ceramics, furniture and saddle making, quilting, tinsmithing, and printinng on a Stansbury Press. In addition, the complex hosts a series of events throughout the year such as Militia Day, Old Home Day, and the Richmond County Fair. Please call in advance to verify the schedule of events.

Philip Schuyler House

648 Rt. 32
Stillwater, NY 12120
(518) 664-9821

Contact: Saratoga National Historical Park
Open: Mid June-Labor Day, Wed.-Sun.
  9 a.m.–5 p.m.
Admission: Free. Guided tours.
Suggested Time to View House: 30 minutes
Description of Grounds: Open grounds

Best Season to View House: Summer
Number of Yearly Visitors: 6,000
Year House Built: 1777
Style of Architecture: Colonial
Number of Rooms: 8
On-Site Parking: Yes **Wheelchair Access:** Yes

Description of House

General Schuyler inherited the 1900 acre estate from his uncle Philip who had been killed in 1745 in the French-Indian raid that destroyed the first house on this site. The estate was originally acquired as part of the great "Saratoga Patent" of 1684 by his great uncle, Col. Peter Schuyler, and six others. During the 1760s, the General turned his estate into a busy center of farming, milling and merchandising, using the labor of farmer tenants and artisans recruited on liberal terms. Here he pioneered the cultivation of flax and used his river fleet to carry the products of the estate as far away as the West Indies.

The house that stands just south of the Fishkill today is not the same house from which Philip Schuyler had overseen the development of his "plantation" during the years prior to the Revolution. The retreating British had set fire to the house three days following the second battle of Saratoga out of fear that the oncoming Americans would use it as cover.

This two-story frame structure was used primarily as a summer residence by Schuyler. The house was restored in the early 1960s. The period furnishings have been provided by the Old Saratoga Historical Association.

Benjamin Long Homestead

24 East Niagara Street
Tonawanda, NY 14150
(716) 694-7406

Contact: Historical Society of the Tonawandas
Open: May 1-Nov.1, Sun. 2–5 p.m.; other times by appointment
Admission: Adults $1; children and school classes free. Guided tours.
Suggested Time to View House: 1 hour
Facilities on Premises: Gift shop
Description of Grounds: large grounds are available for picnics, flea markets, concerts and other outdoor gatherings

Best Season to View House: Summer- fall
Number of Yearly Visitors: 2,500
Year House Built: 1829
Style of Architecture: Early American (Pennsylvania Dutch)
Number of Rooms: 10
On-Site Parking: Yes
Wheelchair Access: No

Description of House

In 1828, Mary Hershey and her husband, Benjamin Long, decided to leave their home in Lancaster County and come to Tonawanda. They arrived here in December of the same year with their five children, all girls, the youngest only six months old. The Longs took residence for the winter in a part log and part block house located on Main Street. In the spring of 1829, Benjamin started the work of building their own house on the location which had been selected by Christian Hershey, Sr. many years before. The site consisted of approximately 200 acres located at the confluence of the Tonawanda and Elliott Creeks.

The walls of the house were constructed of virgin black walnut and the beams are white oak, all hand-hewn and cut from trees growing on the site. Planks two inches thick and some as wide as three feet were nailed vertically to the inside of the black walnut walls. Hand-cut lath strips were then attached to the planking over which a rough plaster made of sand, lime and horse hair or cow hair was applied. In the back of the south west corner of the house, the siding has been left off to show the dove tail contruction and the size of the square cut timbers. The north side was built into an earth bank for winter protection. The collected furnishings are of the same period as the house with the exception of the parlor which is mostly mid and late Victorian.

Notable Collections on Exhibit

The homestead exhibits a wide array of collections including early American carpenter tools, a collection of broken china and pottery pieces excavated from the grounds, a settle bench, splint bottom rocking chair, Windsor chairs, candle sticks and snuffer, candle molds, a cabbage cutter and sauerkraut stomper and other kitchen utensils. Portraits of Mary and Benjamin Long are on the wall over the melodeon (a small reed organ).

Hart-Cluett Mansion

59 Second Street
Troy, NY 12180
(518) 272-7232

Contact: Rensselaer County Historical
  Society
Open: Tues.-Sat. 10 a.m.–4 p.m.; closed
  major holidays
Admission: Adults $2; students and
  children $1. Self-guided tours; guided
  tours by pre-arrangement; special school
  vacation week activities for families.
Suggested Time to View House: 60 minutes
Facilities on Premises: Gift shop and
  adjacent changing exhibition gallery
Number of Yearly Visitors: 10,000
Year House Built: 1827
Style of Architecture: Federal
Number of Rooms: 14

On-Site Parking: No **Wheelchair Access:** Yes

Description of House

The first owners of 59 Second Street were Richard P. Hart and his wife Betsey Howard and their large family of fourteen children. Mr. Hart, a Quaker, was a merchant and entreprenuer as well as Mayor of Troy (1836-38). Mrs. Hart enlarged her husband's business interests after his death in 1843 by investing in railroads, canals, and gas lighting. She was a well-known community philanthropist. In 1893, the property was divided into two lots, the house lot being sold to George and Amanda Cluett, makers of Arrow Shirts. He and his wife lived in the house with their five children until 1910, when the property changed hands for the last time to George's nephew, Albert E. Cluett and his family. Mr. Cluett was involved with Cluett, Peabody & Co.

Built in 1827 by New York City builder John Colegrove for the Harts, this brick and limestone late Federal style townhouse has been a hight point of Troy architecture since it was built. More in keeping with New York City residential architecture of the time, the "Marble House on Second Street" has many unique features including elaborate plaster and woodwork, 19th-century chandeliers and ornamental exterior ironwork.

The mansion is furnished with outstanding 19th-century furniture and decorative arts collection donated to the Society by Rensselaer County residents.

Notable Collections on Exhibit

Today the house is interpreted with all three families in mind. A number of artifacts that the Harts or Cluetts had have been returned to the collection and are on view including furniture by Troy cabinet-maker Glijah Galusha; Federal and Empire-style furniture, and portraits by well-known local artists. The decorative arts collection includes silver, glassware, and porcelain.

Additional Information

Unlike many of the surrounding residences, the Hart-Cluett Mansion has had few changes over time. The visitor is able to see a building that has not been broken up into apartments and offices, but that retains its original character. This is also true of the Carriage House which is an unusual survival in present day Troy. The society's extensive research library is also available to visitors and includes a large photographic collection which is often used to document buildings for preservation purposes. The library is open the same hours as the museum.

McClurg Museum

Westfield Village Park/ P.O. Box 7
Westfield, NY 14787
(716) 326-2977

Contact: Chautauqua County Historical
Society

Open: April 15-Nov., Mon. 1–8 p.m.,
Tues.-Sat. 1–5 p.m.; closed major
holidays

Admission: Adults $1.50; seniors $1;
children (under 6) $.50. Guided tours,
openhouses, musical performances

Suggested Time to View House: 1 hour

Facilities on Premises: Bookstand

Description of Grounds: Village park with
gazebo, bandstand, playground, and
benches

Best Season to View House: Summer

Number of Yearly Visitors: 1,500

Year House Built: 1818

Number of Rooms: 16 and full basement
open to public

Style of Architecture: Federal

On-Site Parking: Yes **Wheelchair Access:** No

Description of House

James McClurg was of Scots-Irish descent. His family settled in Pittsburgh, started the first iron foundry there and amassed a fortune. When James came of age, he received an endowment, and moved on to earn his own fortune. He chose Westfield as his home, and was one of the earliest landowners in the county. He designed the house, made the bricks, fired the lime, and cut timber for the house from the home site. Construction was done in one and a half years. McClurg died here, and his family retained the property.

Three generations of the McClurg family lived in this gracious house. The dwelling has many distinctive features including false doors in the entrance to create the appearance of symmetry, a hand-carved mahogany ceiling, marble-inlaid fireplaces, transom windows throughout, and twelve-foot ceilings. Some furnishings are from the original family, the rest come from county estates, and reflect the 1850 period when family built an addition and modernized the house.

Notable Collections on Exhibit

The McClurg Museum exhibits Fenton paintings by P. Huntington, landscapes by James Hart, the desk of Ulysses S. Grant, early musical instruments, an 1864 Steinway piano, and Native American lithics and pottery.

Additional Information

In 1984, the carriage house was converted to a library which has 2,000 volumes, a local history file, photographs, genealogical records, and archival collections, including the papers of Albion W. Tourgee, Elial T. Foote and Calyburne B. Sampson.

French Castle

P.O. Box 169
Youngston, NY 14174-0169
(716) 745-7611

Contact: Old Fort Niagra Association, Inc.

Open: Daily at 9 a.m. except Thansgiving, Christmas, and New Year's Day; closing hours vary from 4:30–7:30 p.m.

Activities: Guided tours, military and craft demonstations, exhibarits and special events.

Suggested Time to View House: 2 hours

Facilities on Premises: Museum and book shop, food service

Description of Grounds: Entire fort area accessible

Best Season to View House: Summer-fall

Number of Yearly Visitors: 101,000

Year House Built: 1726 (Castle), 1757 to 1771 (others)

Number of Rooms: Castle-18, others-1 or 2

Style of Architecture: Military French Colonial

Description of House

The French Castle, while not a conventional dwelling, has housed several historic residents. As part of Old Fort Niagara, it was located at a vital location at the mouth of the Niagara River, where the fort controlled access to the Great Lakes and the westward route to the heart land of the continent. With the completion of the Erie Canal in 1825, the stategic value of Fort Niagara diminished. It nonetheless remained an active military post well into the 20th century. Army families resided here as late as World War I.

The French Castle was designed by Gaspard-Joseph Chaussegros de Lery, chief engineer of New France. This massive structure has a unique design which combines defensive features with the appearance of a house. The masonry building was constructed as a defensive barrack and storehouse for the French garrison. It includes a chapel (the earliest permanent church in New York), officers quarters, barracks and store rooms. One room was used as a cell for Robert Rogers, the famous ranger of the French and Indian War and hero of the historical novel *Northwest Passage.*

The French Castle was repaired and restored between 1927 and 1933. The layout and details of the building generally conform to its 1727 appearance. The mid-18th century furnishings were reproduced in an effort to make the castle appear substantially as it did during the French occupation.

Pennsylvania

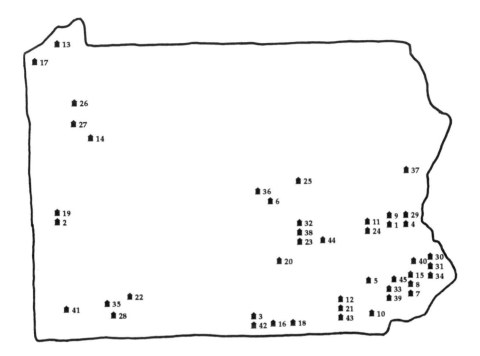

1. Allentown
Trout Hall

2. Ambridge
Baker House
George and Frederick Rapp House

3. Bedford
Old Bedford Village

4. Bethlehem
1810 John Sebastian Goundie House

5. **Birdsboro**
   Boone House

6. **Boalsburg**
   *Columbus Chapel and
   Boal Mansion Museum*

7. **Broomall**
   *Historic 1696 Thomas Massey
   Home*

8. **Bryn Mawr**
   Historic 1704 Harriton House

9. **Catasauqua**
   George Taylor House

10. **Chadds Ford**
    *Gideon Gilpin House
    Brinton 1704 House
    Barns-Brinton House
    The John Chads House*

11. **Egypt**
    *Troxel-Steckel House and Barn
    Museum*

12. **Ephrata**
    *Ephrata Cloister
    Connell Mansion*

13. **Erie**
    Cashiers House

14. **Fairview**
    Sturgeon House

15. **Fort Washington**
    *The Highlands
    Hope Lodge*

16. **Gettysburg**
    Dobbin House

17. **Girard**
    *Battles Museums Yellow House
    Charlotte Elizabeth Battles
    Memorial Museum*

18. **Hanover**
    Neas House

19. **Harmony**
    Bentel House

20. **Harrisburg**
    *Fort Hunter Mansion and Park
    The John Harris/Simon Cameron
    Mansion*

21. **Lancaster**
    *Rock Ford Plantation/ Kauffman
    Museum*

22. **Laughlintown**
    Compass Inn Museum

23. **Lebanon**
    Stoy Museum

24. **Lenhartsville**
    Log House

25. **Lock Haven**
    Heisey Museum

26. **Meadville**
    *Baldwin-Reynolds House
    Museum*

27. **Mercer**
    Magoffin House

28. **Mill Run**
    Fallingwater

29. **Nazareth**
    Whitefield House

30. **New Hope**
    The Parry Mansion Museum

31. **Newtown**
    Court Inn

32. **Northcumberland**
    Joseph Priestley House

33. Paoli
Waynesboro
Wharton Esherick Studio

34. Philadelphia
Cliveden
Mantua House
Cedar Grove
Mount Pleasant
Grumblethorpe
Hill-Physick-Keith House
Powel House
Laurel Hill
Lemon Hill
Strawberry Mansion
Sweetbriar Mansion
Woodford Mansion
Deshler Morris House

35. Scottdale
Overholt Homestead
Henry Clay Frick Birthplace

36. State College
Centre Furnace Mansion

37. Stroudsburg
Stroud Community House

38. Sunbury
Hunter House

39. Valley Forge
Washington's Headquarters

40. Wallingford
The Thomas Leiper House

41. Washington
David Bradford House

42. Waynesboro
*Renfrew Museum
(The Royer House)*

43. Willow Street
1719 Herr House

44. Womelsdorf
Conrad Weiser Homestead

45. Worcester
Peter Wertz Farmstead

Trout Hall

**4th and Walnut Streets
Allentown, PA 18101
(215) 435-4664**

Contact: Lehigh County Historical Society

Open: April-Dec., Tues.-Sat. 12–3 p.m.;
Sun. 1–4 p.m.

Admission: Free. Tour guides available
during scheduled hours and by
appointment.

Suggested Time to View House: 45 minutes

Description of Grounds: A small city park
surrounds the house

Best Season to View House: Spring and
summer

Year House Built: 1770

Style of Architecture: Georgian

Number of Rooms: 7

On-Site Parking: Yes **Wheelchair Access:** Yes

Description of House

Built in 1770, this house was first used as a summer residence by James
Allen, the son of the city's founder, William Allen. Like his father, James was
educated in England and returned to Philadelphia to serve as a councilman,
an alderman, and an assemblyman. Following the practice of other wealthy
Philadelphians, he built Trout Hall as a summer retreat from the city's
swelter and pestilence and used it for his hunting and fishing trips. The
mansion became a full-time residence from 1776 through 1778 when the city
was occupied by the British during the Revolution. Later, after the Civil War,
the house became the first home of Muhlenberg College.

Trout Hall is considered the city's oldest mansion. The limestone structure was restored by the historical society and now houses an impressive
collection of Colonial furniture.

Additional Information

Visitors to Trout Hall are also encouraged to visit the society's other
properties in Allentown–the Frank Buchman House, home of the founder
of the Oxford Group and the movement known as Moral Re-Armament, and
the Old Court Museum where the society's library is located.

Baker House of Old Economy Village

14th Street
Ambridge, PA 15003
(412) 266-4500

Contact: Pennsylvania Historical and
Museum Commission

Open: Tues.-Sat. 9 a.m.–4 p.m,
Sun. 12–4 p.m.; closed winter holidays

Admission: Adults $4; senior citizens $3;
children (7-17) $2. Guided tours with an
orientation film

Suggested Time to View House: 90 minutes

Facilities on Premises: Gift shop

Description of Grounds: The garden
contains historic flowers, vegetable and
herbs based on an 1825 historic site list.

Best Season to View House: Spring,
summer and fall

Number of Yearly Visitors: 35,000

Year House Built: 1826

Number of Rooms: 8

On-Site Parking: No **Wheelchair Access:** Partial

Style of Architecture: Federal with German precedent

Description of House

The Baker House forms part of Old Economy Village, the third and final home of the religious group known as the Harmony Society. The society was one of America's most successful Christian communal groups. The group was comprised of nearly 800 farmers and craftsman who had followed their leader, George Rapp (1757-1847), from Germany to seek religious freedom in America. Romelius Baker, a storekeeper, lived in this unpretentious dwelling. He later became the leader of the Harmony Society, after the death of Father Rapp. Baker lived here with his mother, sister and the famous Hungarian poet Nicholas Lenau.

The house was built in 1826 in the American Federal style otherwise known as "Economy Architecture." The furnishings are part of the 18,000 Harmonist-owned collection at the site. The house is furnished with original objects based upon the 1846 inventory.

Notable Collections on Exhibit

Objects on exhibit Harmonist-made furniture, redware pottery, 19th-century kitchen equipment, and quilts and coverlets from the second half of the 19th century.

Additional Information

The house is part of a seventeen building historic village. Other structures of note include the community kitchen, the feast hall, the cabinet shop, and the blacksmith shop where demonstrations are given.

George and Frederick Rapp House

14th Street
Old Economy Village
Ambridge, PA 15003
(412) 266-4500

Contact: Pennsylvania Historical and Museum Comm.

Open: Tues.-Sat. 9 a.m.–4 p.m, Sun. 12–4 p.m.; closed winter holidays

Admission: Adults $4; senior citizens $3; children (7-17) $2. Guided tours with an orientation film

Suggested Time to View House: 90 minutes

Facilities on Premises: Gift shop

Description of Grounds: Historic garden (c. 1830s) called "Garden of Eden" with a wide variety of plants, an open pavilion and an unusual straw-roofed grotto.

Best Season to View House: Spring, summer and fall

Number of Yearly Visitors: 35,000

Number of Rooms: 25 (2 houses)

Year House Built: 1826; Frederick Rapp addition 1828

Style of Architecture: Federal-German

On-Site Parking: No **Wheelchair Access:** Yes

Description of House

George Rapp was the spiritual leader and founder of the Harmonist Society, one of America's most successful Christian communal groups. Their simple, pietist lifestyle was based on early teachings of the Christian Church. They adopted a celibate lifestyle and were known for their religious devotion and economic prosperity. Frederick Rapp, his adopted son, was the business leader and architect of the society. He designed their two Pennsylvania towns of Harmony and Economy, and New Harmony, Indiana.

This house is actually two houses joined together. For this reason it was once called the "Great House," in addition to it being the home of the society's leaders. The George Rapp House described in 1826 as the "principal building two stories high, with two lower wings standing in the same line." The Frederick Rapp House was added to the rear of Father Rapp's house around 1828. The house is furnished with Harmonist-made artifacts and with period objects added based upon site documentation.

Notable Collections on Exhibit

Various 19th-century artifacts documented by receipts as being purchased by the Harmony Society including furniture, paintings, and decorative objects are on exhibit.

Old Bedford Village

Box 1976
Bedford, PA 15522
(814) 623-1156

Contact: Old Bedford Village Inc.

Open: May–Oct., 9 a.m.–5 p.m.

Admission: Adults $6.50; seniors $5.50; children (6-12) $4; under 6 free. Costumed guides in some buildings; group tours with appointment; special seasonal events, arts and crafts festival, buggy rides, quilt stitching .

Suggested Time to View House: 2 hours for entire complex (approx. 15 min. per house)

Facilities on Premises: Book store and gift shop

Description of Grounds: Entire reconstructed village, including 40 original log homes, work buildings, and shops

Best Season to View House: Spring and fall

Number of Yearly Visitors: 100,000

Year House Built: 5 houses dating from 1762-1800

Style of Architecture: All log houses, styles include: Vernacular German, Georgian, English End Chimney

Number of Rooms: 2-4 in each house

On-Site Parking: Yes **Wheelchair Access:** Yes

Description of House

Very little is known of the original residents of Old Bedford Village; the log houses are noteworthy as a unit, presenting a slice of typical rural life during the 18th and 19th centuries. The homes are named after those who donated them to the village, rather than after those who built them.

All of the houses are reconstructed but maintain their original log walls. Some structures were originally built in neighboring counties and transplanted to Bedford Village in order to be part of this living history museum. The grounds also feature a village jail, a blacksmith shop, a post office, a trading post, and many other reconstructed cabins and barns reflecting local conditions as they changed through history from the pioneer period through the industrial revolution.

Some furnishings are original to individual homes, though most are collected antiques or replica pieces reflecting styles of rural life during the turn of the century.

Notable Collections on Exhibit

There is a tall case clock by Jacob Diehl, who worked locally during the turn of the century on display in the Semanek House. Also exhibited are collections of 19th century Bedford county rifles, Quaker school furnishings, 1850 wagons and farm implements, and Colonial twig brooms; these original pieces are housed in various shop buildings within the village. In addition, the Indian Museum has an eclectic collection of Native American artifacts.

Additional Information

From June through December Old Bedford Village hosts numerous special weekend events such as a Bluegrass Festival, Gospel Music Festival, Pioneer Days Celebration, and the Great Pumpkin Festival. In addition, The Opera House at the Village presents a full season of musicals and comedy. Visitors are encouraged to call the village for more information.

1810 John Sebastian Goundie House

501 Main Street
Bethlehem, PA 18018
(215) 691-5300

Contact: Historic Bethlehem Inc.

Open: Tues.-Sat. 12–2 p.m., Sun. 2 p.m.

Admission: Adults $4; students $2; family $12. Guided tours start at Bethlehem Heritage Center at 509 Main Street.

Suggested Time to View House: 20 minutes

Description of Grounds: The house is located in a 10 acre industrial quarter.

Best Season to View House: Summer and winter

Number of Yearly Visitors: 2,000

Year House Built: 1810

Style of Architecture: Georgian-Federal transitional

Number of Rooms: 8

On-Site Parking: No **Wheelchair Access:** No

Description of House

The house forms part of Historic Bethlehem, a community founded in 1741 by the Protestant group known as Moravians. The community was known for its crafts, trades, and industry which made the town nearly self-sufficient. This attractive dwelling was built for Johann Sebastian Gund (later Goundie), Bethlehem's community brewer.

The house was built in 1810 by George Huber, and is believed to be the first brick, non-Germanic residence built in Bethlehem. Today the house has been restored to its 19th-century appearance. The period furnishing include three items that are original to the house, along with several Goundie family items.

Notable Collections on Exhibit

Exhibits include an 1831 Emma Gund Sampler (Moravian Day School type), an 1818 child's spinning wheel with an ivory inlay and ornamentation, an 1830s child's slat back chair, a 1780s Philadelphia pie crust tilt-top tea table, and an 1840s mahogany veneered Empire sideboard.

Additional Information

Several other buildings in this historic site are of interest to visitors: the 1869 Luckenbach Mill, the 1761 Tannery, and the 1762 Waterworks which has been designated a National Historic Landmark.

Visitors to Bethlehem may also wish to visit the *Kemerer Museum of Decorative Arts* located at 427 North New Street. This Federal vernacular two-story building (c. 1850) is home to a fine collection of furnishings and decorative arts, period rooms, such as a high style Victorian parlor and bedroom suite and a Pennsylvania German room, and quarterly gallery exhibitions. The museum's collection showcases Bohemian glassware, regional oil paintings, locally made furniture and tallcase clocks, and 200 years of decorative and fine arts spanning the period from 1740 to 1940. For further information, contact the Kemerer Museum at (215) 868-6868.

Boone House

400 Daniel Boone Rd
Birdsboro, PA 19508
(215) 582-4900

Contact: Daniel Boone Homestead

Open: Tues.-Sat 9 a.m.–5 p.m.; Sun. 12–5 p.m.

Admission: Adults $3; seniors $2; children (6-17) $1; under 6 free; group rate $2. Guided tours hourly year-round, visitor center exhibits; special programs include crafts presentation, living history, flintlock shoots and talks, holiday programs.

Suggested Time to View House: 1 hour (tour lasts 30 minutes)

Facilities on Premises: Museum shop in visitor center.

Description of Grounds: Land includes 579 acres with trails, bridal paths, a lake, streams, woodland, rural landscape, cultivated fields, woodlots; indoor and outdoor camping available for youth groups

Best Season to View House: All year

Number of Yearly Visitors: 55,000-60,000

Year House Built: 1730-1779

Style of Architecture: Pennsylvania German and English Devonshire

Number of Rooms: 10

On-Site Parking: Yes **Wheelchair Access:** Yes

Description of House

The American frontiersman, Daniel Boone, was born in this simple farmhouse in 1734. His parents, Squire and Sarah Boone, were Quakers from Devonshire, England and owned the site from 1730 to 1750. Daniel was fifteen years old when his family moved to North Carolina. He is best known for later exploring and settling Kentucky. The second resident, William Maugridge, an Anglican from Devonshire, was related to the Boones and worked as a shipwright and carpenter in Philadelphia before owning the site from 1750 to 1766. In addition to being an acquaintance of Benjamin Franklin, Maugridge also served as one of the county's first judges. John DeTurk was the third resident; he occupied the site from 1770 to 1808. He was born in the area in the 1740s. His family was expelled from France in the 1660s.

The house is a two-story fieldstone farmhouse incorporating an English four-bay with front porch with a two-bay Germanic addition, presumably built by the Boone family in 1730. The four-bay English house was built onto the log house in 1750. The English section features a two-room downstairs floor plan (hall and parlor) with gable fireplace and four bedrooms on the second floor. In 1779, John DeTurk built the two-bay addition after removing the log house structure and Germanizing the interior space. The original spring still flows in the cellar.

In the Boone/Maugridge English section, the furnishings are of strong Anglo-style dating from 1720 to 1760. In contrast, the pieces in the DeTurk section show German and Swiss influences.

Notable Collections on Exhibit

The furniture collection includes pieces from the Stodgell Stokes collection and first rate examples of Pennsylvania rural furniture, including Delaware Valley ladderbacks, Windsors, Pennsylvania-German chests, gateleg tables, stretcher tables, chest-of-drawers, beds, and chairs with early Queen Anne characteristics. The site also has a large collection of blacksmith tools.

Columbus Chapel and Boal Mansion Museum

Business Route 322, P.O. Box 116
Boalsburg, PA 16827-0016
(814) 466-6210

Contact: Columbus Chapel and Boal Mansion Museum

Open: May-Oct., Wed.-Mon. 1:30–5 p.m. (spring and fall); 10 a.m.–5 p.m. (summer); other times available to groups by appointment

Admission: Adults $5; group rate $4; children (under 12) $2. Guided tours, special events, festivals.

Suggested Time to View House: 1 hour

Facilities on Premises: Gift shop

Description of Grounds: Allees and paths with a gazebo

Best Season to View House: May-Oct.

Number of Yearly Visitors: 24,000

Year House Built: 1789; 1798; 1898

Style of Architecture: Federal Rowhouse with Classical additions (1898)

Number of Rooms: 40

On-Site Parking: Yes **Wheelchair Access:** Yes

Description of House

Captain David Boal emigrated from Ireland with his family in the 1700s. Since 1789, the Boal Mansion has been home to nine generations of the Boal family who were among the founders of nearby Boalsburg and Penn State University. The most distinctive feature of the mansion is the accompanying historic chapel. In 1909, Col. Theodore Davis Boal removed the chapel from the Columbus Castle in Spain and moved its contents to Boalsburg. His wife, Mathilde de Lagarde, a French-Spanish niece of the Columbus family, inherited the chapel from her aunt, Victoia Columbus, the owner of the castle.

The Boal Mansion has been enlarged considerably over the years with the succession of owners. The structure maintains its fine interior wood-work and contains original, as well as contemporary, American and European furnishings.

The Columbus Family Chapel is in a small stone edifice. The chapel was removed piece by piece from the Columbus Castle in northern Spain, and brought to the United States in 1919. The Chapel contains furnishings and art from the 15th and 16th centuries, including many original pieces from the Columbus Castle. Some objects are over 500 years old. In addition, the chapel has a silver reliquary containing two pieces of the True Cross given to Don Joachim and Don Felix Columbus by the Bishop of Leon in 1817.

Notable Collections on Exhibit

The chapel contains several Columbus family heirlooms and art treasures, the most notable items on exhibit are a choir loft, with an escutcheon of the Columbus family on its railing and colored panels depicting the castle of Castile, the Lion of Leon, Columbus's admiral's anchors, the islands of the Indies and an attendent eagle representing the Alba family; there is also a massive silver crucifix, brocade vestments, carved statues of saints, family swords, and art masterpieces, including "The Sacrifice of Isaac" by Ribera (1615), and a "Pieta" by Ambrosius Benson (1535). Finally, Christopher Columbus's admirals's desk adorns the historic chapel.

Historic 1696 Thomas Massey Home

P.O. Box 18
Lawrence Rd. at Springhouse Rd.
Broomall, PA 19008
(215) 353-3644

Contact: Township of Marple

Open: Mon.-Fri. 10 a.m.–4 p.m.; Sun. 2–4:30 p.m., closed holidays

Admission: Adults $2; children and seniors $1. Guided tours, audiovisual program, junior guide program, candlelight tours, colonial dinners, special events with living history demonstrations.

Suggested Time to View House: 1 hour

Facilities on Premises: Gift shop

Description of Grounds: One acre grounds owned by township and accessible to public

Number of Yearly Visitors: 3000

Year House Built: 1696 with additions

Number of Rooms: 6

Style of Architecture: Rural Farmhouse

On-Site Parking: Yes **Wheelchair Access:** Yes

Description of House

This is one of the oldest English Quaker homes in Pennsylvania. The farmhouse was built by Thomas Massey and his wife, Phebe, and stayed in the Massey family for generations. Massey's son, granddaughter, and great-granddaughter lived in this log cabin. Another relative married into the Smith family; they lived here up until 1925. The Massey House has been continuously rebuilt over three centuries of occupancy. Over seventy percent of the original construction techniques may be seen today. The original house was a log cabin, later the kitchen was rebuilt in stone. A two story addition was also originally made of logs and later rebuilt in stone. The house displays a few original pieces of 17th and 18th-century furnishings, but the majority are period reproductions.

Notable Collections on Exhibit

Very few of the family's belongings have survived, however, there are four pewter plates thought to have belonged to Thomas's son, Mordecai Massey. Descendants have also donated several samplers, bonnets, and quilts for display.

Additional Information

In addition to its historic and architectural interest, the Massey House takes great pride in its living history programs. Visitors are encouraged to touch the artifacts on display to give them a greater experience of the past. There are also a demonstrations of bread baking, open hearth cooking, and other activities which take place on a weekly basis.

Historic 1704 Harriton House

500 Harriton Road
P.O. Box 1364
Bryn Mawr, PA 19010
(215) 525-0201

Contact: Harriton Association
Open: March 15-Dec. 24, Wed.-Sat.
10 a.m.–4 p.m.; other times by
appointment only
Admission: Adults $2; children free. Guided
tours, slide presentation for groups, and
by prior arrangement.

Suggested Time to View House: 1 hour
Facilities on Premises: Small book store
Description of Grounds: 16.5 acre nature
park
Number of Yearly Visitors: 3000-5000
Year House Built: 1704
Number of Rooms: 7 open to public
On-Site Parking: Yes **Wheelchair Access:** Yes

Description of House

The original builder, Rowland Ellis, was a well know Welch Quaker who was important early 18th-century Philadelphia and the surrounding community. The second owner, Richard Harrison (1719 to 1774), grew tobacco on the 700 acre estate using slave labor. The property was named Harriton during his occupancy. The focus of the restoration of Harriton was a later occupant, Charles Thomson. Born 1729 in North Ireland, Thomson was a teacher and merchant in Philadelphia, and the only secretary of the Continental Congress. Thompson lived as a gentleman farmer at Harriton and listed among his notable accomplishments the first translation in North America of the Bible from Greek to English and designing the Great Seal of the United States.

Harriton House is an impressive three-story stone house with tall brick chimneys. The house is configured in a "T" shape with two rooms in the front, a stairhall, and one room in the rear. Several additions were made in 1720 and 1789. Harriton was considered architecturally pretentious for 1704 with its fine stonework including decorative segmental arches and tall brick chimneys. The interior displays superb woodwork, and the original 1704 closed-string staircase. The 18th-century furniture which decorates the house is typical of the late 18th century. Some original Thomson furnishings are included in the collection.

George Taylor House

Front and Poplar Streets
Castasauqua, PA 18032
(215) 435-4664

Contact: Lehigh County Historical Society
Open: June-Oct., Sat.-Sun. 1–4 p.m.; and by
appointment
Admission: Free. Guided tours available
during above hours and by appointment.
Suggested Time to View House: 45 minutes

Description of Grounds: Grounds contain a
small park area
Best Season to View House: Spring and
summer
Year House Built: 1768
Style of Architecture: Georgian
Number of Rooms: 6

Description of House

In 1768, George Taylor, ironmaster, member of the Provincial assembly, and signer of the Declaration of Independence, built this lovely summer residence overlooking the Lehigh River, a few miles north of Allentown. Taylor had worked his way up, while employed by the Warwick Furnace to achieve a position of stature in the community. The property was sold in 1776 to John Benezet, a member of a prominent Philadelphia family, and later to Colonel David Deshler, another patriot active in local government.

This attractive Georgian home features a well-preserved brick exterior. The interior features elegant wood paneling of the kind found in superior houses of the area. The furnishings, while not originally owned by Taylor, have been collected and are appropriate representations of the 18th century.

Notable Collections on Exhibit

The items on display include a framed deed signed by George Taylor, (October 1773), a Chippendale mirror, and a bridal blanket chest (1762).

Gideon Gilpin House

U.S. Highway 1
Chadds Ford, PA 19317
(215) 459-3342

Contact: Brandywine Battlefield Park

Open: Tues.-Sat. 9 a.m.–5 p.m.; Sun.
12–5 p.m.; closed national holidays
except Memorial Day, July 4th and
Labor Day

Admission: Adults $3; seniors and groups
$2; children $1. Guided tours of house,
audiovisual orientation of Battle of the
Brandywine, special events in Sept.,
Dec., and Feb.

Suggested Time to View House: 40 minutes

Description of Grounds: 50 acres set in
rolling southeastern Pennsylvania rural
area, picnic tables available

Best Season to View House: May-Sept.

Number of Yearly Visitors: 60,000

Year House Built: 1745 plus additions (1782
and 1828)

Number of Rooms: 8

Style of Architecture: Penn Plan plus
additions

On-Site Parking: Yes **Wheelchair Access:** No

Description of House

Gideon Gilpin, a Quaker, was a descendant of late 17th-century Quaker settlers from the area. It is widely reported that the Marquis de Lafayette stayed in this house the night before the Battle of Brandywine, September 11, 1777. Washington's headquarters were definitely nearby at the now reconstructed Benjamin Ring House. The last private owner before the house became state property in 1948 was Dr. Cleveland. Noted artist Andrew Wyeth did a portrait of Cleveland on the first floor of the house in 1946. The painting now hangs in the Delaware Museum of Art.

This two-and-a-half story house uses a Penn Plan style of architecture executed in stone. A kitchen addition, also of stone, was built in 1782 and a later wooden addition dates from 1828. The collected period furnishings on display reflect the lifestyle of a typical, large Quaker family of moderate means from the years of the Revolution.

Additional Information

The "Lafayette Sycamore", one of the oldest and largest (in girth) of all North American sycamores, stands beside the Gilpin House.

Brinton 1704 House

Box 1032
Chadds Ford, PA 19317
(302) 478-2853

Contact: Brinton Family Association Inc.
Open: May-Oct., Sat.-Sun. 11 a.m.–6 p.m.;
groups or special appointments by phone
reservation
Admission: $1. Guided tours.
Suggested Time to View House: 1 hour

Facilities on Premises: Book store
Number of Yearly Visitors: 700
Year House Built: 1704
Number of Rooms: 6
On-Site Parking: Yes

Description of House

William Brinton (1636-1700) was born in Staffordshire, England. In 1659 he married Ann Bagley; together they had five children. They were Quakers, and in their struggle for religous freedom they lost considerable property in England. In 1684, William, Ann and their son, William, came to America. They spent their first winter in a cave along the Delaware river. During the summer William built a cabin just north of the present 1704 house (now marked by a silver maple). They then acquired large tracts of farm land beside their home. Both William and Ann died in this house. Their son married Jane Thatcher in 1690; they had six children. In 1704 they built the Brinton home. After William Jr. died, the home was occupied several more generations of the Brinton family until the spring of 1954 when the restoration of the 1704 house was begun.

This sturdy home was constructed of stone from a nearby quarry; the walls are twenty-two inches thick. There is a steep roof and pent eaves over the first floor windows on the north and south sides of the house. The twenty-seven windows are of leaded ash. Most of the original flooring has been preserved and is still in use.

The furnishings are based on inventories taken after the death of the builders. There are a few original items, otherwise all pieces are collected and represent furnishings that William and Jane Brinton might have owned.

Barns-Brinton House

U.S. Route 1, P.O. Box 27
Chadds Ford, PA 19317
(215) 388-7376

Contact: Chadds Ford Historical Society
Open: May-Sept., Sat.-Sun. 12–6 p.m.
Admission: Adults $1; children (under 12) and seniors $.50. Guides in colonial garb interpret tavern and private home; there are also various craft demonstrations.
Suggested Time to View House: 45 minutes
Number of Yearly Visitors: 3,200
Year House Built: 1714
Style of Architecture: Flemish Bond Brick
Number of Rooms: 4 (plus 2 in cellar)
On-Site Parking: Yes **Wheelchair Access:** No

Description of House

Very little is known about William Barnes, the original owner of this gracious home. Barnes married Elizabeth Key at the First Presbyterian Church in Philadelphia on February 16, 1708. Together they had five children named Elisha, Elijah, Emanuel, William and Elizabeth. William petitioned for a license to operate a tavern beginning in 1722 until his death. The license was not always granted. When he died in 1791, his tavern and house were taken to pay his debts. His wife and children stayed in the Chester County area for some years. Elizabeth joined the Friends Meeting of Kennett in 1741; however, she was expelled in 1751 for drinking. The next owners, the Brinton family, lived in the house from 1751 through the mid 1800s.

The tavern has been restored and furnished by the Chadds Ford Historical Society as a historical museum. The tavern and inn were on the right side of the house and the family's private quarters were on the left side, with storage in the cellar. The structure is notable for its fine interior woodwork paneling and its exterior Flemish Bond brickwork accentuated by balsck headers. The kitchen features a walk-in cooking fireplace with cooking equipment which is still used today. There are no furnishings from the original owners; however, the tavern is furnished with tavern tables from the early 18th century. The chairs are reproductions. The rest of the house is furnished with pieces that might have been in a house of its size, including early 18th century antiques.

Additional Information

The house is located one and a half miles west of the Brandywine River museum.

The John Chads House

Route 100, P.O. Box 27
Chadds Ford, PA 19317
(215) 388-7376

Contact: The Chadds Ford Historical Society

Open: May-Sept., Sat.-Sun. 12–6 p.m.

Admission: Adults $1; children (12 and under) and seniors $.50. Guides in colonial garb describe 18th-century life in the Hamlet of Chadds Ford, baking demonstrations in the beehive oven when the house is open.

Suggested Time to View House: 45 minutes

Number of Yearly Visitors: 3,650

Year House Built: c. 1725

Style of Architecture: Chester County Fieldstone

Number of Rooms: 5, including kitchen in cellar

On-Site Parking: Yes **Wheelchair Access:** No

Description of House

This stone building was the home of John Chads, the ferryman and farmer for whom Chadds Ford was named. He started the first ferry service across the Brandywine and operated a tavern and inn. John Chads inherited 500 acres from his father, Francis Chadsey. When he came of age, he hired John Wyeth, Jr. (no relation to the present Wyeths) to build the house. They built the springhouse first and lived in it while they were building the main house. The springhouse was later used as a tenant house and then in the 1850s it was a one room school house. There are copy books in the barn (the new headquarters building) from several students who attended the school. John Chads married Elizabeth Richardson in 1729 and they lived in the house until their deaths (John in 1760, Elizabeth in 1791). His will makes it apparent that for a farmer he was quite well-off when he died.

The houses pleasing proportions, continuous cornice, original oak floors, paneling and woodwork make it a fine example of early 18th- century Pennsylvania architecture. There was never any plumbing or electricity in the house although it was lived in until the 1950s. The house has been restored and furnished with early 18th-century Chester county furniture as a historic house museum by the Chadds Ford Historical Society.

Additional Information

The beehive oven has been restored and bread is baked in it on days when the house is open.

Troxel-Steckel House and Farm Museum

4229 Reliance Street
Egypt, PA 18052
(215) 435-4664

Contact: Lehigh County Historical Society

Open: June-Oct., Sat.-Sun. 1–4 p.m., and by appointment

Admission: Free. Guided tours available during regular hours and by appointment.

Suggested Time to View House: 45 minutes

Description of Grounds: Grounds are accessible in a farm-like setting

Best Season to View House: Spring and summer

Year House Built: 1756

Style of Architecture: German medieval-style

On-Site Parking: Yes **Wheelchair Access:** Yes

Description of House

Built by John Peter Troxell, this stone farmhouse is an excellent example of German medieval style architecture brought to eastern Pennsylvania by German settlers. The Troxell family was of Swiss descent but lived in German for several decades before setting sail for America. John Peter inherited this land from his father and built the farmhouse in 1756. At the time the structure was built, it was the largest building in the area, except for the the Moravian community structures in Bethlehem and Nazareth. This helped to establish the Troxells as one of the most prominent families in the region. A Swiss immigrant, Peter Steckel, purchased the house in 1768. A leading member of the Egypt Reformed Church, he was considered one of the most progressive and ingenious farmers in the area and greatly helped to develop the town.

This large, two-and-a-half story house was based on memories of Troxell's childhood in Germany. The home's fortress-like walls are two-and-a-half feet thick, designed to protect the family from both the Indians and the harsh weather. There are two great fireplaces and a steep gabled roof which extends three feet out over the second story. The interior buildings are made of oak, and the floors of poplar and pine. The furnishings have been collected and and are appropriate for a prominent farming family of the late 18th century.

Notable Collections on Exhibit

The house's furnishings feature a spinning wheel, flint-lock rifle, Chippendale mirror, children's trundle bed, and a five plate cast iron stove dating from 1758 which bears the inscription "Never Despise Old Age". The adjacent barn contains an exhibit of farming implements, blacksmith and carpentry tools, tobacco and cider presses, carriages and sleighs.

Ephrata Cloister

632 West Main Street
Ephrata, PA 17522
(717) 733-6600

Contact: Pennsylvania Historical and
Museum Commission
Open: Mon.-Sat. 9 a.m.–5 p.m, Sun.
12–5 p.m.
Admission: Adults $4; seniors $3; children
$2. Guided tours and visitor orientation
slide program.
Suggested Time to View House: 1 hour
Facilities on Premises: Museum store
Number of Yearly Visitors: 60,000
Year House Built: Mid 18th century
Style of Architecture: Medieval German
On-Site Parking: Yes **Wheelchair Access:** Yes

Description of House

Founded by Johann Conrad Beissel, the Ephrata Cloister was a radical 18th-century religious communal society best known for its original art and music, distinctive medieval Germanic architecture and its significant publishing center. Housed in a unique collection of medieval style buildings, this community of religious celibates practiced an austere life-style which emphasized spiritual rather than material goals. The society declined after the Revolution due to lack of leaderhip and a declining interest in the life of self-denial. By 1800, the celibate orders were practically extinct and in 1814 the remaining married order, known as the householders, incorporated into the Seventh Day German Baptist Church, which used the buildings until 1934. In 1941, the Pennsylvania Historical Society and Museum Commission assumed administration and began its program of research, restoration and interpretation of this important historic site.

Between 1732 and the American Revolution, the Ephrata Cloister constructed log, stone and half timbered buildings largely based on the Germanic architecture of the member's homes in the Rhineland. Today, the surviving buildings include Beissel's house, the chapel, the sisters' house, the Academy or school, and the bake house, where candlemaking demonstrations are performed.

Connell Mansion

249 West Main Street/ P.O. Box 193
Ephrata, PA 17522
(717) 733-1616

Contact: The Historical Society of the
Cocalico Valle
Open: Tues.-Fri. 9 a.m.–5 p.m.
Admission: Free. Guided tours.
Suggested Time to View House: 45 minutes
Facilities on Premises: Publications on sale
Number of Yearly Visitors: 1,360
Year House Built: 1869-70
Style of Architecture: Victorian Italiante
Number of Rooms: 13
On-Site Parking: Yes
Wheelchair Access: No

Description of House

This beautiful mansion was built by Moore Connell, the son of an Irish immigrant, and Rebecca Konigmacher Connell, a descendant of the influential German Konigmacher family, early affiliates of the Ephrata Cloister. Moore Connell, though not born into a wealthy family, became well-to-do as a farmer and as a dealer in livestock and real estate. Moore and his wife Rebecca had eight children, five of whom (all daughters) survived to adulthood. None of these daughters married, and all remained in their parents' home until their own deaths. The youngest, and longest-lived daughter, Nora, died in 1961. A short time later, the historical society purchased the still intact house. All members of the Connell family are buried approximately one mile west of their home, at God's Acre Cemetery, attached to the Ephrata Cloister, because of the Konigmachers' affiliation with that body.

The mansion is a two story, five bay brick house, with a bracketed front porch, double brackets at cornice, hipped roof with polygonal central belvedere, round arch windows, two-over-two sash, marble mantel, and a three story central staircase. Many of the Connell family's furnishings are on display, others are collected and appropriate to period. The second floor of the house is furnished as it was lived in, with modifications. The first and third floors contain museum displays.

Notable Collections on Exhibit

The many period furnishings include plank-bottom chairs painted with 19th-century Pennsylvania German motifs, an original copper-lined wooden bathtub, a display of local hotel furnishings c. 1860 and late 19th-century local church furnishings, oil paintings of Joseph and Cecelia Slaymaker Konigmacher (c. 1850), builders of Ephrata's Mt. Springs Hotel; 18th and early 19th-century Ephrata Cloister imprints, and other items in changing exhibits. The library collection includes manuscripts, photographs, books, and microfilmed items of local historical significance.

Cashiers House

417 State Street
Erie, PA 16501
(814) 454-1813

Contact: Erie County Historical Society

Open: Tues.-Sat. 9 a.m.–4 p.m. for research; Tues.-Sat. 1–4 p.m. for tours; groups by appointment; closed holidays

Admission: Donation. Guided tours, research library and archives, open house Sun. after Thanksgiving.

Suggested Time to View House: 40 minutes

Facilities on Premises: Gift/book shop

Number of Yearly Visitors: 9,675

Year House Built: 1839

Style of Architecture: Greek Revival

Number of Rooms: 15

On-Site Parking: Yes **Wheelchair Access:** Yes

Description of House

Peter Benson of Cincinnati was the cashier of the Erie branch of the United States Bank of Pennsylvania. He and his family were the first occupants, followed by a school for young women run by Louise and Callista Ingersoll in the 1840s. The Erie City Bank operated here in the 1850s, followed by Samuel Goodwin who ran a full boarding house. From 1872 to 1913 the family of Judge Samuel E. Woodruff lived here, including the artist Sarah Woodruff. The Erie Drug Company operated here until the Pennsylvania Historical and Museum Commission purchased the house in 1963. The Erie County Historical Society has occupied the home since its restoration in 1974.

Designed by the Philadelphia architect, William Kelly, the town house is three stories high in front and two stories in the rear, with a full basement. The house's construction features a brick exterior covered with stucco, with plan crowned windows and door. Notable within are the keyhole door and window frames with decorative crowns marked with scroll work on the first floor, and Greek key designs on the second floor. The first floor rooms have coffered ceilings with egg and dart molding. Only two bookcases belong to the Benson family, but the majority of the furnishings date from 1830 to 1880, and were collected to represent the Victorian period.

Notable Collections on Exhibit

Notable collections include the portrait of Judah Colt, agent for the Pennsylvania Population Company, and the cane pictured in the portrait. Also on exhibit are portraits by the area artist Moses Billings, and still lifes by Sarah Woodruff. The china collection includes a platter used to serve General Lafayette during his visit to Erie in 1825. Furnishings span the years 1830 to 1900, American Empire to true Victorian.

Sturgeon House

4302 S. Garwood Street
Fairview, PA 16415
(814) 474-5855

Contact: Fairview Area Historical Society
Open: Mid June-mid Aug., Sun. 1–4 p.m.;
Sept.-June, the first Sun. of each month
Activities: Guided tours; open additionally
for special exhibits
Suggested Time to View House: 30 minutes
Number of Yearly Visitors: 800
Year House Built: c. 1838
Style of Architecture: Saltbox with recessed
porches
Number of Rooms: 5 rooms open to public
On-Site Parking: No **Wheelchair Access:** No

Description of House

The Sturgeon House provides a fine illustration of life in a middle-class family in rural Pennsylvania. The Sturgeon brothers, William and Jeremiah, were drawn to this fertile area of land known as the "Erie Triangle." One of Jeremiah's children, Robert, purchased the land that the house stands on in 1838. The house may have been built by his brother, Samuel, who was a well-known builder in the area. Robert Sturgeon, married twice and had four children by his first wife, Sarah Pollack, and two by his second, Eleanor Jacks. During the 1850s, Robert enlarged the house and extended the dormer on the second floor. Perhaps at the same time he remodeled the parlor on the north end of the house, giving it a more Victorian look.

The Sturgeon House is a Federal-style saltbox structure, unique in that its main entry is through the porch on the low side. This simple farm dwelling consisted originally of two large rooms on the first floor with two smaller bedrooms off to the east, with a storage area behind the fireplace and a dormer-like second floor.

The house is furnished with some original pieces, the remaining furniture is of the same period. The Sturgeon House was placed on the National Register of Historic Places in 1980.

The Highlands

**7001 Sheaff Lane
Fort Washington, PA 19034
(215) 641-2687**

Contact: Highlands Historical Society
Open: Mon.-Fri. 9 a.m.–4 p.m.
Admission: $1
Suggested Time to View House: 45 minutes
Description of Grounds: The grounds
   consist of 44 acres.
Best Season to View House: Spring,
   summer and fall
Number of Yearly Visitors: 12,000
Year House Built: 1795
Number of Rooms: 12

Style of Architecture: Late Georgian
On-Site Parking: Yes **Wheelchair Access:** Yes

Description of House

Anthony Morris, a wealthy Quaker lawyer and merchant from Philadelphia, purchased just over 200 acres of land in Whitemarsh, wishing to provide his family with a refuge from the yellow fever epidemics sweeping the city. Morris immediately started construction of an elaborate country estate which he named "The Highlands". Shortly after the house was finished he suffered extreme financial difficulties and was forced to sell the mansion. Thereafter, "the Highlands" was home to many families.

In June 1795, masons laid the foundation for the grand mansion. The mansion was designed by Timothy Matlack, better known as a politician and ardent patriot. In fact, this was his only recorded architectural commission. The house was designed to blend established Georgian principles of symmetry with a new awareness of neoclassical stylistic details introduced by the Scottish architect, Robert Adams. The house underwent renovations around 1813 including the construction of the verandah on the north side, the addition of the portico on the main south facade, and the replacement of the interior doors and their framing on the first floor. A large garden or "Pleasure Ground", was also installed at this time. By 1844, the landscape architect Andrew Jackson Downing describes it as a "striking example of science, skill, and taste, applied to a country seat". The mansion today remains unfurnished. The focus instead is on the architecture and the beautiful gardens.

Hope Lodge

553 Bethlehem
Fort Washington, PA 19034
(215) 646-1595

Contact: Pennsylvania Historical and Museum Commission

Open: Tue.-Sat. 9 a.m.–5 p.m.; Sun. 12–5 p.m.; closed Mon. and major holidays except July 4th and Labor Day

Admission: Adults $3; seniors, groups of 10 or more, children (6-17) $1; children under 6 free. Hope Lodge offers guided tours and a yearly calender of special events. Visitors should call to find out about special events.

Suggested Time to View House: 1 hour

Facilities on Premises: Museum shop

Description of Grounds: The grounds include a formal garden, an herb garden and a vegetable garden. Picnic tables are available.

Best Season to View House: Spring-fall

Year House Built: 1743-1748

Number of Rooms: 14 on exhibit

Number of Yearly Visitors: 13,000

Style of Architecture: Georgian

On-Site Parking: Yes **Wheelchair Access:** Yes

Description of House

Hope Lodge was built by Quaker businessman Samuel Morris between 1743 and 1748. Morris was a man of many talents; he worked as a farmer, ironmaster, and owner of the mill now known as Mather Mill. He owned the estate until his death in 1770, when it was inherited by his brother, Joshua. Joshua sold the property and dwelling to another Philadelphia merchant, William West. During the Revolution the house was located near the Continental Army's encampment and served as headquarters for Washington's Surgeon General, John Cochran. The house takes its name from Henry Hope who purchased the house as a wedding gift for his ward, James Watmough.

Hope Lodge is an excellent example of early Georgian architecture with the characteristic balance and symmetry reflected in both the exterior and interior of the house. The house is largely original, changing little in its 250 year history. The house is listed on the National Register of Historic Places.

The house is interpreted to both the 18th-century Colonial and the 20th century Colonial Revival periods. Most of the furnishings on exhibit are the collection of the last private owners, William and Alice Degn who purchased the house in 1922. Their furnishings decorate the parlor, dining room, and guest bedroom. The rest of the house is furnished as it would have been during Samuel Morris's time.

Notable Collections on Exhibit

The fine 18th-century furniture makes a notable display. The lodge also holds several paintings by artist Sally Eichholtz.

Dobbin House

89 Steinwehr Avenue
Gettysburg, PA 17325
(717) 334-2100

Contact: Dobbin House Inc.
Open: Mon.-Sun. 11:30 a.m.–12 a.m.
Activities: Guided tours (June-Oct.), the house is open to the public as an authentic colonial tavern
Suggested Time to View House: 1 hour
Facilities on Premises: Gift shop
Year House Built: 1776
Style of Architecture: Georgian stone
Number of Rooms: 9
On-Site Parking: Yes **Wheelchair Access:** Yes

Description of House

Reverend Alexander Dobbin, the original builder of this simple stone house, had many interests. In addition to being a minister, he was a farmer, a theologian, and an educator. Although he was never wealthy, he was considered one of Gettysburg's most prominent citizens and ministered at several area churches. His wife, Isabella, bore him ten children, several of whom died in infancy. The Dobbin family lived in the house until 1825. The property changed owners several times before a butcher, James Pierce, bought it in 1861. More than a dwelling, the house witnessed the Battle of Gettysburg during the Civil War and sustained minor damage from gunfire. Lincoln delivered his famous address in the nearby cemetery.

Built in 1776, the Dobbin House is the oldest house in Gettysburg. This two and one-half story local fieldstone measures fifty-eight feet by thirty-two feet. The Georgian design features seven bay windows and is two rooms deep. The original woodwork is throughout the entire house. In addition, there is an indoor spring which still provides fresh water. The house even has a secret hideaway used as a station in the Underground Railroad. The furnishings correspond with the Dobbin's 1809 inventory.

Notable Collections on Exhibit

The house has a wide and varied collection including an 1818 walnut and chestnut tavern bar, a large collection of dolls from 1850 to 1900, fireplace cooking utensils; a painted Austrian kas (c. 1770); a splay legged table c. 1790; and a poplar hutch c. 1820. In addition, other items discovered in the house and cellar during restoration are on display in the porch room.

Battles Museums–Yellow House

Walnut Street
Girard, PA 16501
(814) 454-1813

Contact: Erie County Historical Society
Open: May-Sept., Tues. and Thurs.
1–4 p.m., call to verify
Activities: Draft horse field day and open
house second Sat. in April; guided tours
of exhibits which change annually;
audiovisual presentation available by
appointment.
Suggested Time to View House: 30 minutes
Description of Grounds: 130 acres of
farmland and woodlands plus the other
buildings included in the Battles
Museum of Rural Life comlex

Best Season to View House: Summer- fall
Year House Built: 1857-58
Number of Rooms: 18, 6 open to the public

Number of Yearly Visitors: 1,500
Style of Architecture: Italianate
On-Site Parking: Yes **Wheelchair Access:** Yes

Description of House

Rush S. Battles, lawyer, farmer, banker and owner of the Climax Manufacturing Company (manufacturer of narrow gauge locomotives), played a crucial role in the development of western Erie County until his death in 1904. He married in 1861 and built a house next door leaving his mother and two unwed sisters to live in the eighteen room home. The last of the sisters died in 1909 and the house was then occupied by several tenant farm families beginning in 1910. The house was occupied until the mid 1960s. Several of the families have been featured in the changing exhibits.

This attractive home uses a square Italianate style of architecture with a back wing. The house is topped by a square cupola and has one-story entry porches and a partial porch ornamented with lattice, and all are topped by a balustrade. The kingpost construction, clapboard frame house has hooded windows and an attached two-story woodshed. The house was restored to its 1860 appearance in 1989, though the interior remains unfinished and is used for changing exhibits dealing with rural life in northwestern Pennsylvania from 1840 to the present. The majority of the items on display came from the Battles family or were used in the house.

Notable Collections on Exhibit

On exhibit are most of the original furnishings, along with the archival material to support the objects, such as purchase receipts, diaries, and photographs. The Battles women were proficient spinners and weavers, and the collections include examples of their handiwork.

Additional Information

The Battles Museums of Rural Life is a new and still developing museum complex funded to interpret life along Lake Erie's southern shore from 1840 to the present.

Charlotte Elizabeth Battles Memorial Museum

Walnut Street
Girard, PA 16501
(814) 454-1813

Contact: Erie County Historical Society
Open: House under renovation, call for hours
Activities: Garden tours, slide shows
Suggested Time to View House: 1 hour, gardens-30 minutes
Description of Grounds: A 1930s garden has been restored and blooms through the summer.

Best Season to View House: Spring-fall
Number of Yearly Visitors: 200
Year House Built: 1861
Style of Architecture: Victorian vernacular
Number of Rooms: 19
On-Site Parking: Yes **Wheelchair Access:** No

Description of House

Industrialist and banker Rush S. Battles and his wife, Charlotte Webster Battles, built this house in 1861. Their surviving child, Charlotte Elizabeth, lived in the house until she died in 1952. She inherited her father's bank and actively managed its affairs until its closing in 1946. It was the only bank to remain open in Pennsylvania through President Roosevelt's banking moratorium. She was an accomplished musician, artist, and gardener, as well as a successful businesswoman, managing the family's extensive farm and investments. Her friend, Georgiana Read, inherited the house and willed it to the Erie County Historical Society to be used as the Museum.

As the primary Battles family residence, the house's structure documents the economic growth of the family, as well as changes in their tastes, styles, and material needs. Beginning as a simple front gable and wing with shuttered windows, the house grew with additions of a wrapped porch with a turkish domed roof supported by Ionic capitals on fluted columns; years later a back wing with a fire-proof garage was added. In its setting of treasured trees and gardens, the house reflects the mores of an upper-class Victorian household continued into the 20th century. The house is full of the accumulated belongings of 150 years of the Battles and Webster families.

Notable Collections on Exhibit

The collection contains fine china and silver, as well as all the known paintings by C. E. Battles, and her art supplies. There is a John Rogers statue and a paper-mache doll with buggy (c. 1868), as well as some unsigned oil portraits from the 1850s. There are Victorian bedroom sets, parlor sets, pianos, and items of historical importance, such as the saddle bags brought by the ancestor who purchased the property in 1823. Notable also are the 1930 LaSalle and the 1942 Cadillac. Included in the furnishings is an extensive archival collection of receipts, diaries, business and personal correspndence, and photographs.

Additional Information

Part of the new and developing Battles Museums of Rural Life, this house was not yet open to the public as of spring 1993. Visitors are encouraged to call and see when it will be open, and to visit the other houses–The Yellow House and the Cashiers House–which are also run by the society.

Neas House

**113 N. Chestnut Road
Hanover, PA 17331
(717) 632-3207**

Contact: Hanover Area Historical Society
Open: May-Oct., Tues.-Fri. 10 a.m.–2 p.m.
Admission: Donations accepted.
   Community history awareness
   programs; special Christmas open house.
Suggested Time to View House: 60 minutes
Description of Grounds: Vegetable and
   herb garden
Best Season to View House: Spring to fall
Number of Yearly Visitors: 1200
Year House Built: 1743
Style of Architecture: Georgia
On-Site Parking: Yes **Wheelchair Access:** No

Description of House

The house was originally owned by Mathias Neas and his family. Neas was an extremely successful tanner. In addition to his cattle and horses, in 1783 Mathias had twelve dependents. His taxes were among the highest in the area, signifying his position in the community. The house was passed to Mathias' eldest son, George, who was the third postmaster of Hanover, its first Burgess, and a legislator for several terms. The house was later used for apartments, commercial enterprises, including a restaurant and a barber shop, until being acquired by the society in 1974.

This large brick house shows the architectural influences of Baltimore, Annapolis and Philadelphia. The house combines Georgian with Federal-style architecture; the Georgian aspect is characterized by a center hall and a symmetry in the placement of rooms, doors and windows. All the original woodwork and floors are in excellent condition. A door on the second floor reveals that, then as now, bored young people were apt to leave their mark on wood with pocket knives. Several sets of initials and dates, as early as 1801, were found during the restoration of the house.

The house is furnished according to inventories taken on the death of Mathias Neas, in 1815, and of his son's widow in 1853.

Notable Collections on Exhibit

The house sponsors changing exhibits related to local history.

Bentel House

Mercer Street
Harmony, PA 16037
(412) 452-7341

Contact: Historic Harmony Inc.

Open: June-Sept., daily 1–4 p.m.; Oct.-May, Mon., Wed., Fri., Sun. 1–4 p.m.

Activities: Guided tours; Dankfest craft festival (last weekend in Aug.) and Horse Trading Days, including a flea market in late July.

Suggested Time to View House: 1 hour (for 3 building tour)

Facilities on Premises: Gift shop

Description of Grounds: The house is part of a larger Mennonite community, including a park with a playground, tennis courts and swimming pools

Number of Yearly Visitors: 8,000

Year House Built: 1809

Number of Rooms: 5 (open to public; 7 others upstairs), plus a wine cellar

Style of Architecture: Harmonist

On-Site Parking: Yes **Wheelchair Access:** Yes

Description of House

The Harmony society was once a thriving religious group whose members, led by George Rapp, immigrated from Germany to settle in Pennsylvania. They adopted a lifestyle of hard work and celibacy in order to prepare for the second coming of Christ. Everyone worked for the good of the society, and in turn, received what he or she needed to live simply and comfortably.

The museum was once lived in by the Bentel family, proprietors of the Harmonist warehouse. The entrance is adorned by a picture of the Virgin Sophia, a religous symbol to the Harmonists, carved by Frederick Reichert. Several of the rooms are furnished with period furnishings including those produced by Harmonists (1804-1814), and other Victorian and Mennonite furnishings.

Notable Collections on Exhibit

In addition to the period furnishings and religious artifacts, the museum also displays Indian artifacts.

Fort Hunter Mansion and Park

5300 North Front Street
Harrisburg, PA 12110
(717) 599-5751

Contact: Dauphin County Parks and Recreation

Open: May-Dec.23rd Tues.-Sat. 10am-4:30pm; Sun. 12–4:30pm

Admission: Adults $3; seniors $2; children (under 12) $1. Guided tours, slide show, nature walks, military re-enactments, candlelight tours, colonial buffets and yuletide celebrations.

Suggested Time to View House: 45 minutes

Facilities on Premises: Gift shop

Description of Grounds: The 35 acre park includes a 19th-century boxwood garden, herb gardens, historic buttonwood trees, and a riverside walking trail

Best Season to View House: May-Oct.

Number of Yearly Visitors: 5,000

Year House Built: 1814 (an original 1786 structure on the same site was incorporated into the mansion)

Style of Architecture: Colonial, Federal, Italiante

Number of Rooms: 20

Description of House

Captain Archibald McAllister built the mansion in 1814, as part of a frontier village he had helped to create on the site. He was a young officer who had served directly under General George Washington in the Revolutionary Army. Years later, Daniel Dick Boas bought the property in 1870 and later willed it to his daughter Helen and her husband John W. Reilly. The Reillys employed the site as a dairy farm, with strutting peacocks and grazing sheep. They left the property to their nieces and nephews. One niece, Margaret Wister Meigs, bought the remaining shares and established the Fort Hunter Museum.

The original structure was a log blockhouse fort, built by the British army when faced with the mounting threat of the French and Indian War (c.1754). In 1763, following the defeat of the Indian Nations, the fort was left to decay. In 1787, Captain Archibald McAllister bought the land, including the old fort, and built up a self-sufficient frontier village on the property. In 1814, McAllister built the stone mansion that now stands in Hunter Park; the rear wooden portion was added by Boas in 1870. In addition to the mansion there are another five outbuildings on the property: an ice house, a tavern, a blacksmith shop, a spring house, and a stable. Furnishings are mostly from original residents, including early American, Empire and Victorian styles.

Notable Collections on Exhibit

In addition to the period furnishings, the mansion exhibits collections of costumes (1820-1920), tools, firearms, and toys.

The John Harris– Simon Cameron Mansion

219 South Front Street
Harrisburg, PA 17194
(717) 233-3462

Contact: The Historical Society of Dauphin County

Open: Mon.-Fri. 11 a.m.–3 p.m.; second and fourh Sun. 1–4 p.m.

Admission: Adults $2.50; seniors $2; children $1; children (under 8 with adult) free. Hourly tours; monthly lectures; public programs and special workshops; all grade level school programs.

Suggested Time to View House: 1 hour

Description of Grounds: Perennial and mum gardens

Best Season to View House: Spring

Number of Yearly Visitors: 10,000

Year House Built: 1740

On-Site Parking: Yes

Style of Architecture: Colonial, Italianate, Colonial Revival

Description of House

The construction of the house was begun in 1740 by John Harris Senior (1691-1748), the first settler in the region. The mansion was completed in 1766 by John Harris Jr. (1721-1791), known as the founder of Harrisburg. The home was modernized by Simon Cameron (1799-1889). Cameron was a United States Senator, and the Secretary of War to Abraham Lincoln.

This lovely 18th-century home has been modernized three times since its original construction. The home now mostly reflects the period of 1863 to 1929. The architecture features a Georgian central block with many additions in the Italianate and Colonial Revival styles. The house maintains a 1929 art deco bathroom and the 1863 restored French wallpaper. The floors were lowered three feet in 1863 as part of Italianate remodeling. None of the original furnishings are present; instead, the house is used as a museum of county history. Each exhibit gallery features a variety of yearly and seasonal exhibitions.

Notable Collections on Exhibit

The society serves as the repository of extensive collections of fine decorative arts (Pennsylvania German, Colonial through Victorian), textiles, tools, military and political memorabilia, and Native American objects. The society's library houses archives of documents, books and newspapers relating to local history. In addition, on exhibit are paintings by Jacob Eichholtz, John Framer, and regional artists.

Rock Ford Plantation– Kauffman Museum

881 Rock Ford Road, P.O. Box 264
Lancaster, PA 17603
(717) 392-7223

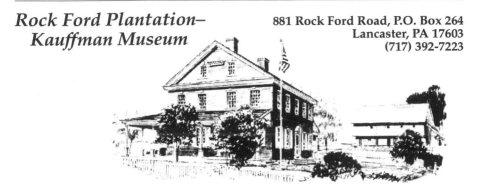

Contact: Rock Ford Foundation

Open: April-Oct. and weekends. in Nov., Tues.-Sat. 10 a.m.–4 p.m., Sun. 12–4 p.m.

Admission: Adults $3; students $1.50; children (under 6) free. Orientation slide show, house tours, June Lobster legacy. (Call for information regarding other events)

Suggested Time to View House: 1 hour-house tour; 30 minutes-museum

Facilities on Premises: Gift counter

Description of Grounds: Grounds are contiguous with Lancaster County Central Park, an open and accessible park atmosphere

Best Season to View House: May-Oct.

Number of Yearly Visitors: 4,500 plus

Year House Built: Completed 1794

Style of Architecture: Georgia

Number of Rooms: 21 rooms (13 open to public)

On-Site Parking: Yes **Wheelchair Access:** Yes

Description of House

Edward Hand was born December 31, 1744 in Clydruff, Ireland. Following medical training at Trinity College in Dublin, he enlisted as surgeon's mate with the 18th Royal Irish Regiment, and was sent to Garrison Fort Pitt in the United States. He resigned from British service in 1774 and came to Lancaster to practice medicine. After having a distinguished military career with the Continental Army, including serving directly under Washington, he returned to Lancaster and entered politics. He moved to Rock Ford in 1793, and died here in 1802. The house was sold in 1810 and occupied by tenants with no physical changes until restoration began in 1958.

This four-story brick gable roof mansion has a restored piazza on three sides. The house maintains 85 percent of its original glass, and 95 percent original interiors. The woodwork is exceptionally well-preserved. The simple exterior is enhanced by pencilled brick. The furnishings are collected and appropriate to period; they were chosen according to an 1805 estate inventory for the period of occupancy from 1794 to 1802.

Notable Collections on Exhibit

On exhibit are furnishings and decorative arts from the period 1794 to 1802. Rock Ford also houses the Henry J. Kauffman Collection of Pennsylvania folk art, which includes rifles, copper, pewter, fraktur glass, pottery, tin, painted furniture, textiles, and carvings.

Compass Inn Museum

Route 30 East, P.O. Box 167
Laughlintown, PA 15655
(412) 238-6818

Contact: Ligonier Valley Historical Society

Open: May-Oct., Tues.-Sat. 11 a.m.–4 p.m.; Sun. 12–4 p.m.; Nov.-mid Dec., Sat.-Sun. 2–5 p.m.

Admission: Adults $4; children (6-12) $2; under 5 free; group tours: adults $3; students $1.50. Open at request for groups of 20 or more; guided tours by costumed docents, living history third weekend in June, July and Aug., Nov.-Dec., candlelight tours

Suggested Time to View House: 90 minutes

Facilities on Premises: Gift shop; inn; working kitchen, blacksmith shop; and barn

Number of Yearly Visitors: 5,000

Year House Built: 1799, additions 1820 and 1862

Number of Rooms: 8

Style of Architecture: Log with random stone addition

Description of House

The Inn was purchased from Phillip Freeman, the original owner, in 1814 by Robert and Rachael Armor. Seven generations of Armor descendants lived in the house until 1962 when the property was sold to the Ligonier Valley Historical Society.

The log structure was built in 1799 by Phillip Freeman, with two rooms downstairs and two or three upstairs. The stone addition of 1820 provided a large common room downstairs and two additional bedrooms upstairs. In 1862, the first indoor kitchen was added and today visitors will see a fireplace and a functional beehive oven. The house has many unique features including a beautiful oak hand tongue and groove, narrow oak floor boards downstairs, an unusually wide stairwell, and two uncommon doors, each with a panel that can be raised to protects the glass panes when locked for the night. After archaeological digs to locate the foundations, the working kitchens, blacksmith shop, with an operational forge, and barn were reconstructed.

The Inn's furnished rooms include the common room, a serving kitchen, the ladies' parlor, and four bedrooms. There are a few pieces belonging to the Armor family. The rest are collected and appropriate to the period.

Notable Collections on Exhibit

Each room and out building is furnished in detail, mostly American primitive. The barn is dominated by a Conestoga Wagon and stagecoach.

Additional Information

The Compass Inn is the only restored inn in what was a busy, commercial site for travelers going either east or west. Thriving towns like Laughlintown died when the railroads by-passed them.

Stoy Museum

924 Cumberland Street
Lebanon, PA 17042
(717) 272-1473

Contact: Lebanon County Historical Society
Open: Sun.-Fri. 1–4:30 p.m.; Mon. evenings, call for times
Admission: Adults $2; seniors $1.75; students (5-18) $1; children under 5 free; group rate (pre-arranged) $1.50. Tours.

Suggested Time to View House: 90 minutes
Facilities on Premises: Gift shop and library
Number of Yearly Visitors: 10,000
Year House Built: 1773
Style of Architecture: Georgian
On-Site Parking: No **Wheelchair Access:** No

Description of House

The original front portion of the Stoy Museum was built in 1773 as a home for Dr. William Henry Stoy, a local minister and prominent Revolutionary War doctor. The upstairs rooms were used as Lebanon County's first courthouse. James Buchanan, fifteenth President of the United States practiced law here as a young attorney.

Notable Collections on Exhibit

Throughout the museum, visitors may view fine examples of Pennsylvania German craftsmanship in such items as furniture, quilting and weaving, fraktur, and redware. Additional collections include war memorabilia and railroading and firefighting equipment, and community industries.

Log House

Lenhartsville, PA 19534
(215) 562-4803

Contact: Pennsyvania Dutch Folk Culture Society, Inc.
Open: April-Nov., call for schedule and rates
Activities: Guided tours; demonstations
Suggested Time to View House: 60 minutes
Facilities on Premises: Gift shop
Description of Grounds: 5 building complex

Best Season to View House: Summer
Number of Yearly Visitors: 5,000
Year House Built: Approximately 1750
Style of Architecture: Log cabin
Number of Rooms: 1½
On-Site Parking: Yes **Wheelchair Access:** Yes

Description of House

This fascinating five building complex illustrates the lifestyle of the early Pennsylvania Dutch. This living history museum features a schoolhouse, a folk culture center, a fashion house with textile exhibits, a library, as well as a log house. The house demonstrates colonial life and includes a working fireplace and bake oven. Moved to its present location from a nearby town, the house is furnished with collected and appropriate pieces used in the colonial period.

Notable Collections on Exhibit

The Log House exhibits a variety of fireplace, cooking and baking utensils; the barn holds horse-drawn equipment and colonial era tools; and the museum features items related to the lifestyle of the Pennsylvania Dutch.

Heisey Museum

362 East Water Street
Lock Haven, PA 17745
(717) 748-7254

Contact: Clinton County Historical Society

Open: Tues.-Fri. 10 a.m.–4 p.m.; other times by appointment

Admission: Adults $2; children $1; group rate $1. Guided tours, visual presentations, special events and programs.

Suggested Time to View House: 1–2 hours

Facilities on Premises: Gift shop

Description of Grounds: Enclosed Victorian grounds, including a lawn, garden, and plantings

Best Season to View House: Summer and early fall

Year House Built: 1831

Style of Architecture: Gothic Revival (from Federal farmhouse)

Number of Rooms: 13

On-Site Parking: Yes **Wheelchair Access:** No

Description of House

The S.D. Ball House—now operated by the historical society as the Heisey Museum—is a two-story brick farmhouse built by Dr. John Henderson for his 200 acre farm along the banks of the West Branch of the Susquehanna. In 1834, Jerry Church purchased the farm and laid out his new town, naming it Lockhaven. John and Walter Devling obtained the property shortly after the Church sale in 1834 and operated a popular tavern for several years. William Fearon Jr. purchased the property in 1853 and proceeded to greatly modernize the house. He was involved with L.A. Mackey and J.W. Quiggle in the Fallon House and Lock Haven Bank adventures. In 1860, physician S.D. Ball bought the property, and after the flood of 1865 altered it to its present form. The house was also used as tavern again in the 1930s and 1940s.

Dr. Ball's alterations transformed the simple Federal farmhouse into an elegant Gothic Revival structure. The vergeboard at the roof's edge comes from a design taken from Sloan's "Model Architect". The Gothic veranda has coupled octagonal columns joined with a lancet arch and trefoil. A 1974 restoration has returned the house to its original 1865 color scheme. Because this is a Gothic Revival remodeling of a Federal style building, the proportions are not as they should be. All furnishings are appropriate to the Victorian period; some are from the original residents, others have been collected and reflect the period.

Baldwin-Reynolds House Museum

848 North Main Street
Meadville, PA 16335
(814) 724-6080

Contact: Crawford County Historical Society
Open: Memorial Day-Labor Day; Wed. Sat. and Sun. 1–5pm
Admission: Adults $2; students (under 16) $1. Guided tours.
Suggested Time to View House: 90 minutes
Description of Grounds: 3 acres of landscaped park, including a herb garden and a spring-fed pond. The grounds also feature a country doctor's office and an ice house.
Best Season to View House: Summer
Year House Built: 1843
Number of Rooms: 27

Style of Architecture: Greek Revival
On-Site Parking: Yes

Description of House

Henry Baldwin (1780-1844) asked local craftsmen to build this home for his retirement based on a Tennessee house he admired. It was completed only a year before his death. A lawyer in Meadville's pioneer days and later a Pittsburgh iron furnace owner, he served three terms in the U.S. House of Representatives, where he became known as the "father" of the American system of protective tariffs. Appointed by Jackson, he served on the U.S. Supreme Court from 1830 to 1844. William Reynolds (1820-1911), Meadville's first mayor, purchased the mansion from his aunt, Mrs. Baldwin. His son, John Earle Reynolds (1864-1947), inherited the house from his parents in 1911. Following in his father's footsteps, he also served a mayor for three terms. His widow lived in the mansion until her death in 1963.

The Baldwin-Reynolds House is an elegant four-story Greek Revival mansion. The first and second floors are highlighted by arched doorways, black walnut and curly maple woodwork, and parquet floors. The interior also includes a plant-filled solarium, an octagonal room and a library with secret panels. The original furnishings of former owners are complemented by appropriate pieces from the 19th century.

The rural practioner's office was moved to the museum grounds in 1976 from its original site at Little's Corners, ten miles to the north. Dr. J. Russell Mosier practiced in this office next to his house until his death in 1938. This small building contains an examining room, a waiting room and a pharmacy. His office contains a medical library, an early typewriter, a galanometer, an examining chair and table, and his personal collection of stuffed porcupines and sea shells.

Notable Collections on Exhibit

The mansion exhibits an unusual collection of carved birds, spoons, paperweights, Staffordshire dogs, Bohemian glass, and Indian artifacts. In addition, the mansion houses a noteworthy portrait collection.

Magoffin House

Contact: Mercer County Historical Society

Open: Memorial Day-Labor Day, Tues.-Sat. 10 a.m.–4:30 p.m.; Labor Day-Memorial Day, Tues.-Sat. 1–4:30 p.m.; closed Christmas and New Year

Admission: Free. Guided tours.

Suggested Time to View House: 1 hour

Facilities on Premises: Sales desk

Number of Yearly Visitors: 1,500

Year House Built: 1821 (oldest section), additions up to c.1910

Number of Rooms: 10, 4 open to public

On-Site Parking: Yes **Wheelchair Access:** Yes

Description of House

The Magoffin family were early settlers in Mercer Borough; their family included many doctors. They also acquired a great deal of real estate in the borough. Research on the family is scanty to this point, however, parts of the family have been identified as leaders in the county's Democratic Party during the Civil War, which earned some of them the label "Cooperheads".

This large, wood frame dwelling is situated in downtown Mercer Borough. The original section, built by Dr. J. Magoffin, dates from 1821. The house is now used as gallery space by the historical society for its growing collections. While the greater part of the house is not furnished as a house museum, there are a few items on display which belonged to the Magoffin family including what is reputed to be the first piano brought west of the Allegheny mountains.

Notable Collections on Exhibit

The historical society's many fascinating collections range from the Dr. Goodsell display related to arctic exploration (he was Admiral Peary's surgeon during the 1908-09 North Pole excursion), to a military gallery and a fashion display. The house also showcases the Dorothea Kaiser collection of antique furniture, Oriental decorative arts, jewelry, and paintings including Kaiser's own work. In addition, the house exhibits collections related to anthropology, natural history, and historic artifacts.

Fallingwater

Route 381, P.O. Box R
Mill Run, PA 15464
(412) 329-8501

Contact: Western Pennsylvania
Conservancy
Open: April 1-Nov. 15; Tues.-Sun.
10 a.m.–4 p.m.; Nov. 15-March, Sat.-Sun.
10 a.m.–4 p.m.
Admission: Adults $8 (weekends), $6
(weekdays); seniors $5 (weekdays);
students (with teacher) $4. Guided tour
through the house with tapes available
for foreign visitors, video available for
those who are unable to walk through
the house.
Suggested Time to View House:
45–60 minutes
Facilities on Premises: Gift shop
Description of Grounds: Walking trails
Best Season to View House: Summer and
fall
Number of Yearly Visitors: 134,000
Year House Built: 1936-1939
Style of Architecture: Modern
Number of Rooms: 14
On-Site Parking: Yes **Wheelchair Access:** Yes

Description of House

Designed in 1936 by Frank Lloyd Wright, Fallingwater has long been considered one of the complete masterpieces of 20th-century art. Constructed of reinforced concrete and native stone, it is dramatically cantilevered over a waterfall. The house was commissioned by Edgar J. Kaufmann, Sr., owner of Kaufmann's Department Stores, a Pittsburgh department store chain. His only son, Edgar Kaufmann, Jr., was an architectural historian and Wright scholar.

Because of its unique location and dramatic architectural style, Fallingwater has received considerable acclaim. Ahead of its time in design and construction, the house was voted the "all-time best work of American architecture" in a 1991 pool of the American Institute of Architects. The furnishings and art collections are of the same period as the house. Many were designed by Frank Lloyd Wright or donated by the residents. Fallingwater is the only major work of Frank Lloyd Wright's to come into the public domain intact with the original site furnishings and art work.

Notable Collections on Exhibit

The collection includes Tiffany pieces, Oriental art, Japanese prints, paintings by Diego Rivera, and work by numerous other contemporary artists. An exceptional outdoor sculpture collection includes pieces by Jaques Lipschitz and Brian Hunt.

Whitefield House

214 E. Center Street
Nazareth, PA 18064
(215) 759-5070

Contact: Moravian Historical Society

Open: Mon.-Fri. 1–4 p.m., and by appointment; closed major holidays

Admission: Free, but donation requested. Guided tours by request, permanent and changing exhibits, special programs, and lectures.

Suggested Time to View House: 30–45 minutes

Facilities on Premises: Specialized books for sale

Description of Grounds: A large lawn plus a garden

Best Season to View House: Spring or summer

Number of Yearly Visitors: 6,000

Style of Architecture: Colonial–mix of English and Germanic

Year House Built: 1740

Number of Rooms: 22, not all open to the public

On-Site Parking: Yes **Wheelchair Access:** Yes

Description of House

This impressive structure has been home to an intriguing array of people and activities. The building has been used as a residence for thirty-three newly married couples, as a school for little girls, as a children's nursery in a communal settlement, as a theological seminary, and as apartments for varying numbers of people, many of whom were Moravian ministers or missionaries and their families.

Whitefield House is one of the oldest extant Moravian buildings in North America (construction began in 1740), and the first building in Nazareth. The German influenced structure is made of limestone and features hand-hewn timbers and a gambrel roof. Although officially only two stories, the house has a double attic which provided additional living space, plus an attic and a basement (not open to the public). The building is not furnished as a house, but instead the large rooms are used as an exhibit space, work space, and storage space. Some pieces in the collection are from the mid-1700s, but are not exhibited in period room settings.

Notable Collections on Exhibit

The collection includes twenty-three oil paintings by Moravian artist, John Valentine Haidt (1700-1780), the first artist in America to do religious paintings in oils. A variety of musical instruments, including brass, strings (the first American-made violin), and keyboards, and period furnishings are also displayed.

The Parry Mansion Museum

45 South Main Street
New Hope, PA 18938
(215) 862-5148

Contact: The New Hope Historical Society
Open: May-Oct., Fri.-Sun. 1–5 p.m.
Admission: Adults $4; groups and seniors $3. Guided tours, and group tours by appointment.
Suggested Time to View House: 30 minutes
Description of Grounds: An early 19th-century town house garden

Best Season to View House: May-Oct.
Number of Yearly Visitors: 3,000
Year House Built: 1784
Style of Architecture: Pennsylvania Georgian
Number of Rooms: 11
On-Site Parking: No **Wheelchair Access:** Yes

Description of House

This gracious home was built by Benjamin Parry, a wealthy Quaker miller and landowner. The property originally extended to the Delaware River. Benjamin Parry was born in 1757, a second generation American. Benjamin was the first in his family to settle in Bucks County. This enterprising man owned and operated mills for linseed oil, flaxseed oil, lumber and flour on both sides of the Delaware. When his mill in Coryell's Ferry was gutted by fire in 1790, he rebuilt the complex and named it the New Hope Mill. He owned almost all of what is now New Hope. He was instrumental in renaming the town, building a bridge to replace the ferry, and constructing the local portion of the canal. Benjamin's mansion remained in Parry ownership until 1966 when Margaret Parry Lang, the last descendant to live in the house, sold it to the New Hope Historical Society.

The mansion is a classic three-story Georgian house built of natural blue and red fieldstone. A central hall with four rooms on each floor, plus a kitchen annex (added in the early 1800s) comprise the interior. Most of the outbuildings on the estate have long since been torn down, except for the barn, which is now an art gallery. Parry's first grist mill still stands but now houses the Bucks County Playhouse.

The house is furnished in five distinct periods from 1775 to 1900, reflecting the five generations of Parrys who lived in the mansion from 1784 to 1966. The furnishings are largely from the original residents; the remaining pieces are collected and appropriate to the periods showcased. The archive room contains a large amount of photographs pertaining to the Parry family, plus old New Hope Borough records dating back to the beginning of the town of New Hope.

Notable Collections on Exhibit

Many notable pieces on exhibit, including a rush seat corner chair, originally belonging to Governor Williamson of New Jersey, an American Sheraton four poster rope string bed, an American Empire bed, four kinds of Windsor straight chairs, a John Henry Belter parlor suite, a James S. Earle gilt pier mirror, and a Raven, Bacon and Company piano. Also on display are numerous utilitarian objects, such as a spinning wheel, slipware plates, a coffee grinder, a Chinese transfer ironstone set, a Victorian tricycle, an eagle-topped coal stove and a Waterford coal oil cut-galss prism chandelier plus many Parry family portraits and other paintings.

Court Inn

Court Street and Centre Avenue
Newtown, PA 18940
(215) 968-4004

Contact: Newtown Historic Association
Open: Thur. 7–9 p.m; Sun. 2–4 p.m.
Admission: Free. Annual Market Day craft fair held in Sept.
Suggested Time to View House: 1 hour
Facilities on Premises: Museum shop

Best Season to View House: Summer
Number of Yearly Visitors: 1000
Year House Built: 1733
Style of Architecture: Colonial
Number of Rooms: 9 open to the public
On-Site Parking: No **Wheelchair Access:** Yes

Description of House

This historic inn comforted many travellers during the 18th century. Joseph and Margaret Thornton originally lived at the Court Inn (originally known as the Half Moon Inn) and ran it as a tavern from 1733 to 1798. The stone and frame inn has a beehive oven in the fireplace in the meeting room used for both warmth and cooking during colonial times. The Newtown Association has restored the inn to its original form.

Notable Collections on Exhibit

The inn displays an extensive collection of primitive painter Edward Hick's artifacts. Also, the famous Hick's hanging sign on Penn's Treaty is on display.

Joseph Priestley House

472 Priestley Avenue
Northumberland, PA 17857
(717) 473-9474

Contact: Pennsylvania Historical and Museum Commission
Open: Fri.-Sun. 12–4 p.m.
Admission: Adults $3; students and seniors $2; children $1. Tours, audiovisual presentations, and special programs.
Suggested Time to View House: 45 minutes

Facilities on Premises: Gift-book store
Number of Yearly Visitors: 5,000
Year House Built: 1795-1798
Style of Architecture: Georgian-Federal
Number of Rooms: 9
On-Site Parking: Yes **Wheelchair Access:** Yes

Description of House

Joseph Priestley, best known as the discoverer of oxygen, built this house in 1794. A recent emigrant from England, Priestly, in addition to being a scientist, was a dissenter, a theologian, and the founder of Unitarianism.

The simple two-and-a-half story frame structure appears much as it did in Priestly's day. The dwelling houses his laboratory which illustrates the workings of an "Enlightenment" scientist, as well as a kitchen and other living areas. Many of the artifacts on display belonged to Dr. Priestly, others are representative of the period.

Additional Information

According to the historical commission, Priestley's library, one of the largest in America of this period, is soon to be reconstructed.

Waynesboro

2049 Waynesboro Road
Paoli, PA 19301
(215) 647-1779

Contact: Philadelphia Society for the Preservation of Landmarks

Open: Tues. and Thurs. 10 a.m.–5 p.m.; Sun. 1–4 p.m.; hourly tours by reservation

Admission: Adults $3; students and seniors $2; group rate (10 or more) $2. Guided tours, slide presentation.

Suggested Time to View House: 45 minutes

Description of Grounds: Several acres of wooded land which serves as a park for the community

Number of Yearly Visitors: 4,000

Year House Built: 1926 with later additions

Style of Architecture: Georgian

Description of House

This stately stone mansion was the home of the Revolutionary War hero, General Anthony Wayne. Wayne was born in this house built on land purchased by his grandfather. He later retired here following his brilliant military career during the Revolution. He left the estate in 1792 when called by President Washington to serve as major general and commander-in-chief of the Legions of America. Through his campaigns, and negotiations with Northwest Indians, he opened the west to settlement. Waynesboro remained in the family until the late 1960s.

The spacious Georgian center block of the house is built on a center passage plan with both an earlier dwelling and later service wing attached. Today the house is restored and furnished to reflect life in the 18th century when General Wayne's family lived here. At the peak of Waynesborough's prominence, the plantation covered more than 1,000 acres of land and included a large tannery located about one-half mile from the house.

Wharton Esherick Studio

Box 595
Paoli, PA 19301
(215) 644-5822

Contact: Wharton Esherick Museum

Open: Sat. 10 a.m.–5 p.m.; Sun. 1–5 p.m.; hourly tours by reservation; studio closed Jan. and Feb.

Admission: Adults $5; children (under 12) $3. Guided tours, slide presentation, traveling photographic exhibition of Esherick's work.

Suggested Time to View House: 45 minutes

Facilities on Premises: Sales desk

Description of Grounds: In addition to the main studio, the grounds contain a unique garage and a workshop (not open to the public)

Best Season to View House: April-July

Year House Built: 1926 with later additions

Number of Rooms: 5 open to public

Number of Yearly Visitors: 4,000

Style of Architecture: Uniquely Esherick

On-Site Parking: Yes **Wheelchair Access:** Yes

Description of House

Wharton Esherick (1887-1970) was the creator and resident of this unusual studio. He was among the vanguard of artists who created a distinctly American sculptural style early in the 20th century. Working in wood, he extended his sculptural forms to furniture, furnishings, and architecture. Esherick has been called the "dean of American craftsman" for his unique melding of art and craft, and for pioneering the way for future craftspeople to create and market original, non-traditional work.

The initial 1926 organic stone sculpture studio, with its tapered walls curving out at the bottom like a tree trunk, expresses the concept of organic architecture. The prismatic living quarters addition, built in 1940, reflects the artist's expressionistic forms. Constructed in 1966, the free form tower frescoed with an abstraction of autumn colors completes this cross section of the development of American art in the mid 20th century. The entire studio is a unique creation, perhaps Esherick's most monumental work of art. The furnishings, furniture, and utensils were all created by the artist between 1920 and 1970. The 1956 workshop was based on a collaborative design by Esherick and his friend, the renowned architect Louis Kahn. The museum has been designated a National Historic Place.

Notable Collections on Exhibit

The studio houses more than 200 of Esherick's works including paintings, woodcuts, ceramics, wood sculpture, furnishings, and unique interiors throughout. They reflect both the evolution of his artistic development and the expansion of his work and living environment.

Cliveden

6401 Germantown Avenue
Philadelphia, PA 19144
(215) 848-1777

Contact: Cliveden of the National Trust Inc.

Open: April-Dec., Tues.-Sat. 10 a.m.–4 p.m.,
Sun. 1–4 p.m.; closed major holidays

Admission: Adults $4; students $3; members
of the National Trust for Historic
Preservation free. Guided tours, lecture
programs, rotating art exhibits, annual
re-enactment of 1777 Battle of
Germantown.

Suggested Time to View House: 45 minutes

Facilities on Premises: Gift shop

Description of Grounds: Six acres of lawns
and shrubs; a small formal garden and
"historic time line" demonstration garden

Best Season to View House: April-July

Number of Yearly Visitors: 10,000

Year House Built: 1763-1767

Style of Architecture: Mid-Georgian

Number of Rooms: 8 open to public

On-Site Parking: No **Wheelchair Access:** Yes

Description of House

Cliveden was built as a country house for Maryland-born Supreme
Court Justice Benjamin Chew from his own architectural drawings. Benjamin Chew was born and raised in Maidsone, a plantation in Maryland,
which he left at age fifteen to study law with Andrew Hamilton, a prominent
Philadelphia lawyer. After Hamilton's death in 1741, Chew worked for his
father Samuel, who was Chief Justice of the lower counties (now Delaware).
In 1743, Chew went to London to study and returned when his father died
the next year. He then established residences in Delaware and Pennsylvania
and began to practice law. He then held a succession of political postions
including Speaker of the Assembly in Delaware and Attorney General, and
councilor to the governor. In 1774, he became Chief Justice of the Supreme
Court of Pennsylvania. The mansion also holds the distinction of having
been captured by the British during the Battle of Germantown. Cliveden
remained in the Chew family until it was acquired in 1972 by the National
Trust for Historic Preservation.

The house is an example of Colonial Georgian architecture that displays many features of the English neo-Palladian style. The two and one-half story rectangle central block is flanked by kitchen and wash-house dependencies older than the house itself. Centrally located on the five-bay facade of cut native Germantown schist stone is a small projected pavillion ornamented with a classic Doric entablature and pediment supported by fluted columns. The design of the stone facade is based on the engraving "A View of the Palace at Kew from the Lawn" published in London in the *Gentleman's Magazine and Historical Chronicle* in 1763. A raised water table, horizontal belt course, modillion cornice, paired dormers, and massive clustered raised chimneys make up the exterior ornamentation. All of the furnishings are from the Chew family; some were brought from London, others were acquired locally.

Notable Collections on Exhibit

Clivedon is decorated with an unusually complete set of furnishings acquired by the Chew family over the course of 200 years. These include a tall-case mahogany clock (c. 1787 by David Evans), an English-style sofa with Marlborough legs (c. 1763 by Thomas Affleck), nine rare Colonial red leather backstools (c. 1763 by Affleck), in addition to numerous Chippendale and Federal-style pieces. The house also exhibits several fine pieces of artwork including "The Battle of Germantown" by artist E.L. Henry, "The Lafayette Reception" by Edward Lamson Henry; and a John Locke bust.

Mantua House

Contact: Elfreth's Alley Museum

Open: 10 a.m.–4 p.m.; except Jan.-Feb., Sat.-Sun. 10 a.m.–4 p.m.

Admission: $.50. Costumed docents; June Fete Days-first weekend in June.

Suggested Time to View House: 30 minutes

Facilities on Premises: Museum store

Description of Grounds: The large garden behind the house is a an attractive place to take a break from city-life

Best Season to View House: Spring, summer and fall

Number of Yearly Visitors: 65,000

Year House Built: 1740

Style of Architecture: Townhouse

Number of Rooms: 4

On-Site Parking: No **Wheelchair Access:** No

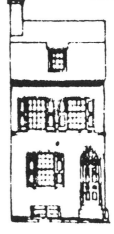

Description of House

Elfreth's Alley, a group of thirty homes built between the early 1700s and the early 1800s, is the oldest residential street in the country. The alley is only six feet wide and appears much as it did during Colonial times. The street offers a unique opportunity to view American, domestic, middle-class architectural styles spanning an entire century. The Mantua House is the only house open to the public; the rest are privately owned. The house has been carefully restored and decorated with furnishings appropriate to the period. In addition to the decorated rooms, there is a permanent display on the history of Elfreth's Alley and 18th and 19th-century artifacts.

Additional Information

Because of Philadelphia's place in our nation's history, the city is filled with historic homes. Visitors wishing to make a complete tour are encouraged to visit the *Betsy Ross House* (239 Arch Street) where the seamstress made our first flag, and *Bellaire* (20th Street and Pattison Avenue), built in 1714 and considered one of the oldest houses in the city.

Cedar Grove

Lansdowne Drive off N. Concourse Drive
East Fairmount Park
Philadelphia, PA 19131
(215) 763-8100 ext. 33

Contact: Philadelphia Museum of
Art/Fairmount Park Commission

Open: Tues.-Sun. 10 a.m.–4 p.m.

Admission: $1.50. Guided tours, special
theme tours, slide presentations,
Christmas tours.

Suggested Length of Time to View House:
1 hour

Description of Grounds: Located near the
concourse of Fairmount Park, the largest
municipal park in the world

Best Season to View House: Spring-fall

Year House Built: c. 1740s

Style of Architecture: Stone cottage

Description of House

Cedar Grove, a Quaker summer cottage, originally stood on Frankfort Road near the Delaware river in a section called Harrowgate, known for its mineral springs. From 1746 to 1888, the house was the summer residence of five generations of the Paschall-Morris family. The fifth generation owner, Miss Lydia Thompson Morris, had Cedar Grove moved, stone by stone, to its present location in Fairmount park.

The house began as a two-and-a-half story, three room house constructed of native stone. In 1799, the house was doubled in size when a new living room and kitchen were added to the first floor and several bedrooms enlarged the second story. At the same time, the gable roof was converted to a gambrel, and the attic was enlarged to accomodate the growing family. The 1848 piazza addition is particularly notable in that every room on the ground floor has a door opening on to the piazza, a detail that suggests easy country living rather than the formality of a great mansion. The house also features a built-in wall oven and a built-in copper cauldron for heating water in the kitchen. Cedar Grove is furnished with original pieces belonging to the Morris and Paschal families.

Notable Collections on Exhibit

The house contains a beautiful collection of family owned furnishings ranging from the William and Mary period through the Federal era. There are many fine examples of American furniture from the 17th, 18th, and 19th centuries including a Philadelphia-made triple chest of drawers.

Mount Pleasant

Mount Pleasant Drive
West Fairmount Park
Philadelphia, PA 19131
(215) 763-8100 ext. 33

Contact: Philadelphia Museum of
Art/Fairmount Park Commission

Open: Tues.-Sun. 10 a.m.–5 p.m.

Admission: $1.50. Guided tours, special
theme tours, slide presentations,
Christmas tours

Suggested Length of Time to View House:
1 hour

Description of Grounds: The house is
located on a rocky promontory
overlooking the Schuylkill River in
Fairmont Park.

Best Season to View House: Spring-fall

Year House Built: 1761

Style of Architecture: Georgian

Description of House

In 1761, Captain John Macpherson, a wealthy Scottish privateer, built this perfect model of Georgian symmetry with his profits made during the Seven Years War. The house has been described as the "most elegant seat in Pennsylvania" and remains one of America's finest surviving examples of mid 18th-century architecture. In 1779, General Benedict Arnold purchased the house but was never able to reside here due to his arrest for treason in the fall of 1780. The house was later home General Jonathan Williams, a descendant of Benjamin Franklin, as well as the first women's automobile club of Philadelphia.

Mount Pleasant has a notable exterior utilizing a contrasting color scheme of light colored trim against darker pattern of smooth brick, a style in opposition to the prevailing aesthetic of the time. The house features an elaborate interior with all of the ornamental carvings and original paneling intact. The rooms are furnished to represent the elegant lifestyle of Philadelphia in the 1760s.

Notable Collection on Exhibit

The fine Chippendale furniture has been described as some of the finest achievements of Philadelphia craftsmen and has been supplied by the Philadelphia Museum of Art.

Grumblethorpe

5267 Germantown Avenue
Philadelphia, PA 19144
(215) 843-4820

Contact: Philadelphia Society for the
Preservation of Landmarks

Open: Tues., Thurs., Sat. 1–4 p.m.

Admission: Adults $3; students and seniors
$2; groups (10 or more) $2. Guided
tours, special tours, tea, and lectures by
appointment.

Suggested Time to View House: 1 hour

Description of Grounds: Recreation of the
original 18th-century garden

Best Season to View House: Spring and
summer

Year House Built: 1744

Style of Architecture: Germantown

Description of House

Built in 1744 as a country home by wine importer John Wister, Grumblethorpe was known through the 18th century as "John Wister's Big House." Originally intended as a summer retreat, the house was occupied during 1793 when the Wister family sought refuge from the raging yellow fever epidemic in Philadelphia. In the early 19th century, Charles Jones Wister, well-known as an astronomer, horticulturalist, and inventor, winterized the house and made many changes and additions, and named it "Grumblethorpe".

Constructed of dressed Wissahickon stone and oak from Wister's lands, the house is a prime example of domestic Germantown architecture of the period. Notable features include the stone coursing of the facade, pent eaves, front and rear balconies, and the double front entrances. The house has been restored and is completely furnished as it might have appeared in 1744. In addition, the Wisters were also well known horticulturists and the society is in the process of restoring the gardens to their original 18th and 19th century appearance.

Notable Collections on Exhibit

Like the society's other properties, Grumblethorpe has a fine collection of period furniture, silver, porcelain, and paintings on display.

Hill-Physick-Keith House

321 South 4th Street
Philadelphia, PA 19106
(215) 925-7866

Contact: Philadelphia Society for the Preservation of Landmarks

Open: Tues., Thurs., Sat. 1–4 p.m.

Admission: $Adults 3; students and seniors $2; groups (10 or more) $2. Guided tours, special tours, teas, and lectures by appointment.

Suggested Time to View House: 1 hour

Description of Grounds: An unusually large city garden with 19th-century plants

Best Season to View House: Spring and summer

Year House Built: 1786

Style of Architecture: Germantown

Description of House

This imposing house was built in 1786 by Henry Hill, an importer of Madeira wine. Dr. Philip Sing Physick took up residence in the house in 1815 and lived here until his death in 1837. Physick was one of the foremost physicians of the time and is known as the "Father of American Surgery". Young Dr. Physick was among the courageous physicians who remained in the city to care for the sick during the yellow fever epidemic. He also counted many notable people among his patients, including the wife of the president, Dolley Madison. Physick was elected to the staff of the Pennsylvania Hospital and within a few years his lectures on anatomy and medicine led to his being named to the first chair of surgery in the United States at the University of Pennsylvania.

This four-story brick house with its formal fanlighted entrance is the only free-standing Federal townhouse remaining in Society Hill. After Physick's death the house was extensively remodelled by members of the family during the 19th and early 20th centuries. After several decades of neglect, the house was given to the society and restored to the Federal period, with fine Federal-style furnishings, and to the time of Dr. Physick's residency.

Powel House

244 South Third Street
Philadelphia, PA 19106
(215) 627-0364

Contact: Philadelphia Society for the Preservation of Landmarks

Open: Tues.-Sat. 10 a.m.–3:30 p.m.

Admission: Adults $3; students and seniors $2; groups (10 or more) $2. Guided tours, special tours, teas, and lectures by appointment.

Suggested Time to View House: 1 hour

Description of Grounds: Formal garden with 18th-century trees and shrubs

Best Season to View House: Spring and summer

Year House Built: 1765

Style of Architecture: Georgian

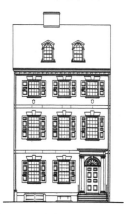

Description of House

This elegant brick house, built in 1765 by merchant and businessman Charles Stedman, was purchased by Samuel Powel in 1769 at the time of his marriage to Elizabeth Willing. Powel, a wealthy, educated man who had toured Europe for seven years before settling donw in Philadelphia, became known as the "Patriot Mayor." He served as the last mayor under the crown and was the first in the New Republic. His wife, Elizabeth, was renowned as a brilliant hostess and her receptions were unrivalled in elegance and distinction of company. Washington, Lafayette, foreign ministers and others of importance in the colonies and, later, the new nation enjoyed the Powels' hospitality.

Located in the fashionable district of Philadelphia, the house presents the three-bay, side-passage plan typical of the city's fine townhouses of the period. The interior appointments of the house are exceptional. The original staircase of Santo Domingo mahogany rises gracefully from a paneled and columned entrance hall leading to the second floor and Mrs. Powel's "parlor upstairs", a spacious, elegant, and finely ornamented room.

Notable Collections on Exhibit

The period rooms of the Powel House displays an excellent collecton of 18th and 19th-century furnishings, porcelain, silver, and paintings.

Laurel Hill

Contact: Women for Greater Philadelphia/Fairmount Park Commission

Open: Wed.-Sun. 10 a.m.–4 p.m., closed major holidays

Admission: $1.50. Guided tours, special theme tours, slide presentations, Christmas tours.

Suggested Time to View House: 1 hour

Description of Grounds: The house is located on a laurel covered hill overlooking the Schuylkill River in Fairmount Park.

Best Season to View House: Spring-fall

Year House Built: 1767

Style of Architecture: Georgian

Description of House

Laurel Hill was one of a chain of summer homes for wealthy city dwellers built along the Schuykill River in the 18th century. Some of the house's notable occupants include Mayor Samuel Shoemaker, William Rawle, founder and first chancellor of the Philadelphia Bar Association, and the distinguished physician, Philip Syng Sick. Laurel Hill was the first of Fairmount Park's houses to be opened to the public as a result of the growing interest in America's colonial past.

The original center portion of the house is Georgian in style. The octagonel, two-story wing was added in the early 19th century. The interior features handsome mouldings and a beautiful mantle in the octagonel room. Laurel Hill is completely furnished with period furniture dating to the early 19th century. Included in the furnishings are several fine musical instruments such as an 1808 Broadwood piano-forte and an 1831 harp.

Additional Information

Visitors to Fairmont park are also encouraged to visit many of the other notable homes including the *Rittenhouse Cottage*, built in 1700 on the site of the first papermill, and the *Ohio House* (c. 1876) constructed originally as an exhibition hall and later converted into a residence. The Ohio House now houses the visitor center for the entire park.

Lemon Hill

Kelly and Sedgeley Drives
East Fairmount Park
Philadelphia, PA 19131
(215) 232-4337

Contact: Colonial Dames of
America/Fairmount Park Commission

Open: Wed.-Sun. 10 a.m.–4 p.m., closed
major holidays

Admission: $1.50. Guided tours, special
theme tours, slide presentations,
Christmas tours.

Suggested Time to View House: 1 hour

Description of Grounds: The house is
located on a hill overlooking the
Schuylkill River in Fairmount Park.

Best Season to View House: Spring-fall

Year House Built: 1799-1800

Style of Architecture: Federal

Description of House

In 1799, Henry Pratt purchased forty-three acres of property once owned by Robert Morris, a signer of the Declaration of Independence. Morris had built a farm and greenhouse on the land but had, unfortunately, overextended himself financially and ended up in debtors prison. Pratt, a successful merchant and philanthropist, built the fine Federal structure that exists today, but never lived here on a permanent basis. Instead, he turned the house into a business enterprise and sold tickets to the public to view the lovely building and surrounding gardens.

Constructed using a Federal design, Lemon Hill features a series of oval rooms on each of the three floors. From each of these rooms, visitors will see a beautiful view of the river and city beyond. A floor to ceiling Palladian window provides another impressive view from above the double door entrance. In addition, the house has a notable entrance hallway made of checkerboard Valley Forge marble.

Notable Collections on Exhibit

Lemon Hill houses a distinguished collection of fine furniture belonging to the Colonial Dames of America as well as several pieces on loan from the Philadelphia Museum of Art. Of particular note are the Louis XVI chairs which were made in Philadelphia in 1790.

Strawberry Mansion

33rd and Dauphin Streets
East Fairmount Park
Philadelphia, PA 19131
(215) 228-8364

Contact: Committee of 1926/Fairmount Park Commission

Open: Tues.-Sun 10 a.m.–4 p.m.

Admission: $1.50. Guided tours, special theme tours, slide presentations, Christmas tours.

Suggested Time to View House: 1 hour

Description of Grounds: In addition to the extensive grounds of the park, the mansion has a sloping lawn which extends to the banks of the Schuykill River.

Best Season to View House: Spring-fall

Year House Built: 1783 plus later additions

Number of Rooms: 20

Style of Architecture: Federal with Greek Revival additions

Description of House

Strawberry Mansion reflects the eras and tastes of its two principal owners, Judge William Lewis and Judge Joseph Hemphill. Lewis purchased the property in 1783 and remodelled an existing stone structure in the Federal style. At that time the house was known as "Summerville". Judge Lewis is best remembered for his defense of Quaker pacifists accused of treason during the Revolution. Judge Hemphill purchased the estate in 1821 and added the Empire style wings in 1828. Hemphill was a great entertainer and traveller who brought many European influences to the house. It has been said that his son added a ballroom to to the mansion in order to entertain first city troops in which he sought membership. Another son imported strawberry plants from Chile: thus, the name became Strawberry Mansion.

This impressive structure is the largest mansion in Fairmont Park. The rooms vary in style from the simple elegance of the Georgian-style entry hall to the Empire bedrooms on the second floor. The mansion contains a unique attic filled with an unusual array of dollhouses, cradles, farm implements, and parlor ornaments. The rest of the house is decorated with a mix of furnishings representing the Federal, Regency and Empire styles.

Sweetbriar Mansion

Fairmount Park West
Philadelphia, PA 19131
(215) 222-1333

Contact: Modern Club/Fairmount Park
Commission

Open: March-Jan., 10 a.m.–5 p.m., closed
Tues. and Feb.

Admission: $1.50. Guided tours, special
theme tours, slide presentations,
Christmas tours.

Suggested Length of Time to View House:
1 hour

Description of Grounds: Located in
Fairmount Park, Sweetbriar has a lovely
lawn and rose garden.

Best Season to View House: Spring-fall

Year House Built: 1797

Style of Architecture: Federal

Number of Rooms: 10

Description of House

Philadelphia was the capital of the new republic when Samuel Breck
(1771-1862) built Sweetbriar in 1797 as a year-round residence.

The mansion is named after the Sweetbriar roses that Breck's father
loved and planted in front of the house. Originally from Boston, Breck was
a leading citizen when he built this lovely Federal-style home. He served in
the state legislature before being elected to Congress. Because of his position, he entertained notable Philadelphians and Frenchmen, including the
Marquis de Lafayette in 1825.

Sweetbriar's delicate ornament over pure geometric lines is a perfect
example of the Adam style of architecture in America. The symmetrical
exterior is enhanced by long French windows with large panes with a single
window over the main door. The symmetry extends to the interior with
double parlors located on the north and south ends of the house. Sweetbriar
features an unusual music gallery on the second floor furnished with a
number of Breck's possessions. Other furnishings and decorations, like the
Wellford-type mantles in the parlors, have been collected and are appropriate for the period.

Notable Collections on Exhibit

There are many Breck family heirlooms and fine Federal furnishings on
display within the house. The south parlor, known as the Johnson Memorial
Room, was installed by Henry P. McIlhenny, the former curator of decorative
arts at the Philadelphia Museum of Art.

Woodford Mansion

33rd and Dauphin Streets
East Fairmount Park
Philadelphia, PA 19131
(215) 229-6115

Contact: Naomi Wood Trust/Fairmount
Park Commission

Open: Tues.-Sun. 10 a.m.–4 p.m.

Admission: $1.50. Guided tours, special
theme tours, slide presentations,
Christmas tours.

Suggested Time to View House: 1 hour

Description of Grounds: Located in
Fairmount Park, Woodford has a
servants' house and stable still standing
on the surrounding grounds.

Best Season to View House: Spring-fall

Year House Built: 1757

Style of Architecture: Georgian

Number of Rooms: 8

Description of House

Woodford is a grand Georgian-style mansion first built as a a one-story structure about 1756. The original owner was William Coleman, a close friend and advisor to Benjamin Franklin who often visited the mansion. Coleman and his wife raised a nephew, George Clymer, who later signed the Declaration of Independence. In 1769, Woodford was sold to Alexander Barclay, the comptroller of customs for the Port of Philadelphia. Barclay's allegiance to the crown made the mansion a Tory center in the years preceding the Revolution. A subsequent owner, David Franks, also had Tory sympathies, and was ultimately forced to leave Woodford when a wave of patriotism swept the city in 1781.

During the period of Franks's ownership, Woodford was transformed from a one-story house to a two-and-a-half story mansion by the addition of a stair hall, a kitchen wing, and a second floor. This was done to make room for their four children and their many guests as they entertained frequently. The mansion is richly furnished in the manner it might have appeared during the 1770s when Woodford was acquired by Franks.

Notable Collection on Exhibit

Woodford contains the Naomi Wood Collection of household furnishings which has been called one of the most important assemblages of its kind in America. The furniture ranges from the William and Mary, Queen Anne and Chippendale periods to notable items from the Federal era. There is also a superb collection of Dutch and English delftware on display as well as a unique collection of miniatures and a large exhibit of boxes made from silver, porcelain, ivory, tortoise shell, and other materials.

Deshler Morris House

5442 Germantown Avenue
Philadelphia, PA 19144
(215) 596-1748

Contact: Independence National Park
Open: Tues.-Sun. 1–4 p.m., other times by
appointment
Admission: Free. Guided tours.
Suggested Time to View House: 30 minutes
Facilities on Premises: Sales shop
Description of Grounds: The house is part
of Independence National Park, a
complex of historic homes and other
structures located in downtown
Philadelphia.
Best Season to View House: Year round
Year House Built: 1752
Style of Architecture: Georgian
Number of Rooms: 10

Description of House

This stately home was built by David Deshler (1712-1792), a Philadelphia Quaker merchant, in Germantown's Market Square in 1752. Deshler
continued to use it as his country resident for two decades. After the Battle
of Germantown in the autumn of 1777, the British commander, Sir William
How, briefly made his headquarters in the building. President George
Washington leased the house in 1793 to escape the yellow fever epidemic
raging in Philadelphia, and met several times with his cabinet members
while living here. The following summer, President Washington returned
with his family to enjoy Germantown's pleasant surroundings. Later, the
house was sold to Samuel Morris; his descendants lived here until it was
acquired for inclusion in the Independence National Park. The house has
been refurnished with period objects to recreate its appearance during the
1790s.

Additional Information

Visitors to Independence National Park and the Deshler-Morris House
are encouraged to visit the many other fascinating historic homes at the site.
These include the restored and refurnished Bishop White House, the home
of the first Episcopal bishop of Pennsylvania, and the Todd House, home to
Dolley Todd who later became the wife of President James Madison. In
addition, visitors may also see the Declaration House (formerly the Graff
House), the site where Thomas Jefferson drafted the Declaration of Independence in 1776.

Overholt Homestead

West Overton Village
Scottdale, PA 15683
(412) 887-7910

Contact: West Overton Museums

Open: May 15-Oct. 15, Tues.-Sat.
10 a.m.–4 p.m., Sun. 1–5 p.m.

Admission: Adults $2; children (7-12) $1;
children under 6 free. House and
museum tour, introductory film.

Suggested Time to View House: 90 minutes

Facilities on Premises: Gift shop, archive

Description of Grounds: 19th-century
historic village

Number of Yearly Visitors: 4,000

Year House Built: 1838

Style of Architecture: Greek Revival
Vernacular

Number of Rooms: 10 plus utility rooms

Description of House

In 1800, a group of German Mennonites from Bucks County, led by Henry Overholt, crossed the Alleghenies and established a farming settlement on the fertile plains just west of Chestnut Ridge. Henry's son, Abraham, had built a three story brick house and was the proprietor of a large gristmill and a distillery by 1838. Both businesses were located in a six story brick structure near the Overholt Homestead. The growing community, consisting of brick homes for Overholt employees, a general store, farm, and other related buildings became known as West Overton Village.

The home is a two-story, five by two bay, red brick building. The basement level constitutes a third floor and is fully exposed except at the rear where it is banked into a hillside. Major architectural features include a full porch across the facade which is reached by a stone stair which is enhanced by an ornamental iron rail. At the roof line a sawtooth pattern cornice provides a subtle design element. There are bridged chimneys at each gable end. The interior retains most of the original walls and doorways. Changes, including a full-wall, walk-in style fireplace was added to the northwest room of the main floor in the late 1920s. The 19th-century furnishings are collected and are of the same period as the house.

Notable Collections on Exhibit

The museums maintain exhibits, and preserve a significant collection of objects, artifacts, and archives.

Additional Information

In addition to the outbuildings–the mill/distillery, the barn, and the carriage house, visitors may also visit the 1849 birthplace of philanthropist Henry Frick.

Henry Clay Frick Birthplace

West Overton Village
Scottdale, PA 15683
(412) 887-7910

Contact: West Overton Museums
Open: May 15-Oct. 15, Tues.-Sat.
10 a.m.–4 p.m., Sun. 1–5 p.m.
Admission: Adults $2; children (7-12) $1;
children (under 6) free. House and
museum tour, introductory film.
Suggested Time to View House: 1 hour
Facilities on Premises: Gift shop, archive
Description of Grounds: 19th-century
historic village
Number of Yearly Visitors: 4,000
Year House Built: 1849
Style of Architecture: Greek Revival
Vernacular
Number of Rooms: 8
On-Site Parking: Yes

Description of House

Henry Clay Frick, the industrialist and philanthropist, was born in this former springhouse in 1849. His mother was the daughter of Abraham Overhalt, the owner of the local distillery. Although Frick only lived in this humble stone cottage during his infancy, he spent a great deal of time with the Overholt side of the family. As a young man, Frick went to work in the family's second distillery and, while there, he became interested in the coke business and eventually began building ovens to produce coke for the Pittsburgh market. By 1881, Frick was a millionaire living in Pittsburgh with his wife, Adelaide Howard Childs.

The Frick birthplace is a one story, two by two bay structure with a shingled, gable roof. The central doorway is paneled and recessed and is an excellent example of the Greek vernacular style. The interior was reconstructed in the early 1970s and although original materials were reused, the original appearance of the house was not restored. Frick family artifacts are exhibited in two of the rooms.

Centre Furnace Mansion

1001 East College Avenue
State College, PA 16801
(814) 234-4779

Contact: Centre County Historical Society

Open: Sun., Mon., Wed., Fri. 1–4 p.m., other times by appointment, closed major holidays

Admission: $2 (or donation); children under 12 free. Guided tours; special programs, workshops, exhibits and social events. The house is available for small private functions.

Suggested Time to View House: 45 minutes

Facilities on Premises: Books on local history

Description of Grounds: Two acres are being landscaped to create a miniature version of the grounds at Centre Furnace for the period 1850 to 1870

Best Season to View House: Spring-fall

Number of Yearly Visitors: 5,000

Year House Built: c. 1830s, additions (1846 and 1860)

Number of Rooms: 15

Style of Architecture: Georgian and Victorian with Italiante features.

On-Site Parking: Yes **Wheelchair Access:** Yes

Description of House

In 1791, Samuel Miles and John Patton, two Revolutionary War officers, founded Centre Furnace Ironworks. Miles was a member of the Colonial Assembly of Pennsylvania, and later the mayor of Philadelphia. Patton was a member of George Washington's life guard. Sixty years later, two Centre ironmasters who lived in the mansion, General James Irvin and his brother-in-law Moses Thompson, donated 200 acres of furnace land to the Pennsylvania Agricultural Society for a new farmer's school, now Penn State University. In the 1920s, David B. Garver became the new owner of the mansion and renamed it "The Evergreens". In 1978, The Centre County Historical Society received the property by bequest.

This five-bay Pennsylvania Georgian mansion was originally one of a series of buildings comprising the Centre Furnace Ironworks, the county's first ironmaking center. Many of the furnishings are from the original residents, they are combined with donated antiques, many of which have Centre County origins. The rooms have been furnished to reflect the period of the Thompson residency, 1842 to 1891.

Notable Collections on Exhibit

A growing collection of artifacts and historic documents relating to the iron industry are on exhibit. Also a Benjamin Franklin signed document and a fine crafted miniature version of the house are on display. The mansion's library features materials on historic preservation and the Victorian age.

Stroud Community House

900 Main Street
Stroudsburg, PA 18360
(717) 421-7703

Contact: Monroe County Historical Association

Open: Tues.-Fri. 10 a.m.–4 p.m.; Sun. 1–4 p.m.; closed Christmas, New Year's Day, Easter, and Thanksgiving

Admission: Adults $1 donation; groups, students, and senior citizens $.50. Guided tours of the house and museum collection; Christmas open house-first Sun. in Dec.

Suggested Time to View House: 90 minutes

Facilities on Premises: Book store

Number of Yearly Visitors: 3000

Year House Built: 1795

Style of Architecture: Georgian

Number of Rooms: 12 (3 used as research library)

On-Site Parking: No **Wheelchair Access:** No

Description of House

The Stroud Community House was built by Jacob Stroud, founder of Stroudsburg, for his son, John. John lived in the house from 1795 to 1800. In 1800, Jacob's younger son, Daniel, took residence and helped his father sell the lots. Daniel Stroud, a Quaker, lived here until 1840. He helped organize the first schools, as well as worked for the formation of the borough in 1815. He had practiced law before joining the Society of Friends. The house also served as a boarding house and tavern. Reverend Theophilus Heilig, a Lutheran minister, and his family lived in the house for ten years. The Strouds sold their interest in the structure in 1892. In 1920, the house was again for sale. The community purchased it at this time to run as a historical museum.

The house includes the original cellar kitchen, three floors with four rooms each. The double-wall stone construction is plaster-covered. The house maintains many of its original features including wide plank floors, a fanlight, a cellar kitchen and blacksmith hinges on the doors. At the time of its construction, the house was considered an impressive effort, because the area was still a frontier. The collections include pieces of the Stroud family and later furnishings from local county residents. The house has had several changes in its 200 year history. Other museum exhibits reflect Monroe County history. The house is listed on the National Register of Historic Places.

Notable Collections on Exhibit

Collections include portraits of the Stroud family and other local residents; furniture made in the county (two tall case clocks, dower chests, chairs, sofa); a weapon and tool room (with Pennsylvania-made rifles) with some Civil War pieces; a children's room with furniture, toys, and a large doll house from 1890. There are also two Cullen Yates oil paintings on view, as well as old lithographs of the Delaware Water Gap.

Hunter House

1150 North Front Street
Sunbury, PA 17801
(717) 286-4083

Contact: North Cumberland Historical Society

Open: Mon., Wed., Fri.-Sun. 1–4 p.m.; closed weekends in Jan. and Feb.

Admission: Free. Guided tours; meetings six times per year featuring programs relating to local history.

Suggested Time to View House: 45 minutes

Facilities on Premises: Gift shop

Description of Grounds: Lawn and small garden, including original powder magazine from Fort Augusta cemetery

Best Season to View House: Spring and fall

Number of Yearly Visitors: 3,000

Year House Built: c. 1820

Number of Rooms: 6

Style of Architecture: Late Federal

On-Site Parking: Yes **Wheelchair Access:** Yes

Description of House

The Hunter House gives the visitor a glimpse into an extraordinary authentic setting of colonial merchant-class domestic life. After the Revolutionary War, Colonel Samuel Hunter continued to reside in the commandant's quarters of Fort Augusta, the headquarters for the American forces in the upper Susquehanna Valley during the War. The land had become his property. His descendants continued to live there until 1848 when a fire destroyed his log quarters. The present Hunter house was built at that time by the Colonel's grandson, Captain Samuel Hunter. In 1931, the Commonwealth of Pennsylvania purchased the large tract of land which included the Hunter House.

The house is made of brick, with five front windows on the second floor, and two on each side of the front door on the first floor. The many additions made from 1876 to 1895 were removed during restoration and now the building looks as it did when it was first built.

The Hunter House contains a historical and genealogical library containing thousands of records of early families, church records, and cemetary records, not only for Northumberland County, but for many surrounding counties as well.

Notable Collections on Exhibit

The furniture includes one of the country's finest collections of Townsend and Goddard furnishings made in Rhode Island, other parts of New England, and Great Britain.

Washington's Headquarters

Valley Forge National Park
Valley Forge, PA 19451

Contact: National Park Service
Open: Mon.-Sun. 9–5 p.m.
Admission: Free. Guided tours.
Suggested Time to View House: 30 minutes
Facilities on Premises: Sales shop
Best Season to View House: Year round

Description of Grounds: The house is part of a lovely park which contains a bakehouse, a reconstructed soldiers' hut, and other outbuildings.
Year House Built: 1773
Style of Architecture: Stone cottage
Number of Rooms: 8

Description of House

This simple stone building played a crucial role in the Revolution while serving as General Washington's headquarters from December 1777 to June 1778. The house was built by Issac Potts, a prominent local businessman and mill owner, in 1773. Potts was a man of considerable means due to his family wealth and hard work work in the milling and iron business. Potts rented the furnished house to another family member who, in turn, rented the dwelling and furnishings to General Washington. Washington was facing a difficult period after recently suffering defeats at battles in Brandywine and Germantown. From this house, he coordinated and directed the daily activities of the forces, and oversaw the political, organizational, and military actions of his entire command in the North. The house soon proved to be too small to accomodate all of his military duties and social obligations, and a log cabin was built near the house for dining functions. The house today is furnished with period furnishings including several which belonged to the original owners, the Potts family.

There are many other historic structures located on the grounds at Valley Forge which will give visitors a sense of the winter encampment. In addition to Washington's headquarters, the buildings which housed the headquarters of General Varnum and Baron Von Steuben are also open for viewing as is a reconstructed soldiers' hut and bake house.

The Thomas Leiper House

521 Avondale Road
Wallingford, PA 19086
(215) 566-6365

Contact: Friends of the Leiper House Inc.
Open: April-Dec., Sat.-Sun. 1–4 p.m.; other times by appointment for groups
Admission: Adults $1; children free. Guided tours, lectures, slide presentations for off-premises locations; candlelight open-house in Dec.
Suggested Time to View House: 45 minutes

Description of Grounds: Four outbuildings (three open to public).
Best Season to View House: Summer
Number of Yearly Visitors: 1,500
Year House Built: 1785
Style of Architecture: Federal
Number of Rooms: 7 open to public
On-Site Parking: Yes **Wheelchair Access:** No

Description of House

The house was the country home of Thomas Leiper, a wealthy Philadelphia merchant. It later became the manor house for his stone quarry and mill village. Thomas Leiper was born in Strathaven, Scotland in 1745. He came to America in 1763, and settled in Philadelphia in 1765. He was an organizer of the First City Troop of Philadelphia (1774); he engaged in action in battles at Trenton, Princeton, Brandywine, Germantown, and Monmouth, and in special service at Yorktown. Leiper was also president of the Common Council of Philadelphia in the early 19th century. Among his other accomplishments, he constructed and operated the first railroad in Pennsylvania from 1809 to 1810. For sixty years he was active and successful in business; as merchant and manufacturer and was honored by his city and state for patriotic services and devotion to the cause of liberty and his country. He died in Philadelphia in July of 1825.

The Federal-style house is part of a 700 acre estate. The house features a cooking fireplace in the basement, a dumb waiter, and jib doors on the porch. Antique furnishings reflect the early 19th century; included are some original family pieces. There is also a bank building on the grounds, said to be the first private bank in Pennsylvania as well as a smoke house/spring house building.

David Bradford House

175 South Main Street, P.O. Box 537
Washington, PA 15301
(412) 222-1374

Contact: Bradford House Historical
Association
Open: May 1-Dec. 15, Wed.-Sat.
11 a.m.–4 p.m.
Admission: Adults $3; seniors $2.50;
children (6-16) $1.50. Costumed guides,
living history representing life in the
18th century.
Suggested Time to View House: 1 hour
Facilities on Premises: Gift shop
Best Season to View House: Summer
Number of Yearly Visitors: 2,000
Year House Built: 1786-88
Style of Architecture: Georgian
Number of Rooms: 6

On-Site Parking: Yes **Wheelchair Access:** Yes

Description of House

This stone house was home to David Bradford, a frontier lawyer and businessman, who left his mark on history by leading a a revolt against excessive taxes in 1791 known as the Whiskey Rebellion. Bradford felt that the new taxes imposed on distilleries were unjust, and organized a massive resistance to the law. He was ultimately forced to leave Pennsylvania as a result of his actions.

The Bradford house has a simple stone exterior and an elegant interior appropriate for his standing in the community. The original mahogony staircase still stands, and the house is completely furnished with period furnishings. Most of the furnishings were Pennsylvania-made.

Renfrew Museum (the Royer House)

1010 East Main Street
Waynesboro, PA 17268
(717) 762-4723

Contact: Renfrew Museum and Park

Open: Last weekend in April–last weekend in Oct., Thur., Sat.–Sun. 1–4 p.m.

Admission: Adults $3; seniors $2.50; children (6-12) $1.50; bus tours $1.50 per person. Guided tours; Spring Fest last weekend in April (demonstrations of blacksmithing, quilting, open hearth cooking, soapmaking); Yuletide program.

Suggested Time to View House: 35 minutes

Facilities on Premises: Visitor's center

Description of Grounds: 107 acres with 3 hiking trails, nature areas with picnic facilities

Best Season to View House: Year around

Year House Built: 1810-1815

Number of Rooms: 8 for viewing

Number of Yearly Visitors: 11,000-20,000

Style of Architecture: Federal style

On-Site Parking: Yes **Wheelchair Access:** Yes

Description of House

The Renfrew Museum—also known as the Royer House—provides a fascinating view of German heritage and traditions in Pennsylvania. Daniel Royer moved to this stone farmhouse at the beginning of the 19th century and members of his family, and their descendants, lived here for several generations. In 1942, the home was purchased by Edgar Nicodemus and his wife, Emma, left the house to the town when she died in 1973.

The farmhouse has a traditional interior arrangement of a center passage with two rooms flanking on eash side. The parlor amd dining room mantles were conceived in Neo-Classical taste. The exterior of the house is notable because the front faces north; most Pennsylvania homes were built with a southern exposure because of the extremely cold winters. The house is filled with early 19th-century period furniture including many large Federal-style pieces. The grounds contain a number of outbuildings including a smokehouse, milkhouse plus restored barn and the Fahnestock house where classes ranging from pre-school to adult are offered to enhance knowledge of German heritage of this community.

Notable Collections on Exhibit

The museum holds a number of unique collections including a large collection of Shenandoah pottery—the majority of the pieces were made by the Bell Family of potters, several of which are considered fine pieces of folk art. There are also over 300 pieces of Cantonware on display along with a group of Pennsylvania hand-decorated towels and hooked rugs.

1719 Herr House

**1849 Hans Herr Drive
Willow Street, PA 17584
(717) 464-4438**

Contact: Hans Herr House

Open: April-Dec., 9 a.m.–4 p.m.; closed Sun. and major holidays

Admission: Adults $3; children (7-12) $1; groups (10 or more) $2. Guided tour through house and other self-guided interpretive exhibits, Mennonite Folk Festival in Aug., October Apple Fest, and other special events.

Suggested Time to View House: 45–60 minutes

Facilities on Premises: Gift shop and book store

Description of Grounds: 11 acres of rural wooded grounds with picnic tables

Best Season to View House: April-Oct.

Year House Built: 1719

Number of Rooms: 6

Number of Yearly Visitors: 12,000

Style of Architecture: Pennsylvania-German

On-Site Parking: Yes **Wheelchair Access:** No

Description of House

Mennonite minister Hans Herr led several Mennonite families to the "Conostago" region in 1710. They became the first European settlers to the area. The house was built nine years later by his son, Christian Herr. The Herr family occupied the house and owned the land until 1860; they continued farming until 1869.

The Hans Herr House is the oldest building in Lancaster County, Pennsylvania. The house uses stone and half timber construction and features a medieval German "flurkuchen" floor plan. In addition to being a home, the structure was also used as a church meeting place until 1860. The furnishings represent the period from 1719 to 1750. They include a mixture of original pieces, some period pieces, and some 18th-century reproductions.

Notable Collections on Exhibit

The grounds feature an interpretive exhibit reflecting Lancaster County Mennonite rural life from 1710 to 1920. Periodically, there are living history demonstrations carried out in the museum's blacksmith shop, smoke house, bake oven, and in the house itself.

Additional Information

There are many festivals held on a regular basis: the Mennonite folk festival held the second Saturday in August; an apple festival held the first Saturday in October; and Christmas candlelight tours held the first Friday and Saturday nights in December.

Conrad Weiser Homestead

RR 2-Box 28
Womelsdorf, PA 19567
(215) 589-2934

Contact: Pennsylvania Historical and
Museum Commission
Open: Wed.-Sat. 9 a.m.–5 p.m.; Sun.
12–5 p.m.
Activities: Guided tours; special events
Suggested Time to View House: 30 minutes
Facilities on Premises: Book store

Description of Grounds: Beautiful 26-acre
park designed by Frederick L. Olmstead
Best Season to View House: Spring-fall
Number of Yearly Visitors: 25,000
Year House Built: c. 1730
Style of Architecture: Colonial Revival
Number of Rooms: 2
On-Site Parking: Yes **Wheelchair Access:** No

Description of House

Conrad Weiser was an 18th-century German pioneer who served as diplomat, judge, church leader, community planner, farmer and soldier. He is best known as Pennsylvania's foremost treatymaker who kept peace with the Iroquois along the frontier.

Weiser built this tiny, limestone house around 1730. The structure originally contained only one room with a loft; another was added in 1751. The house displays collected period furniture.

Peter Wertz Farmstead

Shearer Road, P.O. Box 240
Worcester, PA 19490
(215) 584-5104

Contact: Montgomery County Dept. of
History and Culture
Open: Tues-Sat. 10 a.m.–4 p.m.; Sun.
1–4 p.m.; Last tour begins at 3:30 p.m.
Admission: Free, donations accepted.
Guided Tours, slide presentation.
Suggested Time to View House: 45 minutes
Facilities on Premises: Museum sales shop

Description of Grounds: Gardens, barns,
orchard, demonstration fields
Best Season to View House: Spring-fall
Number of Yearly Visitors: 18,000
Year House Built: 1758
Style of Architecture: Georgian with
German features
Number of Rooms: 10
On-Site Parking: Yes **Wheelchair Access:** Yes

Description of House

This stately mansion was home to a wealthy German farmer during the American Revolution. Peter Wertz Jr. received the property as a part of his inheritance from his father in 1743. In 1777, General Washington used the mansion for his headquarters before and after the fateful battle of Germantown in which he lost over 1000 men. In 1784, Peter Wertz Jr. sold the property to Devault Bieber who, ten years later, sold it to Melchior Schultz. The farm stayed in the Schultz family until 1970 when it was purchased by Montgomery County. The mansion utilizes English Georgian architecture with German features. The interior has unique paint work, referred to as *daclous*, which has been well preserved. The furnishings have been collected to represent the culture and region of the late 1700s. The farmstead grounds also feature an 18th-century garden, pigsty, and crop demonstration areas.

Washington, D.C.

Anderson House

Bethune Council House Museum and Archives

Cedar Hill

Christian Heurich Mansion

Decatur House

Dumbarton House

James Monroe House

The Octagon

Old Stone House

Sewall-Belmont House

The White House

Woodrow Wilson House

Anderson House

2118 Massachusetts Avenue, N.W.
Washington, DC 20008
(202) 785-2040

Contact: The Society of the Cincinnati

Open: Tues.-Sat. 1–4 p.m.; closed major
holidays; library open Mon.-Fri.
10 a.m.–4 p.m.

Admission: Free. Docent guided tours,
concert series, library.

Suggested Time to View House: 1 hour

Description of Grounds: Outdoor
sculpture garden (only open during
moderate weather)

Best Season to View House: Year round

Number of yearly visitors: 10,000 plus

Year House Built: 1902-1905

On-Site Parking: No

Wheelchair Access: Partial

Style of Architecture: Beaux Art

Description of House

This impressive mansion was built between 1902 and 1905 by Ambassador and Mrs. Larz Anderson to be used as their private residence for entertaining during the "Washington season", from December through February. Anderson was a career diplomat who served in London, Rome, and Tokyo, among other places. He was also a member of the Society of the Cincinnati, a group whose membership is composed of the direct male descendants of the officers who served in the Continental Army during the American Revolution, including the descendants of the French officers who served in the War. After Anderson's death in 1937, his wife, Isabel, presented the house, along with most of its original contents, to the society to use as their headquarters.

This distinguished house was well suited for Anderson's formal entertaining of foreign and national statesmen and politicians. The second floor remains decorated with beautiful Belgian tapestries and furnished largely as it was during the days of the Anderson's occupancy. Many of the furnishings are from the 20th century, but a number date from an earlier period. The house is listed on the National Register of Historic Places and also functions as a museum of the American Revolution.

Notable Collections on Exhibit

Because of Anderson's many travels throughout the world, the house is filled with exquisite paintings and decorative objects which reflect his position. The French Salon exhibits a forest of jade trees from China and Japan while the Olmstead Gallery holds 17th-century French and Italian religious paintings and numerous Oriental art objects. The first floor's museum of the Revolution holds many personal letters and manuscripts, medals, swords, and other objects of historical importance as well as portraits of members of the society by Gilbert Stuart, George Catlin, Ezra Ames and other early American painters.

Bethune Council House Museum and Archives

1318 Vermont Avenue
Washington, DC 20005
(202) 332-9201

Contact: National Park Service
Open: Mon-Fri. 10 a.m.–4:30 p.m.
Admission: Free. Photography gallery and library.
Suggested Time to View House: 1 hour

Description of Grounds: Garden and courtyard, carriage house now houses archives
Year House Built: 1874
Style of Architecture: Victorian
Number of Rooms: 6
On-Site Parking: Yes

Description of House

Mary McLeod Bethune, a leading activist in the struggle for black women's rights, lived in this townhouse while consulting with national leaders on their policies. Born in South Carolina in 1875, Bethune was the fifteenth of seventeen children of former slaves. She became a powerful force in the emerging struggle for civil rights—as a counselor to four Presidents, director of the Division of Negro Affairs under the Roosevelt administration, and founder of the National Council of Negro Women. The house served as the headquarters for the Council from 1943 to 1966; it now houses the Bethune Museum and Archives, a center for black women's history.

This four-story Victorian townhouse stands in the Logan Circle Historic District. The area began as a fashionable white residential area, by 1940 it was occupied by prominent black political and social figures. While not furnished as a typical house museum, the building does display an extensive and fascinating photographic exhibition devoted to black women's history. There are, however, several furnishings on exhibit which belonged to Mary McLeod Bethune.

Additional Information

The Bethune House is located on the Black History National Recreation Trail. Other notable structures include Frederick Douglass's home Cedar Hill, the Metropolitan A.M.E. Church, and the Mt. Zion Cemetery, where many famous black leaders from the city's past are buried.

Cedar Hill

1411 West Street, S.E.
Washington, DC
(202) 426-5960

Contact: National Park Service
Open: Daily
Admission: Free. Guided tours,
   audiovisual programs
Suggested Time to View House: 1 hour
Facilities on Premises: Book store in
   visitor's center
Year House Built: 1855
Style of Architecture: Victorian
Number of Rooms: 9
On-Site Parking: Yes
Wheelchair Access: Yes

Description of House

This lovely brick home on the heights overlooking Anacostia with a view of the Capitol, was home to Frederick Douglass, the noted abolitionist, author and lecturer. A former slave, this self-educated man worked tirelessly for abolition and, in the years following the Civil War, also spoke out on behalf of women's rights. Douglass wrote several autobiographical volumes as well as numerous essays and articles. In purchasing the home called Cedar Hill, he broke the "whites only" covenant of the hill. He spent the last years of his life reading and writing at Cedar Hill and died on February 20, 1895. His wife, Helen Pitts Douglass, immediately began efforts to convert the home into a museum devoted to his life and work.

In addition to the nine rooms open for viewing in the main house, the property also contains a small, one-room structure known as "the Growlery" located a short distance behind the house. The building, where Douglass used to work, was reconstructed in 1981. Inside this special place, visitors will see a fireplace, a desk filled with papers and books, and a leather couch where Douglass used to rest and contemplate his work. All of the furnishings on display were owned or used by Douglass during his lifetime.

Christian Heurich Mansion

1307 New Hampshire Avenue, N.W.
Washington, DC 20036-1507
(202) 785-2068

Contact: Historical Society of
Washington, D.C.
Open: Wed.-Sat. 12–4 p.m.
Admission: Adults $3; seniors $1.50; access
to library and exhibit gallery free.
Guided Tours (starting at 1 p.m., 2 p.m.,
3 p.m.), for special tours please inquire
Suggested Time to View House:
45 minutes-1 hour

Facilities on Premises: Library, book store,
exhibit gallery
Description of Grounds: Victorian garden
(open Tues.-Fri., 10 a.m.–4 p.m.)
Best Season to View House: Spring-summer
Year House Built: 1894
Style of Architecture: Victorian
Number of Rooms: 31
Wheelchair Access: Yes

Description of House

The mansion was the home of one of the city's leading businessmen.
The German immigrant brewer Christian Heurich (1842-1945) hired John
Granville Meyers, an architect known for his experience with poured concrete construction, to design this elegant house in keeping with his growing
wealth and social standing. While Heurich achieved his success in the
United States, he never forgot his homeland as evidenced in the thematic
design of the woodwork in the dining room and the furniture which incor-
porate historical figures from Heurich's native village in Thuringa.

The Heurich mansion is a fine example of the lavish domestic lifestyle
of the wealthy merchant class at the turn of the century and is the only house
museum of this period in Washington. The house reflects the grandeur of
the "Gilded Age" with its opulent interior decor and furnishings. The New
York decorating firm of Charles Huber and the Washington firm of August
Grass carved the splendid mahogany and oak woodwork.

The furnishings reflect the revival tastes of the time with delicate gold
leaf parlor sets "in the French manner" and heavily carved oak pieces of
northern Italian Renaissance design.

Notable Collections on Exhibit

The historical society houses an extensive research library at the mansion which includes photographs, prints, maps, and manuscripts, and
newspaper clippings. The Thomas G. Machen print collection features 535
engravings, lithographs, and woodcuts which depict public buildings and
sites, street scenes, landscapes, and Civil War scenes. In addition, the print
holdings contains the William Newton collection of pencil sketches (1859 to
1880) and the Richard "Dick" Mansfield Cartoon Collection (1921 to 1960).

Decatur House

748 Jackson Place, N.W.
Washington, DC 20006
(202) 673-4210

Contact: National Trust for Historic
Preservation

Open: Mon.-Fri. 10–3 p.m., Sat.-Sun.
12–4 p.m., closed major holidays

Admission: Adults $3; students and seniors
$1.50; members of National Trust, free.
Guided tours, annual quilt show and
craft show, concerts, special exhibits.

Suggested Time to View House: 30 minutes

Facilities on Premises: Gift shop

Description of Grounds: Formal garden

Best Season to View House: Year round

Number of yearly visitors: 20,000

On-Site Parking: No **Wheelchair Access:** Yes

Year House Built: 1816

Style of Architecture: Federal

Description of House

This handsome brick house was built for Stephen Decatur, a U.S. Navy Commodore, who was the toast of the nation when he moved to Washington in 1816. Decatur was killed in a duel with Commodore John Baron in 1820 and his wife rented the house to a number of notable tenants including the Baron Hyde de Neuville (the French minister to the United States) and three Secretaries of State– Henry Clay, Martin Van Buren, and Edward Livingston. In 1842, millionaire-hotelier John Gadsby purchased the home; subsequently it was rented by his family to a number of politicians. During the Civil War, the house was confiscated by the Federal government and used as a clothing depot and offices. The Beale family, later occupants, made substantial renovations to the house in 1871 and returned to to its former status as the center of Washington's social activity.

The Decatur house was designed by Benjamin Henry Latrobe, the first professionally trained architect to practice in the United States. The house features the beautiful, Federal-style interiors which made Latrobe famous, and include a formal entrance hall and stairway leading to an elegant second-floor drawing room. Of note is an unusual parquet floor made of rare and native woods which incorporates the state seal of California.

The furnishings on display reflect two different periods of the house's history. The family rooms on the ground floor look much as they did from 1818 to 1820 when Stephen Decatur lived in the house. The formal parlors on the second floor are furnished to represent the period from 1871 to 1956 when the Beale family owned the house.

Notable Collections on Exhibit

Decatur House exhibits a fine collection of period furniture ranging from Chippendale side chairs to American rococo revival chairs by Belter. The house also displays impressive artwork including a series of Florentine paintings, and portraits by American artists.

Dumbarton House

2715 Que Street, N.W.
Washington, DC 20007
(202) 337-2288

Contact: National Society of Colonial Dames
Open: Tues.-Sat. 9:30 a.m.–12 p.m.,
  afternoons by appointment
Admission: Adults $3; students free; group
  rates available, please inquire. Guided
  tours.

Suggested Time to View House: 1 hour
Year House Built: c. 1799
Style of Architecture: Federal
Number of Rooms: 10

Description of House

Today home to the National Society of Colonial Dames, the Dumbarton
House has had a series of owners over the years. The original tract of land
was patented by Ninian Beall in 1703, however, this substantial residential
structure was not built until 1799 by Samuel Jackson. The first residents to
live here for a length of time (1805 to 1813) were the Nourse family, headed
by Joseph Nourse, register of the U.S. Treasury. Subsequent owners include
Charles Carroll, member of a prominent Maryland family, who lived here
from 1813 to 1820. Several other families occupied the dwelling before the
house was obtained by the Colonial Dames in 1923. Dumbarton House is
listed on the National Register of Historic Places.

The main facade of Dumbarton House resembles other structures of the
same period designed by architect William Thornton, as well as other area
houses with its use of cut and dressed stone as a complement to fine
brickwork. The house features stone lintels above the windows, a cut stone
belt course between the first and second stories, and a stone coping at the
water table. The entrance doorways are both topped by arch cut stone
openings and fanlights. The interior of the house is equally as impressive;
the graceful stairway is lighted on the landing by the Palladian window on
the garden facade.

The furnishings correspond to the period of the house's construction and are predominantly in the Hepplewhite and Sheraton styles. There are also earlier pieces from the Chippendale period which have been included because of their historical importance.

Of chief architectural interest is the plaster cornice in the entrance hallway which extends for the first half of the hallway to the dividing classical arch. The beautifully executed frieze contains a wealth of Adamesque designs composed of arabesque and classical urns.

Notable Collections on Exhibit

Dumbarton House showcases an impressive collection of 18th and 19th-century furnishings. Some of the more notable items include a large a large English Chippendale linen press as well as a few examples of Louis XVI French furniture. The furnishings also include more decorative pieces such as early 19th-century Dresden urns and a silver tea service made by W.G. Forbes of New York. The second floor gallery displays a series of objects with historical associations with Dumbarton House, as well as other artifacts related to local and national history.

James Monroe House

2017 I Street N.W.
Washington, DC 20002
(202) 546-3839

Contact: Arts Club of Washington

Open: Tues. and Thurs. 10 a.m.–5 p.m.;
Wed. and Fri. 2–5 p.m. Sat. 10–2 p.m.;
Sun. 1–5 p.m.

Admission: Free. Frequent gallery
exhibitions, performances, recitals, and
lectures.

Suggested Time to View House: 1 hour

Facilities on Premises: Gift shop

Description of Grounds: Formal garden

Best Season to View House: Year round

Number of yearly visitors: 10,000

Year House Built: 1802

On-Site Parking: No **Wheelchair Access:** No

Style of Architecture: Federal

Description of House

Many prominent people have passed through this gracious Federal-style mansion and several have even called it home.Timothy Caldwell built the house known today as the James Monroe House. Caldwell first leased this beautiful townhouse to Monroe while he was Secretary of State and Secretary of War under President Madison. The house served as the executive mansion while President Monroe waited for the White House to be rebuilt after its partial destruction by fire during the War of 1812. The Monroe House later served as a home for many other prominent people including Charles Francis Adams and General Silas Casey and several Congressman before it was acquired in 1881 by Professor Cleveland Abbe, founder of the U.S. Weather Service. The house is officially known on the National Register of Historic Places as the Caldwell-Abbe House.

Notable Collections on Exhibit

The townhouse has been carefully restored to its original splendor by the Arts Club of Washington. Paintings, drawings and sculpture from the club's permanent collection are displayed in the stairhalls and in the second and third floor rooms. Most of the these works are by Washington artists and represent the many styles that have been popular over the years. The adjoining MacFeeley House provides space for rotating exhibitions, which typically change every three weeks.

Additional Information

Standing adjacent to the Monroe House is the smaller MacFeeley House, built around 1870, and later purchased and remodeled (with an octagonel bay addition) by General Robert MacFeeley.

The Octagon

1799 New York Avenue, N.W.
Washington, DC 20006
(202) 638-3105

Contact: American Institute of Architects
Open: Tues.-Fri. 10 a.m.–4 p.m.; Sat.-Sun.
12–4 p.m.; closed major holidays.
Admission: Adults $2; students and seniors
$1; children (under 12) $.50. Guided
tours, tours for the hearing impaired by
special arrangement
Suggested Time to View House: 1 hour
Best Season to View House: All
Year House Built: 1801
Style of Architecture: Federal
Number of Rooms: 8 open to public

Description of House

This unusual dwelling was built in 1801 for Colonel John Tayloe III, a wealthy plantation owner from Virginia. Tayloe selected Dr. William Thornton, winner of the competition for the design of the U.S. Capitol, to be the architect for his new city residence. The Octagon, with its graceful and unusual design immediately became a center of official and non-official business; some of the guests included James Monroe, Thomas Jefferson, Daniel Webster and the Marquis de Lafayette. Other notable residents included President James Madison and his wife, Dolley, during the winter of 1814 to 1815. It was here that Madison signed the Treaty of Ghen on February 17, 1815, establishing peace with Great Britain.

The unusual geometric shape of The Octagon (which actually has six sides, not eight) was determined by the size of the plot of land Tayloe was able to acquire in the rapidly growing city. An excellent example of Federal period architecture, the building also illustrates the late 18th-century preference for curved areas with its circular entry hall, oval staircase and diagonally placed rooms. Functional features such as the service stairway, dressing rooms and closets take advantage of the odd corners in the design. The unique floor plan also satisfied the desire for symmetry and is a masterpiece of fluid space within a compact geometric design.

Many of the Federal and Chippendale furnishings which decorate the house belonged to the Tayloes and other residents, while others have been collected and are appropriate for the period. The stairhall contains the settee and armchairs which Tayloe ordered from London.

Notable Collections on Exhibit

The Octagon exhibits many rare items including the circular table where President Madison signed the Treaty of Ghent. Also of interest are two orignal coal-burning stoves, a Chippendale breakfront, and two portraits by French artist Charles de Saint-Memin of Colonel Tayloe and William Thornton, the architect. The second floor museum galleries feature changing exhibitions on architecture and the decorative arts.

Old Stone House

3051 M Street, N.W.
Washington, DC 20007
(202) 426-6851

Contact: National Park Service

Open: Wed.-Sun. 8 a.m.–4:30 p.m.; closed
major holidays

Admission: Free. Guided tours, craft
demonstrations.

Suggested Time to View House: 1 hour

Description of Grounds: English-style
garden

Best Season to View House: Spring and
summer

Year House Built: 1765

Style of Architecture: Georgian

Number of Rooms: 6

Wheelchair Access: Yes

Description of House

Little is known of Christopher Layman who built what is believed to be
the oldest surviving building in the city. Layman came to Washington from
Pennsylvania with his wife, Rachel, and their two sons. Layman was a
woodworker and it appears that his store was located on the the first floor
of the house. Layman died soon after the house was finished in 1765 and his
widow sold the home to Cassandra Chew, companion to Georgetown's
leading businessman and first mayor, Robert Peter. Members of the Chew
family lived in the house well into the 19th century. Legend has it that
George Washington used the house for his headquarters in 1791 when
choosing land for the nation's capital, although this has never been substan-
tiated.

Located in historic Georgetown, the Old Stone House offers a view of
middle-class life in colonial days. The house today reflects the changes of
the different occupants. The first floor contains Layman's carpenter's shop
and the kitchen. The winding staircase at the back of the house leads to the
living quarters. Mrs. Chew may have added the lovely room with attractive
paneling in 1775 as a place to receive visitors. The east front room, where
visitors also came to call, exhibits a delicately carved mantel of 1790s Adams
style. The third room served as a bedroom and the third floor contains the
children's bedrooms. Although none of the objects in the house is original
to the Layman family, the furnishings are based on an inventory taken at the
time of his death. These include period bedsteads, a table, blanket chest, and
two Pennsylvania Dutch Bibles. Mrs. Chew's rooms feature built-in cupboards displaying platters and utensils.

Sewall-Belmont House

144 Constitution Avenue, N.E.
Washington, DC 20002
(202) 546-3839

Contact: National Park Service
Open: Tues.-Fri. 10–3 p.m., Sat.-Sun.
  12–4 p.m., closed major holidays
Admission: Free
Suggested Time to View House: 1 hour
Facilities on Premises: Gift shop

Best Season to View House: Year round
Number of Yearly Visitors: 10,000
Year House Built: c. 1800
On-Site Parking: No **Wheelchair Access:** No
Style of Architecture: Georgian

Description of House

The American women's movement got its start from this unpretentious building located on Capitol Hill. The house was originally built by Robert Sewall in 1800, and was one of the few buildings burned by British troops in 1814. The dwelling stayed in the Sewall family until 1922. The National Women's Party bought the house, with funds from supporter Alva Belmont, to use as their headquarters in 1929. The National Women's Party was founded in 1913 by Alice Paul, a young social worker, in order to press for women's right to vote. Members of the Party even chained themselves to the White House fence in order to demand change. Finally, they achieved their objective when the 19th Amendment was ratified in 1920.

One of the oldest houses in Washington, the house now serves as a museum and art gallery commemorating the history of women's suffrage and the women's rights movement. The house displays paintings and sculpture of notable women including, among others, Elizabeth Cady Stanton, Lucretia Mott, and Joan of Arc.

In 1974, Congress passed a bill to restore the Sewall-Belmont House and declared it a National Historic Site. Today, the house stands as a testament to Alice Paul and her struggle for women's rights.

The White House

1600 Pennsylvania Avenue, N.W.
Washington, DC 20006
(202) 456-7041

Contact: National Park Service

Open: Tues.-Sat. 10 a.m.–12 p.m., closed holidays and for official functions

Admission: Free. Guided tours.

Suggested Time to View House: 1 hour

Description of Grounds: Garden tours available on selected weekends in April and October, call in advance

Year House Built: 1792 to 1800

Style of Architecture: Classical Revival

Number of Rooms: 9 open to public

On-Site Parking: No **Wheelchair Access:** Yes

Description of House

No visit to the historic houses of Washington would be complete without a visit to the White House. Home to every American president since John Adams, the White House has been extensively renovated and enlarged over the years to suit the needs of the residents and the demands of the growing country. Following the British burning of 1814, the house was rebuilt between 1815 and 1817 using the same walls. Despite the numerous modifications and additions, the White House has remained recognizable for 200 years.

The guided tour of the White House includes visits to the rooms that have shaped so much of our nation's history. The East Room, the largest in the building, has been used for receptions and ceremonies, and is elaborately decorated with glass chandeliers which date from 1902. The Diplomatic Reception Room, where Franklin Roosefelt broadcast so many of his fireside chats, still has the original 1834 wallpaper with scenes of the United States on the walls. The rooms contain a magnificent array of period furnishings which rival many major museums. The Blue Room, often said to be the most beautiful room in the White House, is furnished the represent the period of James Monroe and contains the original French furnishings. The Green Room, which was once Thomas Jefferson's dining room, features an Italian white marble fireplace mantle and furniture made by Duncan Phyfe in the early 19th century. The Red Room, a favorite of many First Ladies, is decorated as an American Empire parlor of the period 1810 to 1830.

While many of the rooms are not open to the public, the few on tour offer a fascinating view of American history as seen through the lives of the Presidents who have resided at the most famous address in the United States.

Notable Collections on Exhibit

The most notable portrait on display is Gilbert Stuart's 1797 portrait of George Washington (the one Dolly Madison saved from the 1814 fire). In addition to the splendid period furnishings and paintings, the White House exhibits a collection of Presidential china and glassware in the China Room.

Woodrow Wilson House

2340 S. Street NW
Washington, DC 20008
(202) 387-4062

Contact: National Trust for Historic
Preservation

Open: Tues.-Sun. 10 a.m.–4 p.m.

Admission: Adults $4; students and seniors
$2.50; under 7 free. Guided tours, films,
educational programs.

Suggested Time to View House: 1 hour

Facilities on Premises: Book store

Description of Grounds: Town house with
garden

Number of Yearly Visitors: 16,000 plus

Year House Built: 1915

Style of Architecture: Georgian Revival

Number of Rooms: 10 perod rooms on view

On-Site Parking: No

Wheelchair Access: Yes

Description of House

Woodrow Wilson began his long and varied career as a university professor, writing nine books and more than thirty-five articles on politics and history. After serving as president of Princeton University, he was elected governor of New Jersey. In 1912, he was elected president of the United States, and won re-election to a second term in 1916.

The Woodrow Wilson House Museum is the only former President's home open to the public in the nation's capital. Woodrow Wilson, twenty-eighth President of the United States (1913-21), retired directly to this house after completing his second term of office, and resided here for nearly three years until his death in 1924. Mrs. Wilson continued to live in the residence for nearly forty more years. Upon her death in 1961, the property became a historic house museum. Filled with mementoes of Wilson's long and varied career as both scholar and statesman, the house and its original furnishings today appear much as they did during the former President's residency. The rear garden overlooks Embassy Row.

Notable Collections on Exhibit

The house displays a varied collection of family furnishings, presidential gifts, and memorabilia related to Wilson's distinguished career. Notable items include his inaugural Bible, his White House cabinet chair, a framed mosaic from the Vatican, and portrait photographs of British and Belgian royal families. In addition, the house exhibits objects associated with the Paris Peace Conference and the League of Nations.

Additional Information

The Wilson House sponsors the annual Kalorama House and Embassy Tour on the first Sunday in September.

Index

🏛 Pennsylvania

🏛 Washington, D.C.

🏛 Delaware

	Photo or illustration courtesy of
Eleutherian Mills	Hagley Museum and Library
George Read II House and Garden	Historical Society of Delaware
John Dickinson Plantation	Delaware State Museum
Lombardy Hall	Lombardy Hall Foundation
Rockwood Museum	Rockwood Museum
Historic House s of Odessa	Winterthur Museum and Gardens
Winterthur	Winterthur Museum and Gardens
Woodburn (The Governor's House)	Woodburn

🏛 Maryland

Ballestone Manor	Ballestone Preservation Society
Carroll County Farm Museum	Carroll County Farm Museum
Carroll Mansion	Baltimore City Life Museums
Chase-Lloyd House	Chase-Lloyd Corporation
Evergreen House	Johns Hopkins University
Geddes-Piper House	Historical Society of Kent County
Hammond-Harwood House	Hammond-Harwood House Association, Inc.
Historic St. Mary's City	Historic St.Mary's City
Home of Chief Justice Taney	Francis Scott Key Memorial Foundation, Inc.
John Evans House-Robert Strawbridge House	Strawbridge Shrine Association
Jonathan Hager House & Museum	City of Hagerstown
Joseph Neall House & James Neall House	The Historical Society of Talbot County
Ladew House & Topiary Gardens	Nancy Boye/Ladew Topiary Gardens Inc.
London Town Publik House	London Town Publik House & Gardens
Marietta	Maryland National Capital Park Commission
Meredith House	Dorchester County Historical Society
Montpelier Mansion	Larry Zimmerman/ Maryland National Park & Planning Commission
Sotterly Mansion	Sotterly Mansion Foundation, Inc.
Surratt House Museum	Maryland National Park
The Rectory	Preservation Maryland

🏛 New Jersey

Bainbridge House	Historical Society of Princeton
Ballantine House	Armen/The Newark Museum
Captain James Lawrence House	Burlington County Historical Society
Centennial Cottage	Historical Society of Ocean Grove
Cooper House	Burlington County Historical Society
Craig House	Department of Enviromental Protection
Dey Mansion/Washington's Headquarters Museum	Passaic County Parks Department
Dr. William Robinson Plantation House	J. D. Mumford/Clark Historical Society
Emlen Physick Estate	Mid-Atlantic Center for the Arts
Johnson Ferry House	Washington Crossing State Park
"Lakeview" The Buckelew Mansion	Jamesburg Historical Association
Lambert Castle	Passaic County Historical Society

	Photo or illustration courtesy of
Macculloch Hall Historical Museum	Macculloch Hall Historical Museum
Miller-Cory House Museum	Miller-Cory House Association
Pearson-How House	Burlington County Historical Society
Ringwood Manor	Elbertus Prol/State of N.J. Dept, Env. Prot. & Energy.
Risley Homestead	Atlantic County Historical Society
Smith-Cadbury Mansion	Historical Society of Moorestown
The Steuben House	Bergen County Historical Society
Thomas Clarke House	Princeton Battlefield State Park

🏛 New York

1890 House	Museum and Center for the Victorian Arts
Abigail Adams Smith Museum	Abigail Adams Smith Museum
Alice Austen House Museum	Simon Benepe/NYC Dept. of Parks & Recreation
Bartow-Pell Mansion Museum	NYC Dept. of Parks & Recreation
Boscobel	Boscobel Restoration, Inc.
Bowne House	Bowne House Historical Society, Inc.
Caleb Smith House	Franklin Abbott/Smithtown Historical Society
Campbell-Whittlesey House	Richard Margolis/Landmark Society of Western New York
Coe Hall at Planting Fields	H. Leigh/Planting Fields Foundation
Conference House	NYC Dept. of Parks & Recreation
Constable Hall	Constable Hall Association, Inc.
Cottage Lawn	Madison County Historical Society
David Conklin Farmhouse	Huntington Historical Society
Dr. Daniel Kissam House	Huntington Historical Society
Dyckman House Museum	Eva Jakubowski
Epenetus Smith Tavern	Smithtown Historical Society
Franklin O. Arthur House	Smithtown Historical Society
Fraunces Tavern	Fraunces Tavern Museum
French Castle	Old Fort Niagara Association, Inc.
Garibaldi Meucci Museum	Garibaldi Meucci Museum
Genesee Country Museum	Genesee Country Museum
Gibby House	Arcade Historical Society
The Glebe House	Dutchess County Historical Society
Gould Mansion	Lewis County Historical Society
Granger Homestead	Granger Homestead Society Inc.
Hallock Homestead	Hallockville Museum Farm
Hart-Cluett Mansion	Rensselaer County Historical Society
Historic Richmond Town	Staten Island Historical Society
Huguenot Street	Huguenot Historical Society
The Jacob Blauvelt House	The Historical Society of Rockland County
James Vanderpoel House	Columbia County Historical Society
John Hanford House	Hanford Mills Museum
John Jay Homestead	John Jay Homestead State Historic Site
Johnson Hall	Johnson Hall State Historic Site
Jonathan Hasbrouck House	Washington's Headquarters State Historic Sit
Judge J. Lawrence Smith Homestead	Smithtown Historical Society
Kent-Delord House Museum	Kent-Delord House Corporation
King Manor Museum	Simon Benepe/NYC Dept. of Parks & Recreation
Kingsland Homestead	Queens Historical Society

Lefferts Homestead	Prospect Park Admin. Office and Park Alliance
Le Roy House	Le Roy Historical Society
Lindenwald	Martin Van Buren National Historic Site
Locust Lawn	Huguenot Historical Society
Lower East Side Tenement Museum	Eva Jakubowski
Luykas Van Alen House	Columbia County Historic Society
The Manor of St. George	Estate of Eugene A. T. Smith
The Mansion House	Oneida Community Mansion House, Inc.
McClurg Museum	Chautauqua County Historical Society
Mills Mansion	Mills Mansion State Historic Site
The Mills Mansion	Mt. Morris Historical Society
Miss Amelia's Cottage	Amagansett Historical Association
Morris-Jumel Mansion	Eva Jakubowski
Mount Lebanon Shaker Village	Cheryl Bell/Mount Lebanon Shaker Village
Mynderse-Partridge-Becker House	Seneca Falls Historical Society
Obadiah Smith House	Barbara Banks/Smithtown Historical Society
Olana	Olana State Historic Site
Old Fort House Museum	Fort Edward Historical Association
Old Merchant's House	Eva Jakubowski
Oliver House Museum	Ruth Brown/Yates County Historical Society
Oysterponds	Oysterponds Historical Society
Parishville Museum	Parishville Historical Association Inc.
Philip Schuyler House	Saratoga National Historical Park
Pieter Claeson Wyckoff House	Wyckoff House & Association Inc.
Poe Cottage	The Bronx County Historical Society
Pratt House	Historical Society of Fulton
Prouty-Chew Museum	Geneva Historical Society
The Pruyn House	Town of Colonie Cultural Center
Queens County Farm Museum	Colonial Farmhouse Restoration Society of Bellrose
Raynham Hall Museum	Friends of Raynham Hall
Richardson-Bates House Museum	Oswego County Historical Society
The Robert Jenkins House	Hendrick Hudson Chapter-NSDAR
Rose Hill Mansion	Geneva Historical Society
Schuyler Mansion/ The Pastures	Schuyler Mansion State Historic Site
Seward House	Foundation Historical Society Assoc. Inc.
Sonnenberg Gardens Mansion	Sonnenberg Gardens
Square House	Rye Historical Society
Stone-Tolan House	Hans Padelt/The Landmark Society of Western New York
Theodore Roosevelt Birthplace	National Park Service
Van Cortlandt House	Eva Jakubowski
Vander Ende-Onderdonk Farmhouse Museum	Greater Ridgewood Historical Society
Walt Whitman House	Walt Whitman Birthplace Association
Whitney-Halsey Museum	The American Manse
William Floyd Estate	National Park Service
Woodside	Rochester Historical Society
Zim House	Daniel Sturika/Horseheads Historical Society

	Photo or illustration courtesy of
1719 Herr House	Hans Herr House
1810 John Sebastian Goundie House	Historic Bethlehem Inc.
Baker House of Old Economy Village	Pennsylvania Historical and Museum Comm.
Baldwin-Reynolds House Museum	Crawford County Historical Society
Barns-Brinton House	Theodore Brinton Hetzel/ The Chadds Ford Historical Society
Battles Museums Yellow House	Erie County Historical Society
Bentel House	Historic Harmony Inc.
Boone House	Daniel Boone Homestead
Brinton 1704 House	The Brinton Family Association Inc.
Cashiers House	Erie County Historical Society
Centre Furnace Mansion	Centre County Historical Society
Charlotte Elizabeth Battles Memorial Museum	Erie County Historical Society
Cliveden	Cliveden of the National Trust Inc.
Cedar Grove	Philadelphia Museum of Art
Columbus Chapel and Boal Mansion	Columbus Chapel and Boal Mansion Museum
Compass Inn Museum	Ligonier Valley Historical Society
Connell Mansion	The Historical Society of the Cocalico Valley
David Bradford House	Bradford House Historical Association
Dobbin House	Dobbin House Inc.
Ephrata Cloister	Pennsylvania Historical and Museum Comm.
Fallingwater	Western Pennsylvania Conservancy
George and Frederick Rapp House	Pennsylvania Historical and Museum Comm.
George Taylor House	Lehigh County Historical Society
Gideon Gilpin House	Brandywine Battlefield Park
Grumblethorpe	Philadelphia Soc. for the Preservation of Landmarks
Henry Frick Birthplace	West Overton Museums
The Highlands	Highlands Historical Society
Hill-Physick-Keith House	Philadelphia Soc. for the Preservation of Landmarks
Historic 1696 Thomas Massey Home	Fletcher MacNeil/Township of Marple
Hope Lodge	Friends of Hope Lodge
Hunter House	North Cumberland Historical Society
The John Chads House	The Chadds Ford Historical Society
The John Harris/Simon Cameron Mansion	The Historical Society of Dauphin County
Laurel Hill	Philadelphia Museum of Art
Lemon Hill	Philadelphia Museum of Art
Magoffin House	Mercer County Historical Society
Mantua House	Elfreth's Alley Museum
Mount Pleasant	Philadelphia Museum of Art
Neas House	Hanover Area Historical Society
Overholt Homestead	West Overton Museums
Old Bedford Village	Old Bedford Village Inc.
The Parry Mansion Museum	The New Hope Historical Society
Powel House	Philadelphia Soc. for the Preservation of Landmarks
Renfrew Museum (the Royer House)	Renfrew Museum and Park
Rock Ford Plantation/ Kauffman Museum	Rock Ford Foundation
Strawberry Mansion	Philadelphia Museum of Art
Stroud Community House	Monroe County Historical Association

	Photo or illustration courtesy of
Sturgeon House	Fairview Area Historical Society
Sweetbriar	Philadelphia Museum of Art
Trout Hall	Lehigh County Historical Society
Troxel-Steckel House and Farm Museum	Lehigh County Historical Society
Waynesboro	Philadelphia Soc. for the Preservation of Landmarks
Washington's Headquarters	Ken Block/National Park Service
Whitefield House	Moravian Historical Society

🏛 Washington, D.C.

Anderson House	Society of the Cincinnatti
Cedar Hill	Bill Clark/National Park Service
Decatur House	National Trust for Historic Preservation
Dumbarton House	National Society of Colonial Dames
Old Stone House	National Park Service
James Monroe House	R. Kruger/Arts Club of Washington
The Octagon	John Tennant/American Institute of Architects
Sewell-Belmont House	Bill Clark/National Park Service
The White House	Bill Clark/National Park Service
Woodrow Wilson House	National Trust for Historic Preservation

Notes